D1599713

# Arab Guerilla Power

The Middle East around Israel

# EDGAR O'BALLANCE

# Arab Guerilla Power
## 1967-1972

ARCHON BOOKS
1973

*First published in 1973
by Faber and Faber Limited, London
and in the United States of America
as an Archon Book
by The Shoe String Press, Inc.,
Hamden, Connecticut 06514*

*Library of Congress Cataloging in Publication Data*

O'Ballance, Edgar
    Arab Guerilla Power, 1967-1972

    1.   Fedayeen.   I.   Title.
DS119.7.022   1974        322.4'2'09174927        74-4306
ISBN  0-208-01436-5

# Contents

# *Maps*

9

# *Acknowledgements*

The following works have been consulted in compiling this book, and grateful acknowledgement is made to the authors, contributors, reporters and publishers.

Heikal, Mohammed, *Gamal Abdul Nasser*, Doubleday, New York (1972)

Kimche, David & Bawley, Dan, *The Sandstorm*, Secker & Warburg (1968)

Laqueur, Walter, *The Road to War*, Weidenfeld & Nicolson (1970)

Shukairy, Ahmed, *Dialogues and Secrets with Kings*, Published in Beirut, May 1971

Institute for Strategic Studies—Various papers, particularly The Military Balance and Strategic Survey series.

# *Preface*

This is a comprehensive account of the rise, expansion, principal activities and general decline of Arab Guerilla Power which, occurring mainly between 1965 and 1972, took the world by surprise. Instead of abjectly waiting, as Palestinian refugees and exiles had been doing since 1948, for Israel to collapse, Arab guerilla power sought to solve the Palestine problem by violent means, first unsuccessfully attempting to put into practice Mao Tse-tung's theory of the 'fish' (the guerilla fighter) swimming safely in the 'sea' (of the 1·3 million Arabs under Israeli control) and to emulate the Viet Cong. When this failed, Arab Guerilla Power turned to a war of attrition, with guerilla, commando and terrorist tactics, to reduce the Israelis to such a state of apprehension that they would agree to demands for an Arab-controlled Palestine.

It is a fascinating story of the rise and internal conflicts of several guerilla groups, whose rivalries overshadowed idealism, and of a struggle to gain power without responsibility in host Arab countries that developed into a three-sided contest— with the Fedayeen, the Arab states and Israel fighting against each other. The Fedayeen also fought a propaganda war amongst themselves for prestige, carried out dramatic hi-jackings, assassinations and acts of terrorism, and set up where they could autonomous sectors such as Fatahland in the Lebanon, until their rising power vied with that of Arab governments, when arrogance and bad judgement provoked civil war in Jordan and fighting in the Lebanon, that swung the guerillas back on the waning defensive.

The Arab guerilla struggle against the Israelis is a continuing one. This, the main and vital phase, is brought to a close with the Munich killings of September 1972, and the subsequent rescue of the three surviving members of the Black September Group from German hands, because these incidents mark the commencement of another phase in which other means are employed. Since this book was written there has, for example, been fighting in the Lebanon between the Fedayeen and the Government forces but this is part of the expected aftermath of subsiding rumbles; even more spasms may follow, but they are not of sufficient significance to warrant dragging out this narrative to include an account of them. Also the death of President Nasser and the exodus of most of the Russians from Egypt changed the balance of power in the Middle East. Arab guerilla power had been supported and kept viable by Nasser who tried to use it to 'divide and influence' Arab states. After his death it became apparent that it had no discernible strategy, only a vague, clouded purpose; it went into a decline, as did pan-Arabism. The guerilla fighter always had a mystique that attracted admiration and sympathy for him as the underdog, regardless of his purpose, his real successes and failures being shrouded in the mists of propaganda, as were those of the Fedayeen. I have tried to blow away those mists and examine their activities in clear detail. Only time will tell whether Arab guerilla power was the start of an Arab awakening and revival, or merely a transient phenomenon.

EDGAR O'BALLANCE

# *Abbreviations*

Unfortunately initials or abbreviations are necessary to avoid repetition of lengthy titles. The main ones are given below.

| | |
|---|---|
| *AAS* | Association of Arabs in Sinai |
| *ACLP* | Action Committee for the Liberation of Palestine |
| *ALF* | Arab Liberation Front |
| *AMLP* | Arab Movement for the Liberation of Palestine |
| *ANM* | Arab National Movement |
| *AOLP* | Action Organization for the Liberation of Palestine |
| *APO* | Arab Palestine Organization |
| *BSG* | Black September Group |
| *DPF* | Democratic Popular Front for the Liberation of Palestine |
| *FPPS* | Front for the Popular Palestine Struggle |
| *ILP* | Islamic Liberation Party |
| *JDL* | Jewish Defence League |
| *PASC* | Palestine Armed Struggle Command |
| *PF* | Partisan Forces |
| *PFLP* | Popular Front for the Liberation of Palestine |
| *PLA* | Palestine Liberation Army |
| *PLF* | Popular Liberation Force |
| *PLO* | Palestine Liberation Organization |
| *PNC* | Palestine National Council |
| *POLP* | Popular Organization for the Liberation of Palestine |
| *PPS* | Parti Populaire Syrien |
| *R-PFLP* | Revolutionary Popular Front for the Liberation of Palestine |
| *UNEF* | United Nations Emergency Force |
| *UNRWA* | United Nations Relief and Works Agency |
| *VPLW* | Vanguards of the Popular Liberation War |

13

# 1. *The Cult of the Fedayeen*

The first Arab-Israeli War, of 1948, brought two new factors on to the Middle East scene—the Palestine problem and the Arab refugee problem; these have given birth to, and sustained at varying degrees of intensity and application, the cult of the Fedayeen, of the vaunted Arab guerilla 'freedom' fighter. The Palestine Arabs had no national entity as such and, indeed, from World War I onwards had grown up under the heavy overtones of bi-nationalism, so that when the state of Israel appeared and by force of arms displaced some 700,000 of them, they had no centrally inspired cohesion with which to exploit national ideals. Suggestions and even attempts to form a Palestine government-in-exile were quashed by Arab governments which were far more interested in occupying and annexing parts of Palestine, or preventing other Arab states from doing so, than altruistically working to establish an independent Arab Palestine. Huddled together in miserable refugee camps in the Gaza Strip, Jordan, Syria and the Lebanon, Palestinians were callously neglected by the Arabs, who blatantly used them as international and pan-Arab pawns. The Palestine problem and the Arab refugee problem at this stage were inseparable and merged into each other.

The years immediately after 1948 were lawless ones in which terrorist groups raided into Israel from adjacent Arab states, which they were able to do with comparative ease, as much of Israel's 591-mile frontier was open, and for a while stretches of it were even unmarked. The Palestinian Arabs had developed a tradition of raiding and terrorism between the two World Wars, when the Mandate for Palestine was held by the British, during which, in protest against the number of Jews arriving, the Arab revolt broke out in the 1930s; it was only just brought under control when World War II commenced. The Arab terrorist was not a dedicated guerilla fighter in the sense in which we tend to think of one today, motivated like the Viet Cong by a clear political objective. He was one who either raided into Israel for a criminal purpose, or who was instigated to do so to the vague political advantage of the host Arab country concerned or to the detriment of his rival—but any detriment to Israel was only an after-thought. Not all the raiders were Palestinians, although most were. The Arabs still hated each other more than they hated anyone else, and age-old traditional feuds lingered on, exacerbated by current ambitions and jealousies.

There was no disguising the fact that the Arabs had been badly defeated by the Israelis in 1948, their ego punctured and their boasts proved empty: their Jihad, their Holy war, in which all Arabs were to unite against the Jews, had failed to materialize. Wallowing in a plethora of recrimination, both with other Arab states and themselves, they sat back to lick their wounds and salve their pride. All Arab governments were badly shaken, and some fell. To the north, tiny Lebanon, traditionally half Christian and half Arab in population, had joined in the war against Israel hoping for some morsel of territorial spoils, but it badly burnt its fingers and, glad when the Israelis withdrew from Lebanese territory, was content to accept the old Mandate boundary as its frontier with Israel. The Lebanon did not want any trouble, and was relieved to have got off so lightly; its continuing cries to destroy Israel were merely con entional platitudes, at times barely audible. To the north-east was Syria, whose army had done comparatively well in the war, but it was inward looking, convulsed with violent political spasms and beset by frequent coups. A line of strong, static defences was constructed on its frontier along the 'Syrian Heights'[1] overlooking the Huleh and Upper Jordan Valleys in Israel, manned by about one-third of its standing army, where from time to time the Syrians periodically fired on Israeli workers in the fields. Despite internal pre-occupation, the

[1] Later to become better known as the Golan Heights.

Syrians loudly sang the anti-Israeli song, quarrelled with other Arab states and encouraged terrorists to raid into Israel.

To the south of Syria and to the east of Israel lay Jordan, ruled by King Abdullah, whose British-officered Arab Legion (of then Trans-Jordan) had entered the war against Israel to occupy and hold many Arab populated areas of Palestine, including the Old City of Jerusalem, which were eventually annexed to form the new Hashemite Kingdom of Jordan. King Abdullah, until he was assassinated in 1949, reputedly for trying to make peace with Israel, was mainly pre-occupied with consolidating his expanded country and exerting his influence over one and a half million people, of whom about one-third were Palestinians or 'West Bankers' not reconciled to his authority, one-third were Palestinian refugees also not regarding themselves as owing him any allegiance, and one-third were a mixture of 'native Trans-Jordanians', of whom a large proportion were Bedu, upon whom the King basically relied for his solid support. The Israeli-Jordanian border lent itself to infiltration tactics and Arab terrorists frequently raided across it into Israel.

The Egyptian army, with ramshackle, cast-off British arms and equipment, had put up a poor show during the war. Jostled out of most of the Arab inhabited parts of Palestine it had entered, Egypt managed only to hang precariously on to the small, thin Gaza Strip, where about half-a-million people, including refugees, were crammed. Back in Egypt proper, under a corrupt government, there was economic chaos, squabbling politicians and the lingering elements of British military occupation that hurt Egyptian pride. Hate against Israel was on all Egyptian lips but their thoughts were elsewhere. In July 1952 a coup by young officers forced King Farouk to abdicate and brought a revolutionary council to power, headed by General Neguib. In June 1953 Egypt was declared a republic, and in November the following year Gamel Abdul Nasser displaced Neguib and took control of the Government, which he retained until his death in 1970.

In Iraq, physically separated from Israel, Nuri Said, the pro-Western premier, continued to ride the storm of internal political turmoil for a little while longer.

For many months the displaced Arab refugees were stunned and lifeless, the majority soon accustoming themselves to inactivity and existence on meagre UNRWA rations. Living in squalid conditions in scattered tented camps, they sank into lethargy, a mood of hopelessness overtaking most of them as in traditional Arab form they philosophically waited for something to happen and for someone to do something for them. Had it not been for UNRWA there would have been mass starvation. The negative attitude of Arab governments was that time was on their side and against the Israelis; frequently they recalled that the old Crusader Kingdom, which at its height encompassed a greater area than modern Israel, did not survive a hundred years before being swept away, and they asserted that soon the same fate must inevitably overtake Israel. In all Arab countries there was a 'hate-Israel' campaign, of varying intensity, but no sign of a 'pro-Palestine Government' one. The Palestinian refugees were tolerated by the Arab countries and used politically, but they were not helped as their miserable conditions made them a continuing bargaining counter.

A few Palestinian intellectuals, politicians and students working in the refugee camps, endeavoured to raise spirits and awaken feelings, but they themselves were divided, lacking national identity, they sought in vain for a definite purpose and a constructive political programme to put to the apathetic refugees. The only purely Palestinian leadership was that of Haj Amin al-Husseini, the ex-Mufti of Jerusalem, and the Arab Higher Executive Committee of the pre-World War II Arab revolt days, but, discredited and unacceptable to many as they were, they had little influence. Para-military youth units were formed and financed by the ex-Mufti, who had some funds at his disposal, to give training to youngsters in camps, but because of lethargy they never prospered. Some Palestinians, especially students, organized lectures and meetings, but they gave no positive lead as they concentrated on former Arab glories and the rights and wrongs of the Palestine problem.

Arab terrorist raids into Israel increased in frequency in the early 1950s. The Israelis claimed that there were 3,742 illegal border crossings in 1952, which resulted in 60 Israelis being killed and over 70 wounded. The precise degree of implication of the Arab governments was hard to determine, and probably ranged from inability to prevent them and passive approval to active aid. Through lack of manpower the Israelis were unable to seal off their borders effectively against the terrorists, and an Israeli request through the UN to construct a wire fence along the eastern side of the 20-mile long Gaza Strip, which contained over 200,000 refugees, was blocked by Egypt. The Israeli counter was to hit back at terrorist camps near its frontiers in reprisal raids, which usually had the effect of quietening down a particular sector for a short while.

For several weeks after ousting Neguib and assuming power, Nasser was preoccupied with consolidating his position, and he had little time for other matters, but the impact of the many raids Arab terrorists were making into Israel from the Gaza Strip was sharply brought to his attention in February 1955, when an Israeli brigade group, taking Egyptian frontier guards by surprise, crossed the border to fight a three-hour battle on the outskirts of Gaza, in which Israelis blew up buildings, killed 38 Egyptians and wounded 31. From this moment Nasser gave encouragement to Arab raiders, quietly allowing them to use military training camps. Raiding into Israel was stepped up in the first half of 1955, but there was no Egyptian official support until August, when the first public mention was made of the Fedayeen—the freedom fighters. Roughly, Fedayeen means 'self sacrifice' and is sometimes translated as 'men of sacrifice'. The Israelis continued to refer to them as terrorists, the word guerilla had not then come into common usage. It was admitted that the Fedayeen were controlled and paid by the Egyptian army. Overnight their deeds were glorified and they became heroes in the Arab world.

The Israeli reply, a sharp reprisal raid against Khan Yunis, a Fedayeen training centre, in which 40 Egyptians were killed and 40 wounded, ignited a whole section of the border, and UN observers only dampened down the situation with difficulty. Two Egyptian Vampires had been shot down. Fedayeen raids from the Gaza Strip continued during the first part of 1956, causing other Israeli reprisal attacks, notably one in April, when Israeli artillery bombarded Gaza, killing 40 Egyptians

19

and wounding another 100. Radio Cairo boasted that Fedayeen were penetrating Israel and causing a reign of terror there. Arab terrorist raids from Jordan multiplied after March 1956, when Glubb Pasha, the British commander of the Arab Legion, who was a restraining influence, was dismissed. Again they were countered with reprisal raids on terrorist camps and staging areas. In September, for example, the Israelis assaulted Dhariya, killing 16 Jordanians. Jordan allowed the Egyptian Fedayeen to raid into Israel from Jordanian territory, which provoked a reprisal assault on Kalkilya, a terrorist staging post overlooking the Sharon Plain in Israel. Further north spasmodic artillery fire, sniping and terrorist activities continued along the Syrian-Israeli border. Although it had its small share of incidents, the Lebanese frontier was the quietest of them all.

To carry out their threats to eliminate Israel, the Arab governments required more, and modern, arms, but had difficulty in obtaining them in any quantity. The only three major countries able to supply them, Britain, America and France, alarmed at the prospect of renewed war in the Middle East, agreed to limit arms sales to keep the military balance between Israel and the Arab states and to ensure that no one Arab state became militarily powerful enough to attack or dominate the others. This was known as the Tri-partite Agreement of 1950, which worked creakingly until 1955.

Nasser strove to build Egypt up into a powerful nation, and for Cairo to be the centre of the pan-Arab, pan-African and pan-Islamic worlds—his famous 'three circles'. As a first step he required large modern armed forces to impress, dominate and conquer. Baulked by the Tripartite Agreement, he turned to the Soviet Union then deeply involved in the cold war with the West, and successfully concluded an arms deal with that country in August 1955, which became for convenience known as the Czech arms deal. As this happened at the time of the Geneva summit on Vietnam, the Soviet Union was not yet ready to supply arms openly, so the talks were conducted in Prague by the Czechs on behalf of the Russians.[1] At the next Independence

[1] *Gamal Abdul Nasser* by Mohammed Heikal, Doubleday (New York, 1972).

20

Day parade in Cairo in July 1956, Nasser was able to put his
Soviet weapons on display for all the world to see. Already, on
the 13th June, the last British troops had left the Suez Canal
Zone, and on the 23rd Nasser had become President of Egypt.
In July America refused a loan to the Egyptians to complete
the Aswan Dam project, and on the 26th of that month President Nasser nationalized the Suez Canal, thus beginning his
confrontation with Western powers that was to end in war. In
the months from August to October his preoccupation with
Israel was secondary.

On the 29th October 1956 the Israelis launched their forces
against the Egyptians in the Sinai, driving them back to the
Suez Canal,[1] a campaign that was fought concurrently with
Anglo-French attacks on Egypt. One of the main Israeli
objectives was to eliminate the Fedayeen bases in the Gaza
Strip. In his adversity Nasser stood alone. Not a single Arab
government put a soldier in the field or fired a shot to help him;
they all timidly withheld their trembling trigger fingers. The
following year under UN and American insistence the Egyptians
were allowed to return to their pre-Sinai campaign boundaries,
and were shielded from the Israelis by the newly formed UN
Emergency Force, positioned and strung out on the Egyptian
side of the Egyptian-Israeli border.

This sudden, brilliant Israeli victory temporarily subdued
the Arabs and caused their anxious governments to keep
Fedayeen activities down to a minimum. President Nasser
hastily disbanded his army-sponsored Fedayeen units, and for
some months there was comparative quiet along the Israeli
frontiers, but the Fedayeen idea and ideal had caught the
imagination and given the rising generation in refugee camps
an inspiration. Impatient with current Arab governmental
policy of waiting for Israel to collapse, some of the young
refugees began to advocate violent means to solve the Palestine
problem, which did not please Arab countries adjacent to Israel
as they were neither ready nor willing to face Israeli reprisal
punches. There arose a restless discontent in the refugee camps
which caused political groups and organizations to be formed,
but few lasted long. It was variously estimated that between

[1] Officially, the Israelis halted 10 miles from the Suez Canal.

1956 and 1967, 40 to 50 clandestine political organizations appeared on the Middle East scene, most of them briefly, but none amounted to much until the dramatic emergence of Fatah in 1965.

There was a constant grouping and regrouping of Palestinian intellectuals who, having to rely upon the good will of their host country to exist and operate, inevitably became involved in Arab rivalries, changing governments and changing policies. Often for expediency they had to switch allegiances and modify ideologies. These intellectuals remained divided amongst themselves. Some were for an Arab Palestine, some for a bi-national Palestine, some for wresting the West Bank from King Hussein, who had succeeded to the throne of Jordan in 1952,[1] some were Nasserites and yet others were Baathists; there were many divergent Palestinian views but not a united one. A few Fedayeen organizations adopted a mercenary role, being employed by their host country to engage in subversive and terrorist activities for its own selfish national ends; as such they were regarded as dangerous by other Arab countries, which would not let this type operate on their territory if they could prevent it. At the best the Palestinian Fedayeen were tolerated by reluctant hosts, only their immense popular acclaim in the Arab world retarding government action against them.

Meanwhile President Nasser, who never won a military battle, gained the peace, and was soon using his confrontation with Israel as an aid to help him dominate Arab states. In 1958 he engineered the United Arab Republic, the UAR, by linking Egypt with Syria, and he planned greater unions and federations, but in September 1961 Syria broke away.[2] The Arab states remained as disunited as ever. The next item of major significance was information, gained in 1963, that Israel was to commence work the following year on its projected national water carrier, which would draw off water from the River

---

[1] King Hussein became king on the 11th August, 1952, just after his father, King Talal, had been deposed for insanity, and assumed full powers on the 23rd May, 1953, his 18th birthday.

[2] Egypt retains the title of the United Arab Republic, but will be referred to by either name in this book.

Jordan and its tributaries. The Jordan waters were a constant source of friction in an arid region, not only between the Arabs and Israel but among the Arab riparian states themselves. Israel desperately needed more water to develop agriculturally and economically, but the Arabs did not want it to have any at all from this source.

In January 1964 an Arab summit meeting, chaired by President Nasser, discussed what should be done to prevent the Israelis from going ahead with this project, but nothing positive was decided, and although Syria was for open war with Israel, Nasser was not. This summit produced only the false-fronted Unified Arab High Command, headed by an Egyptian general, which was to direct and co-ordinate all Arab military action against the Israelis. Work began on the national water carrier in July (1964), and the same month the Egyptian-sponsored Palestine Liberation Organization, the PLO, came into being as a face-saver. Nasser chose Ahmed Shukairy, a Palestinian Arab, who had served at the UN, first as a Syrian representative and then as a representative of Saudi Arabia, to lead it. Shukairy had always spoken up loudly for the cause of the Palestinian refugees and was considered to be a safe Nasserite.[1] The PLO was to be financed by the Arab League (on which Shukairy was given a seat) and certain other Arab states.

President Nasser would not tolerate a Palestine government-in-exile, but he allowed Shukairy to recruit small military units from amongst the refugees, mainly in the Gaza Strip, which were led and trained by regular Egyptian officers and which became known as the Palestine Liberation Army, the PLA. Controlled by the PLO, the aim of the PLA was to harass the Israelis by constant Fedayeen raids, and its purpose was to be the 'vanguard for the liberation of the usurped parts of Palestine'. It was formed and trained on the lines of the Algerian Front de Libération Nationale, the FLN, which then enjoyed a high reputation and was extremely popular in revolutionary circles.

The Soviet Union disapproved of guerilla movements and gave no help, so, disillusioned by poor Arab financial and other

[1] In his book *Dialogues and Secrets with Kings*, published in Beirut in May 1971, Shukairy stated that he made no move or statement of any importance without first consulting Nasser.

23

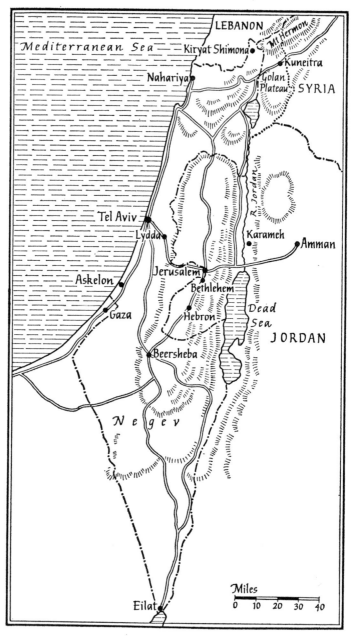

Israel

support, Shukairy turned to China to see what he could get. The PLO had become a member of the Afro-Asian People's Solidarity Organization, which had its headquarters in Cairo, and through this body he was able to make contact with China. In March 1965 Shukairy was invited to Peking, where he met Chou En-lai, the Premier, who thought he might be the type of independent guerilla leader who could be used to further Chinese policy in the Middle East, which at this stage was to export 'guerilla-type revolution'. Chou En-lai stressed that crushing right-wing reactionary personalities and elements was more important than the reconquest of Palestine.

The PLO was allowed to open an office in Peking, and soon Shukairy was boasting that China had offered arms and money and that training of 'PLA shock troops' would begin as soon as equipment arrived. During 1966 and 1967 he claimed that Chinese weapons were reaching him and that 'several dozen' PLA members were being trained in China. In fact, Chinese assistance was extremely slight, and the majority of arms, usually cast-off Soviet models, and money came from the Arab League, Egypt and Kuwait. It should be remembered that at this period China was entering the ghastly throes of its great cultural revolution, and had little time for anything else. The PLA eventually had a few small units of artillery and a few armoured vehicles in Egypt and the Gaza Strip. Shukairy carried out recruiting in the refugee camps in Syria, and two small PLA units were formed in that country.

Ahmed Shukairy soon fell out with King Hussein of Jordan, who had initially granted the PLO some facilities in the refugee camps in his country. Hussein would not agree to Shukairy's demands that the PLO be allowed to tax the Palestinian refugees, enlist them in his PLA, train the PLA in Jordan, or let the PLA man the frontier villages. Shukairy alleged that Hussein had denuded the Jordanian border defences when in 1965 he disbanded the 30,000-strong National Guard, a part-time force formed to protect the frontier with Israel, because of its potential unreliability (being composed of West Bank Arabs) to himself. This had caused discontent, which mounted as Israeli reprisal raids increased. In February 1966 Hussein allowed the PLO to have offices in Jordan, but as they seemed to be primarily used to stir up dissidence against him, he closed them all down again in April, arresting many PLO members. This caused Shukairy, egged on by Syria—which was particularly anti-King Hussein at this moment—to turn his hatred and propaganda fully against King Hussein, almost to the exclusion of all else, a policy he maintained right up until Hussein's surprise pact with Nasser on the 28th May 1967.

The Fedayeen organization, Fatah, commenced terrorist raids into Israel in 1965, and within months became the foremost guerilla group of its kind—one that at last appeared to be achieving something. The full title of Fatah was 'Tahir al Hatani al Falestini', the Movement for the National Liberation of Palestine. The initials HTF form the Arabic word for 'death', and when reversed to FTH, the Arabic word for 'conquest'— hence Fatah. The nucleus of Fatah consisted of Palestinian students at foreign universities, and was probably formed in the late 1950s.[1] The students were disillusioned with the attitudes of Arab Governments towards the Palestine problem, and they decided that an Arab Palestinian organization should be formed that would not be tied to, or influenced by, any Arab government. The first elements of Fatah were formed in Germany by (Yasir) Mohammed Arafat, Hani al-Hassan and Khalil al-Wazir, all Palestinian students, and they looked to the FLN, then fighting in Algeria, for inspiration and guidance, defining the primary aim as being to liberate Palestine, with all other matters secondary. Arafat had attended the Cairo (then Fuad I) University, gaining a degree in civil engineering. In 1955 he went to an officers' school in Cairo, being commissioned a year later as a reserve lieutenant. Posted to the PLA in the Gaza Strip for a short period, he watched Nasser's Fedayeen operating into Israel, which made him determined to have a Palestinian force, sympathetic to but outside Nasser's direct control.

From 1960 onwards the small Fatah core concentrated on developing secret cells on the Communist pattern, collecting funds and distributing pro-Palestinian literature. Both Arafat and Wazir visited Peking and received some encouragement. In

[1] *The Sandstorm* by David Kimche and Dan Bawley.

26

1962, when Algeria became independent, Khalil al-Wazir set up a Palestine office in Algiers, and with the approval of the new Algerian Government all Palestinians in Algeria had to register there to obtain work permits, which immediately gave Fatah great influence as there were numbers of Palestinians, especially teachers, in that country. Training camps were established to which Fatah sent Palestinians studying in Europe and Algeria. Arafat went to Kuwait, ostensibly to edit a magazine, where many Palestinians worked, but really to recruit guerilla fighters, the Emir giving approval and money. However, the Fatah training camps in Algeria and Kuwait were not a great success, and most of the students who attended courses at them, after returning to their universities to qualify, took jobs away from the Middle East, having little heart for such tough, selfless revolutionary activities.

The Fatah view had come to be that as no reliance could be placed on Arab leaders, and that as the Palestinians alone could not defeat Israel, it must work for an Arab-Israeli war (which it was sure the Arabs would win), by carrying out acts of terrorism inside Israel that would provoke ever larger reprisal raids, which must inevitably escalate into full-scale war. In early 1964 Fatah decided to move over to the offensive. First it looked for a country adjacent to Israel from which it could operate. It chose Syria, then an outcast among Arab nations and currently engaged in a power tussle with Nasser. Wishing to impress all Arabs that the Syrian Baathists were the real leaders, the Government allowed Fatah to establish itself in its territory. The Syrian Government wanted to outshine Egypt in the Palestine liberation cause, and it also believed unusually, as did Fatah that time was working against—and not for—the Arabs. It also thought falsely that Fatah approved the Syrian belief in the need to work for a revolutionary war in the Middle East. President Nasser did not want war with the Israelis, as he knew that he was not yet militarily strong enough.

Fatah determined to remain independent, but the move to Syria caused it to modify its principles in this respect for the time being. It wanted a strong guerilla arm, which so far had failed to emerge, and as the Syrians had good contacts in the

27

refugee camps,[1] not only in Syria but also in the Lebanon and northern Jordan, Fatah reckoned it could use them to recruit one. The Syrians were also prepared to allow Fatah freedom of movement, training facilities, money and some arms, which enabled Fatah to form its military arm, which became known as Kuwat al-Asifa, or storm troops, generally referred to as Asifa.[2] Asifa was given special sabotage and commando training by the Syrian regular army and provided with explosives and small arms, many of Soviet and some of Chinese origin. Money and arms continued to be received by Fatah from other sources too.

Recruitment for Asifa was slow, and Fatah had to hire thugs, devoid of all ideological motivation, from refugee camps to carry out terrorist raids into Israel, the first of which occurred in January 1965. For secrecy and security the Fatah leaders adopted aliases; Arafat's was Abu Amar and Khalil al-Wazir's was Abu Jihad. The first Fatah raid into Israel had been planned for the 31st December 1964, when four small groups were to cross from the Lebanon to strike at four targets on the northern Israeli road network, but the Lebanese Government got to know of this and prevented the operation.[3] It was not until the 14th January 1965 that Fatah had its first success, operating from Jordan, when explosives were placed beneath the national water carrier near the village of Eilabun. Not wanting to attract reprisal raids, the Syrian Government insisted that guerillas must not cross into Israel from its territory: Fatah was, of course, the main and only effective guerilla force at this stage. On the 28th February a grain silo at Kfar Hess was destroyed by explosives. On the 3rd March

[1] UNRWA figures for Arab Palestinian refugees in camps in June 1966 were 700,000 in Jordan (400,000 on the West Bank), 300,000 in the Gaza Strip, 160,000 in the Lebanon and 136,000 in Syria. High birth rate and concealment of deaths, so that the family could retain the ration card, tended to cause confusion. Totals were reckoned to be somewhere between 1 million and 1·3 million.

[2] Fatah was the sponsoring and controlling political organization, and Asifa was its military, or guerilla arm, but the two terms gradually became synonymous. Both will be used, but latterly the word Fatah has been more usual for both.

[3] *The Sandstorm.*

Fatah attacked the desert village of Arad, and again on the following night. On the 25th May, in a Fatah raid on Ramat Hakovesh in the Sharon Valley, three Israelis were killed, and during the next night Fatah blew up a house in Afula. Arafat stated later that this was an experimental era, when Israeli defences and Arab public opinion were tested. According to Israeli sources, during 1965 there were 31 Fatah raids into Israel, of which 27 were from Jordanian territory, the remainder being from the Lebanon.

On the 27th May an Israeli force crossed into Jordan and destroyed Fatah staging camps in the area of Jenin and Kalkilya, allegedly in reprisal for a series of nine terrorist attacks from Jordanian territory. The Government had been unable to prevent Fatah establishing bases in Jordan near the Israeli border. Syria was jubilant, thinking that although the Israelis knew full well that the Syrians were sponsoring Fatah activity, the Israelis did not dare to attack their strong defences along the Syrian Heights, but instead chose weaker Jordan. This was the first Israeli reprisal raid into Jordan since the 1956 war, and the Syrian Government was delighted to embarrass King Hussein in this way. Relations between Syria and Jordan deteriorated badly over guerilla activities and reprisal raids.

Fatah's propaganda department worked hard and to good effect, claiming many fictitious successes for its Asifa, which were widely believed in the Arab world. The reputation of Fatah suddenly blossomed—here at last was a Fedayeen organization actually doing something other than making empty boasts.

In the early months of 1965 distrust and suspicion arose between Fatah leaders and the terrorists they employed, which made secrecy and aliases more than necessary; many of the hired thugs simply took their pay, went close to the Israeli border, buried their explosives and stayed where they were all night, returning the following dawn with glowing accounts of successes, of people killed and of damage done. This made Fatah communiqués even more false than was intended, causing such claims to be ridiculed by the Israelis, who frequently produced photographic proof of their total lack of foundation,

29

but the degree of Arab credulity was high as they were being told what they wanted to hear.

However, enough terrorists did infiltrate into Israel to cause its Government concern. They were countered by a network of warning devices and ambushes on the many footpaths near the borders, backed by strong fighting patrols. These measures proved to be reasonably effective, and of the terrorists who actually entered Israeli territory, few returned. Most were killed, often when they ran into ambush while trying to slip back across the frontier to safety. Others were captured, and having no special loyalty to Fatah ideals, willingly told all they knew in the hope of lenient treatment. In January 1965 the Syrian Government sponsored Fatah, which was placed under the wing of the Second Bureau, the main contact being a Palestinian, Mohammed Araka. For some months the Syrian Government had been undecided whether to back Fatah fully. With Araka's help more and better recruits, with ideological motives, were gained from the refugee camps and were drafted into Asifa units as they were trained, to replace the unreliable thugs. The Fatah doctrine remained firmly one that all joining must give up any political affiliations, that Fatah should stay outside all inter-Arab quarrels, and that it should have only one aim—to liberate Palestine.

Fatah raids continued at intervals from Jordan, but on the 1st June 1965, Asifa personnel crossed from the Lebanon for the first time to blow up a house in Yiftah. Generally, Fatah chose random targets of no strategic importance. Often little damage was done and loss of life and injuries were comparatively small, the object being to strike at the enemy to keep tension high and to provoke retaliation. In 1966 Fatah went from strength to strength, raiding into Israel with increasing frequency and provoking more reprisals. Its popularity rating with the Arab masses rose even higher. In February 1966, in Syria, a coup by General Salah Jadid brought to power an extreme left-wing government, which decided to give Fatah more support and more freedom of movement. In July Fatah came completely under Syrian control, there being just one small armed clash in protest, in which four Fatah men were killed. For the time being at least Arafat and his colleagues thought it best to forget some of their principles of independence from all Arab governments. Fatah remained under the Second Bureau, the Syrian Chief of Staff took a special interest in it, and during the summer and autumn regular officers organized Asifa units, planned their missions and supplied arms, explosives and intelligence. A sabotage training school was established near the Sea of Galilee. The fighting strength of Asifa rose to about 500 by the eve of the third Arab-Israeli War.[1] The majority of the terrorists still penetrated Israel by way of Jordan, the mood of the people in that country and their enthusiasm for the Fedayeen mystique deterring King Hussein from ordering his army to take strict preventive measures.

In October a unit of Fatah moved briefly into the Judean Hills, just south of Jerusalem, and in a series of sorties blew up a house near Jerusalem, derailed a train, mined roads and shot up settlements. The Syrian Government anxiously expected that this time Israel would at last strike at the Fedayeen camps in Syrian territory, the basic source of the terrorist campaign. But this did not happen, and once again the Israelis struck at Jordan. On the 13th November they assaulted the small southern town of Samu, about four miles from the border, near where two days previously two Israelis had been killed by a mine. The Israelis' primary objective was to destroy buildings, but a company of Jordanian soldiers in trucks, supposing that the Israelis were attacking a village a short distance away, ran into the assaulting force and 15 Jordanian soldiers were killed. A six week lull followed, but Syria's hope to embroil Jordan and expose it to Israeli retaliation was being realized. During the last week in December and the first week of January (1967) there was a series of explosions in Jordanian Government buildings, which King Hussein suspected were caused by Syrian-based Fedayeen. At the subsequent elections in April he did not allow any party groupings, except for the Muslim Brotherhood, still dominated by the ex-Mufti of Jerusalem, who was antagonistic to Ahmed Shukairy's PLO.

For months President Nasser ignored Fatah activities as he felt that the major task of uniting the Arabs and launching

[1] Frequently referred to as the Six Day War, as it was of that duration, or as the June War.

them against the Israelis should be his alone; eventually he too had to praise them cautiously, but he refused to allow Fatah to establish itself or to operate from Egyptian territory. He also kept a tight rein on his Egyptian-sponsored PLA units in the Gaza Strip, holding them in check. The only element of this organization to make a few timid forays into Israel was the Syrian-based one, probably over 100 strong, operating through Jordan with negligible success. But the governments of the Lebanon and Jordan pronounced against Fatah activities, both were unwilling to have them on their territory, and both detained Fatah personnel, but the Jordanian Government was forced to release its prisoners because of popular outcry in their favour in Amman. Both governments slowly began to lose control of the Fedayeen movement within their territories. Since February 1966 Fatah had been openly publishing its own newspaper, *Saut al-Asifa*, the 'Voice of the Storm', in Damascus, which was widely distributed and eagerly read in the Arab world.

Endeavouring to cash in on the wave of hysterical Fedayeen popularity, other groups tried to emulate Fatah and form guerilla arms. Syria, which now, apart from harbouring a detachment of Shukairy's PLA and Fatah, also had elements of the National Liberation Front, a Baathist-sponsored organization[1] which believed that the Palestine problem could only be solved by first overthrowing reactionary Arab régimes, which in its view meant most of them. Other Fedayeen groups in Syria included the Abdul Kader Commando,[2] the Heroes of the Return to the Homeland, and one or two others—all small and ineffective. When the Syrian Government took control of Fatah, the head of Military Intelligence became associated with the National Liberation Front, and an army officer was appointed to co-ordinate the movements of all Fedayeen in Syria to ensure some measure of control. Efforts to bring unity of purpose and action amongst the Fedayeen groups had little success. By the end of the year (1966) Fatah had become so popular that it heavily overshadowed all other organizations, causing President Nasser to become anxious in case its activities

[1] Led by Ali Bushnak, Ahmed Jabril and Fadil Shrur.
[2] Named after a hero who was killed in the 1948 war.

should provoke the war he did not want. On the other hand, Ahmed Shukairy, of the PLO, saw Fatah in the light of an ally in his personal, bitter feud that had arisen with King Hussein, and so in December he went to Damascus where he succeeded in obtaining an agreement for co-operation between his PLA and Fatah.

After the Samu Raid, Fatah incursions into Israel recommenced on the 28th December, and became more frequent. Eventually the Israelis were provoked into hitting back at the Syrians. On the 7th April 1967, after an exchange of fire between artillery and tanks on both sides, an air battle developed in which six Syrian aircraft were shot down. By this time a Fatah incident was occurring inside Israel almost every day; during the first fortnight in May, while President Nasser was practising his fatal brinkmanship, there was at least one every day.

Much to Fatah's delight, war seemed fast approaching, and during the last days of May its representatives toured universities in Europe urging Palestinian students to report for training to camps in Algeria. Many did, but conditions there were chaotic, and most students slipped back to their universities as soon as they could. Only about 100 stayed on to complete this military training, after which they were sent to Syria, to arrive just too late for the third Arab-Israeli War. The conflict between the Israelis and the Arabs, which Fatah had deliberately set out to provoke, erupted suddenly, but Fatah calculations that the Arabs would win were wrong—on the contrary, they lost with disastrous results.

When the third Arab-Israeli[1] war broke out, Shukairy put his PLA (which he falsely claimed to be 8,000 strong) under 'national command' of the countries the personnel happened to be in, which in practice meant Egypt and Syria. He specifically excepted Jordan. The Syrians sent their detachments, still about 100 strong, into Jordan with the Iraqi brigade on the 5th June, the first day of the war, to be attacked and scattered by Israeli aircraft during the first afternoon. In far off Peking Chou En-lai was able to do little more than send cables of congratulations to President Nasser, President Atassi of Syria, and Ahmed Shukairy, Chairman of the PLO.

[1] See *The Third Arab-Israeli War*, by Edgar O'Ballance.

C 33

In its 18 months of operations Fatah had been of great nuisance value to the Israelis, and of great morale value to the Arabs, carrying out sufficient real raids to give a degree of credence in Arab eyes to all its false claims, and so raised enthusiasm for the cult of the Fedayeen to a colossal height. It revived the dejected and depressed spirits of the Palestinian refugees, giving them fresh hope and new ideals—but all this was instantly quashed by the swift and unexpected (to the Arabs) Israeli victory. None of the other Fedayeen groups made any significant contribution to the escalation.

It is of interest to speculate that if it had not been for the Samu Raid and the April 1967 air battle with the Syrians there might not have been a war between the Arabs and the Israelis until a later date,[1] or possibly not at all. Some feel that the Israeli reprisal raids simply caused the Arabs momentarily to forget their own differences and turn together to face the common enemy, although there is not much evidence to support such a premise, but had there been no Israeli reprisal raids it is possible that the Arabs might have become so involved in squabbling and fratricidal strife that eventually Israel might have been pushed into the background, been overlooked and even forgotten. It is odd to think how the Fedayeen, and especially Fatah, might have developed into a sword that turned in the Arabs' hands.

[1] *The Road to War 1967*, Walter Laqueur.

# 2. The 'Fish' and the 'Sea'

It is an understatement to say that the swift, crushing defeat by the Israelis in the third Arab-Israeli War left the Arabs numbed, aghast and astonished. In their wildest moments of despair none had thought such a catastrophe would befall them and for a while, as if in a coma, they struggled for breath. As the shock began to wear off a few Arab intellectuals and leaders perceived, in view of the amount of territory the Israelis had forcibly occupied, that there might be a distinct probability of unlimited guerilla activity. Encouraged by the distant Chinese certain Arabs visualized emulating Mao Tse-tung and putting into practice his now-famous guerilla precepts, using the Arab cadres and guerilla fighters as the 'fish' that would be able to swim in the large 'sea' of the occupied Arab population, which would shelter, hide and supply them. Hitherto unable to assert much influence in the Middle East, the Chinese Government urged the Palestinian Arabs to take up Vietnam-type guerilla warfare, but as China was in the throes of the great cultural revolution it was not able to spare much time or attention or give any active assistance.

Israel now controlled almost 1·3 million Arabs, as owing to the speedy advances of the Israeli armed forces comparatively few had been able to escape, and indeed practically all the Arabs, both inhabitants and refugees, in the Gaza Strip had to remain where they were as there was no convenient Arab territory to which they could flee. To the east the much-publicized exodus of refugees from the West Bank into Jordan proper, across the broken Allenby Bridge, had been over-emphasized by the Israelis. Shortly afterwards an Israeli-held census revealed that only about 150,000 had fled across the River Jordan, and that the majority of these were already refugees from the 1948 War, who had come to be known by the Israelis as 'professional refugees'. Comparatively few of the inhabitants of the West Bank had left.

Guerilla aspirations were encouraged by political decisions taken at the Khartoum Conference, held from the 31st August to the 2nd September 1967, attended by President Nasser and other Arab heads of state. The main decisions were that there should be no recognition of Israel, no negotiation with Israel and no peace with Israel. To these widely accepted Arab principles Nasser added (in November) another, of 'no (outside) interference in the Palestine issue'. Defeat heightened disunity among the Arab states, and in particular there was a division over how the lost territories should be regained. The Algerian and Syrian view was that a 'people's revolutionary war' should be launched, but this was opposed by Nasser, who was an ardent, if unsuccessful exponent of conventional warfare. The Syrian Baathist Party insisted that 'Popular revolutionary war was the only way to counter the Zionist challenge ... that traditional wars exhausted the material resources of the Arabs, while popular war exhausts the enemy'. Nasser persuaded the majority to reject this view, and the Syrians abruptly left the conference. Despite President Nasser's repudiation, it was fairly obvious that some form of guerilla warfare was the only means the Arabs had of hitting back at Israel, as their armies were shaken and ineffectual.

Anxious to find a peaceful Middle East solution, after much argument the Security Council of the United Nations, on the 22nd November 1967, passed a resolution which aimed at bringing together the Arabs and the Israelis at the conference table; it also vaguely asked the Israelis to withdraw from the Arab territory they had occupied in June, in return for Arab recognition of Israel. A Swedish diplomat, Gunnar Jarring, was appointed UN representative charged with this task, but neither the Israelis nor the Arabs would make the first move, or even give a sign of slackening their rigid attitudes. The 'November Resolution'[1] was a sterile talking point for many, many months. In November President Nasser made his first major speech after the June War over Radio Cairo: he was bellicose and reiterated the Four Principles.

Backed by the Arab League, and led by Ahmed Shukairy, the PLO had been singularly ineffective during the June War, and its Arab League subsidy of about £15 million was abruptly cut off after it. Both the PLO and its military arm, the PLA, were discredited; they had taken no effective action, had no influence on events at all, issued many irresponsible statements, and now the leaders quarrelled amongst themselves. Shukairy's conduct in the June War was undistinguished: on the first day (5th June) he quickly left the Old City of Jerusalem, going first to Amman, where he lingered hardly at all, and then to Damascus where he stayed. After the war he advised all Arab states to leave the UN, and said that the headquarters of the PLA would be transferred to the Israeli-occupied territories so that Israel would have no excuse for attacking any Arab country which harboured elements of it. But this was merely for public consumption and did not mean anything as he was fast losing control and any influence he had.

The PLO began to fall to pieces. Towards the end of the year Shukairy was ousted from its leadership, as were the majority of his nominees within the organization, by pressure from various Arab governments which felt he had badly let them down. His place was taken provisionally by Yahya Hamouda, who was strongly influenced by Algerian methods. Shukairy sank into obscurity, and later (in May 1971) published his apologia, which he called Dialogues and Secrets with Kings (in Beirut in Arabic). In it he defended his notorious demand 'to liquidate the state of Israel and throw the Jews into the sea'[2] as being the accepted view then of the Arab heads of state, Arab politicians, who had since turned on him and prised him from office and the Arab press.

The PLA, which once boasted a strength of over 8,000, decayed and splintered. The larger element, which was in Egypt, remained inert in the Suez Canal region, under control

[1] Also referred to as (Security Council) Resolution 242.
[2] The New Middle East, July 1971.

of Egyptian officers, while that in Syria split into two parts. One was dissolved briefly, but reappeared shortly afterwards as the Popular Liberation Force, which for a time was vaguely under Arab League influence, but gradually came under Syrian dominance. The other part, retaining the title of PLA, was placed under the command of a Syrian officer, Major Abdul Razzak Yahya; Egyptian officers were removed from it. Both parts were small, totalling less than 300 men, but after a few months the strength increased. The Egyptian element of the PLA, which remained about 4,000 strong, and that in Syria, were both nominally under the control of the PLO.

Favouring Vietnam-style guerilla warfare, despite disapproval from other Arab states, the Syrian Government, concluding that no Arab country would be militarily strong enough to defeat Israel in open battle for at least five years, took the lead in recruiting, training and launching guerillas into the occupied territories—but the concept and aim were changed. The pre-June policy, of using guerillas to provoke open war by escalation, ceased; there were to be no more 'hit and run' commando raids, but instead the guerillas were to infiltrate into the occupied territories and carry out subversive warfare on the Viet Cong pattern. Discussions were held between the Syrian Chief of Staff and Yasir Arafat, the Fatah leader, and plans were evolved for future operations.

Fatah still had only a small number of trained and armed guerilla fighters, perhaps less than 500, and so large-scale recruitment was carried out in the Palestinian refugee camps in Syria, sponsored by the Syrian Government. Training camps, staffed by regular Syrian military personnel, were established near Damascus, Fatah members scattered abroad in Europe and Algeria were recalled, and arms, ammunition and equipment were provided by the Syrians. Fatah was quick off the mark in one respect, and during the last two weeks in June (1967) its personnel went into parts of the Sinai desert collecting arms and ammunition abandoned by the retreating Egyptians, before the Israeli salvage squads even got to work. Quantities collected included machine-guns, bazookas, grenades and explosives. Fatah also established contact with the Bedu and professional smugglers, and bought from them abandoned weapons they discovered—a traffic that continued for some years.

June and July were months of preparation and infiltration into the occupied territories, during which Fatah endeavoured to establish new guerilla underground networks to replace those which had been swept away in the June War. Dozens of trained Fatah members moved into the West Bank. Some, it was reported, carried translations of Viet Cong training manuals. They tried to set up in villages cells designed to provide information and food for small groups, whose task was to attack Israeli forces and to disrupt life generally, which they next wanted to maintain in the hills. Fearing armed Israeli retaliation, Syria took care not to implicate itself openly, and blatantly used next-door Jordan as a guerilla route to the occupied territories. A unit of the Iraqi army,[1] formed of Palestinian recruits, had been infiltrated by Fatah members anxious to obtain military training and experience, and immediately after the June War it had moved into northern Jordan as part of the Iraqi expeditionary force. Its trucks were used to transport Fatah men, weapons and stores from Syria into Jordan, from where they slipped across the river into the occupied West Bank by night. Several hundred Fatah members travelled along this underground route in July and August.

By August Fatah was ready to act. Its primary aim was to instigate revolt among Arabs on the West Bank, but such guerilla activity as occurred in the occupied territories until September was merely of minor irritation to the Israeli security forces. At the end of that month more Fatah members had arrived. The number of subversive incidents increased, causing the Israelis to mount a security offensive, which lasted for three months, with the aim of rooting out the guerillas. In their swift advance the Israelis had seized Jordanian intelligence and police files and records, and so were able to detect many agents as they were sent back to the West Bank. A few resident Palestinians had been involved in these Fatah cells, but not so many. Deprived of the support of the cells in the villages the

---

[1] According to *The Sandstorm* it was the 421st Battalion.

small guerilla groups hidden away in the hills not only found it difficult to operate but difficult to escape capture and survive the constant sweeps made by the Israeli security forces. Generally the villagers wanted nothing to do with the guerillas as they feared and were inconvenienced by Israeli retaliatory measures, which included demolitions, curfews and restriction of movement, and so they were reluctant to pass on information, provide food or give shelter to the Fedayeen. By November the majority of Fatah personnel on the West Bank had been either killed, captured or driven back across the River Jordan. This projected Fedayeen 'second phase' of the 'fish and the sea' concept of establishing guerillas in the hills to terrorize the security forces never really got going.

The Israeli method of governing the occupied territories was to ignore all who derived their authority from Amman, such as ministers, senators, members of parliament and appointed officials (all of whom incidentally continued to draw their pay from the Jordanian Government) and instead to deal directly with such mayors (mukhtars) and municipal councils remaining at their posts. Especially on the West Bank the Israelis allowed them the maximum freedom to govern within the security restrictions, as moderate security measures kept the Arabs docile for a while. Conservative and practical, the West Bank inhabitants in particular were not keen on forming the 'sea' envisaged by the Fedayeen leaders; all wanted to be allowed to continue farming and trading as before and to avoid any Israeli blows of retribution. Many were collaborators, and many Fatah guerillas at this stage were given away by West Bank residents. One of the most prominent 'moderate' personalities was Sheikh Mohammed Ali Jabari, Mayor of Hebron, who was in favour of a West Bank state of some kind, although he prudently refrained from political comment. A former Jordanian Minister of Justice, he was early in contact with the Israeli authorities and would have liked to have been able to negotiate freely with them for his people, but the current Arab climate was unfavourable and he risked assassination.

Although the Israelis announced that they would permit certain refugees to return, generally under a 'uniting families' scheme, in practice they were extremely selective and would not allow any 'professional refugees' to come back into the occupied territories, as they were a disturbing factor. The Israeli Government considered only farmers, craftsmen, shopkeepers, traders and others who might contribute to the economy. By the end of September some 20,000 applications had been approved, although a great many more than that number had been received. In this way the Israelis were able to prevent many Fatah personnel entering the West Bank. However, at this juncture many refugees were reluctant to return, partly because they thought that the Arabs might soon drive the Israelis back again, when they would be branded as collaborators, and partly because they thought that they might be cut off from their money remitted by relatives who had jobs in the oilfields of Kuwait, Qatar and Saudi Arabia. There was a certain amount of formal contact and cross-frontier traffic between the occupied West Bank and Jordan. The Israelis encouraged the West Bank Arabs to farm and trade, but forbade them to sell their produce to the Israelis, who would have paid a higher price. Instead, the produce had to be exported to Jordan.

When the Egyptians hastily evacuated the Gaza Strip they left behind them not only fear and chaos, as with them went government officials, teachers and doctors, but economic collapse, as there was sudden and massive unemployment outside the refugee camps. Such organizations as the Egyptian army, the PLA and the UNEF had employed many local Arabs and spent sums of money locally. Even the previously profitable and tacitly permitted smuggling, which had become big business across the Israeli border, was abruptly terminated. Money received from relatives abroad helped to sustain many Arab families, but it had to be channelled through Israeli banks, and Israeli currency had to be used. The Arabs were encouraged to seek work on the West Bank, whose economy was left in much better shape after the June War, and indeed even farther afield.[1] This was the first occasion when they were allowed to travel outside the Gaza Strip, as the Egyptians had strictly controlled such movement.

About half of the approximately 300,000 refugees were

[1] To prevent them going to the East Bank, Jordan closed its bridges over the River Jordan.

41

clustered into eight main camps,[1] the remainder in smaller, scattered ones and on the fringes of the towns and villages. They were still under their local leaders (mukhtars) who had been responsible for them since before the 1948 War, and who retained considerable influence as it was they who received and distributed UNRWA ration cards. Since 1948 these refugees had sunk deeper into a mood of hopeless despair and lassitude. No one seemed to care about them, little was done for them, they had no social life and no newspapers, their only information and stimulation coming from Radio Cairo. However, Fatah had more success in penetrating the Gaza Strip than the West Bank, and managed to establish cells in this crowded area. During the latter part of 1967 there were demonstrations and terrorist incidents, mainly of a minor character, which the Israelis countered by curfews, arrests and by occasionally demolishing houses.

The Israelis announced that in the six months following the June War they killed 63 armed guerillas and captured over 350, while in the month of December they arrested another 54 Fedayeen agents operating in the West Bank. During this period there had been many incidents, and a degree of terrorism lingered on, but the Israelis claimed that owing to the measures they had taken there had been no major street demonstrations or civil disobedience campaigns, and that acts of terrorism had been isolated and sporadic, all of which was largely true. It was painfully obvious to Fedayeen leaders that the 'sea' was unwilling to allow the 'fish' to swim in it, and also that the 'fishermen' were quite expert. The Fedayeen attempt to instigate Viet Cong and Algerian-type revolutionary warfare in the occupied territories had failed, and the Israeli appreciation was that despite advantages, the failure was due to the fact that the guerillas had not been able to win the minds of the resident Palestinian Arabs and convert them to their cause whole-heartedly.

The Fatah leadership, never keen on revolutionary or people's warfare and tending to favour infiltration or commando tactics,

[1] These were (from north to south) Jabalia (36,000); Shati or Beach Camp (27,000); Nuseirat (16,000); Burej (9,000); Maghazi (7,000); Deir el-Balah (7,000); Khan Yunis (24,000) and near Rafah (39,000).

saw that it was time to change strategy. Already in November it had established staging camps close to the east bank of the River Jordan, from which small groups of guerillas slipped over into the occupied territories by night to carry out acts of terrorism and sabotage and then return. The Israelis erected wire fences, put up detection devices on known crossing routes, and patrolled the west bank of the river, but they were unable to seal the border completely. For example, on one occasion guerillas penetrated far enough into Israel to lob mortar bombs into Petah Tikva. With only the River Jordan to cross to be in Israeli occupied territory, most of the infiltrations were in that sector; small, crude rafts on tractor tyres or oil drums were frequently used, while the frontiers with Syria and the Lebanon were comparatively quiet. In the extreme south a few Fedayeen made the journey across the northern Negev along smugglers' trails to raid towards Beersheba, but not so many, as most of the incidents in the southern part of Israel and Israeli occupied territory emanated from refugee camps in the Gaza Strip or by way of the Hebron area.

In retaliation the Israelis began to hit back with artillery fire at the Fedayeen staging camps on the east bank of the river, unleashing a particularly heavy barrage in the last week in November because Israeli patrols had been sniped at from Jordanian territory. After this, as the Jordanian army frequently provided covering fire to enable returning guerillas to recross the river, artillery duels developed and became commonplace. During December Fatah incidents included sabotaging a reservoir in a Galilee kibbutz, cutting the railway line near Jerusalem and derailing a passenger train near Beersheba, while two guerillas were killed resisting arrest in a cave near Jerusalem and a small group shot it out with the Israeli security forces near Lydda airport. Houses that harboured guerillas, or were used by them, were demolished by the Israelis, a small village on the West Bank, a suspected guerilla staging point, being levelled to the ground, while in the Gaza Strip, for the murder of an Israeli, ten houses were demolished in the village of Deir el-Balah.

Fatah issued boastful communiqués, making many fictitious claims of casualties inflicted and damage done. Its threat that

Christians would not be safe in Jerusalem and Bethlehem at Christmas time caused the Israelis to take extra precautions, but all passed off without incident and, indeed, some 40,000 Israelis visited the Tomb of the Patriarchs[1] in Hebron.

In Jordan King Hussein was trying to rebuild and re-equip his armed forces after his disastrous defeat. Early in October he visited Moscow to make contact—a ploy to encourage more aid from the West—but nothing happened and he returned with neither arms nor a pact of any sort.[2] In November he visited America but the result was similar, and indeed he did not have a single operational combat plane. To assist him in case of Israeli aggression an Iraqi expeditionary force of divisional strength[3] had moved into northern Jordan; it was composed of four brigades, one of which was camped outside Amman for a while. Among Arab leaders there was talk of forming an eastern front against Israel, based on Jordan and Syria, to which Arab states would send contingents of troops, but there was hesitation. Only Iraq moved soldiers in number, although there were two Saudi Arabian brigades in southern Jordan. Along the border, within sight and shot of the Israelis, the Jordanian Army was in position and patrolling. With nervous trigger-fingers on both sides there were several incidents and spasmodic rumbles of gunfire across the River Jordan. During the latter half of 1967 the Jordanian soldiers were in sympathy with the Fedayeen who infiltrated into Israel, and frequently used their weapons to help them return.

King Hussein had lost the richer half of his kingdom, and his tourist trade. His economy came to a halt, but he still had a good currency reserve, estimated to be over £100 million, and he had been promised another £40 million annually by Saudi Arabia, Kuwait and Libya. Despite the fact that he was burdened by an extra 150,000 refugees from the West Bank, who had flooded into his country in a disorganized mass, adding

[1] The traditional tombs of Abraham, Isaac and Jacob, which had been a mosque.

[2] A Soviet-Jordanian trade agreement was signed on the 20th January 1969.

[3] Reports of its strength vary from 12,000 to 15,000; it probably fluctuated between these two estimates.

unproductively to the some 300,000 who had been there since 1948, he slowly got the economy moving again. At first most of the fresh refugees were herded into tented camps, many around the capital, but in the autumn a number were moved down into the Jordan Valley to avoid the harshness of winter, where they suffered from unusual storms and floods, so many drifted back to their original makeshift camps.

Hussein's additional problem became that of the Arab Fedayeen organizations whose members, encouraged by Syria, then hostile to Jordan, began to move into Jordan, openly setting up headquarters and offices in the capital, towns and refugee camps, collecting funds and recruiting. Fatah already had staging and training camps in Jordan, and was gaining a grip on certain refugee camps. The Syrian Government encouraged Fatah, which it heavily influenced, to expand and raid into Israel from Jordan, which gave Hussein anxious moments. During 1967 he was able to keep Fedayeen activities within bounds, but owing to the ever-growing popularity of the Fedayeen mystique, restrictions had to be applied discreetly. Fatah refused to become involved in Arab politics or quarrels, and so was in a fairly strong position, Arafat at this period often saying: 'One enemy at a time is enough'.

In the first weeks of 1968 Fatah infiltration into Israel sharply increased until by the end of February the Israelis alleged that there had been 91 incidents that year. Although they claimed that 80 per cent of the guerillas were either killed or captured, enough real damage was done to cause alarm. This provoked the Israelis to retaliate along a 60-mile front, stretching from Jericho to the Sea of Galilee, with mortars, guns and tanks firing into Jordan, and in the resulting seven-hour battle Israeli aircraft came into action using rockets, phosphorous bombs and napalm. Alarmed, and fearing this could escalate, King Hussein asked for a ceasefire as his army was in no state to stand up to that of Israel in battle, and one was arranged by the American Ambassador to Jordan. The Israelis claim to have destroyed a Fatah base, damaged several towns, terrorized refugee camps and knocked out Jordanian guns as far inland as Irbid, 20 miles from the border.

Moshe Dayan, the Israeli Defence Minister, said that the

object had been to teach the Jordanians that a 'cease-fire was a cease-fire and that it applied to Jordan'. The inference was that the Jordanian Government must control the guerillas within its borders or suffer the consequences. Chastened, King Hussein announced over Radio Amman[1] that he would try to prevent the Fedayeen using Jordanian territory as a base, saying that 'I shall not allow anyone to supply the enemy with pretexts and justification for aggression'. This was easier said than done and almost immediately, prompted by the Syrian Government (which would still not allow the guerillas to operate across its own border with Israel), Fatah announced from Damascus that it would continue raiding into the Israeli occupied territories. Fatah still had only a few hundred armed and trained fighters, but thousands were volunteering for service with the Fedayeen.

Terrorist incident followed terrorist incident until the 21st March 1968, when the exasperated Israelis mounted a large operation against the Fatah base at Karameh, with a subsidiary thrust south of the Dead Sea. A few days previously a bomb had exploded in Jerusalem and a school bus near Eilat had run over a mine, when two adults were killed and 28 children injured. Moshe Dayan had again warned that Israel would hit back if King Hussein could not control the guerillas in his country. At dawn Israeli helicopters moved off from near Jericho carrying troops who were put down in blocking positions around Karameh, and then the main body, of brigade strength in half-tracks and supported by Centurions, advanced into Jordan across the Damiya and Allenby Bridges, under a creeping artillery barrage. When barely a mile inside Jordan the Israeli tanks were met and held by Jordanian armour, and half the attacking force was pinned down. The other half sheered off and raced towards Karameh, a further two miles where, forewarned, some 2,000 guerillas, the majority in training, were quickly pulled back from the town to take up positions in the surrounding hills, while a hardcore of about 200 others stayed in Karameh and fired back at the Israelis as they approached. Unable to advance, after several attempts the attackers were forced into a fighting withdrawal. The result

[1] Television did not start in Jordan until June 1968.

46

of the 15-hour battle at Karameh was that while the Israelis claimed to have killed about 110 guerillas, they lost 23 dead and suffered 70 wounded, as well as losing one aircraft[1] and 'several tanks and half-tracks'. Although the main clash was with the Fedayeen, the Jordanian army took part, and its tanks had halted those of Israel.

The smaller, southern thrust from the area of Sodom was also preceded by troops lifted forward by helicopters and put down in blocking positions, while three small units in half-tracks and also supported by Centurions made respectively for the large villages of Safi, Feifa and Dahal, all Fatah bases, just inside Jordanian territory south of the Dead Sea, which they overran, killing in the process about 20 guerillas before withdrawing.

The battle of Karameh was an early and prominent milestone in the Palestinian Arab struggle for power, and the event has since been commemorated as a national day in Jordan. Fatah claimed it as an outstanding victory, and made great propaganda capital from it. Two days later foreign journalists were invited into Karameh by Fatah, where they saw hundreds of guerillas dressed in the soon-to-become-familiar camouflaged combat suits, carrying arms, and openly and casually walking about the town. After this battle King Hussein was compelled to praise the Fedayeen and their aims, which he had not done so far, and to restrain his criticism of them. He uttered the words 'I am becoming a guerilla', but perhaps without much conviction.

King Hussein had not wanted to clash with the Israelis and some Jordanian gunners had opened fire during the battle against orders. It is doubtful exactly what part he intended his armoured unit to play, if any, as he was still not sure of the loyalty of certain elements of his army. Probably it was there only to deter the Israelis and contain the guerillas training at Karameh, and its involvement in the fighting was involuntary. Only a fortnight previously the Jordanian army had tried to persuade Fatah to leave Karameh, but the soldiers had been warned off at gun point, so the Jordanian tanks may have been more anxious about the guerillas than the Israelis. Fatah was

[1] At this time the Jordanians had no combat aircraft, while the Israelis made ample use of theirs in this battle.

doubly jubilant, partly because it had met and held the Israeli army in battle, being the first Arab force to do so since the June War, and partly because it had won its first clash with Jordanian authority. Basically the Fatah victory had been one of prestige and morale, as it quickly moved its staging and training camps, which had been just inside the Jordanian frontier, back some distance beyond the immediate reach of such massive Israeli reprisal raids.

On the Israeli side there was disappointment and criticism, as they had failed to wipe out a Fedayeen base, which had been their objective, and the raid had been far more costly than anticipated. A crack had appeared in the smooth military reputation of the Israeli soldier, continually advancing against the Arabs, which reached its peak in the June War. Also, the Israelis had to admit that their estimate that massive retaliatory raids would compel Arab governments to control guerilla activities in, or from, their territories, was not realistic, if only because weak military régimes, such as that of Jordan, were incapable of physically bringing them under control. Because of the amount of force used, the raid at Karameh cost the Israelis a degree of world sympathy.

# 3. Fedayeen Expansion

The battle of Karameh was a significant turning point, marking the end of the initial stages of the Fedayeen struggle. The first, that of revolutionary guerilla warfare, had failed; the second, which had been one of preparation, had been more successful. In this latter phase the guerillas had concentrated upon establishing training centres, obtaining money and arms, gaining political influence and searching for freedom of movement in host Arab countries. The third phase, one of rapid expansion, was about to begin. Dressed in a camouflaged combat suit, with an obsolescent Soviet AK-47 rifle in his hands the Fedayeen fighter became the instant hero of the Arab world. A blaze of publicity exploded and journalists were invited to the headquarters of the various Fedayeen organizations, especially to Fatah where Arafat showed a flair for publicity and an ability to take full advantage of the hysteria of the moment.

Money poured in from well-wishers in such volume that Fatah had to employ accountants to handle it. More arms were purchased as well as other equipment, such as medical supplies, although much of the latter was donated. Such was the financial strength of Fatah that it was able to give pensions to dependants of Fedayeen fighters killed in action. In the month of March (1968) alone a drive for funds in the Lebanon brought in over £200,000, while in Kuwait a 5 per cent tax was levied on the salaries of all Palestinian employees and handed over to the Fedayeen; even Saudi Arabia contributed, mainly because it hoped that Fatah was above inter-Arab squabbles. Algeria gave cash to Fatah because it seemed to be the only guerilla organiza-

D

tion that was achieving anything, and also because at first its methods were modelled on those of the Front de Libération Nationale, the FLN.

This sudden popularity and publicity caused a rush of volunteers to join the Fedayeen movement, more than the organizations could absorb and train, and for a while only limited numbers were accepted according to the arms and training facilities available. Large numbers were nominally put on a 'waiting list', and pressed into a supporting body to carry out non-combatant tasks until there were vacancies in the training camps. Thus gradually developed the Fedayeen militia, vaguely resembling the Chinese civilian militia. The Fedayeen descended on the Palestinian refugee camps, especially in Jordan, and certain organizations began to gain influence in, and then to dominate individual ones. As they became stronger and more confident they took over the running of the camps, even to the point of excluding UNRWA officials and the Jordanian security forces. Although throughout 1968 the guerillas were not anxious for a test of strength with the Jordanian Government, they pushed as far as they could, and then demanded more freedoms. Guerilla strengths were always suspect, frequently being grossly inflated for political reasons. Accurate estimates are almost impossible to make, but it is thought that up to the battle of Karameh there were little more than 600 armed and trained fighters. The majority were under Fatah control, with perhaps just over 3,000 (again the majority being Fatah) more in training or actively participating in some way. These figures excluded the PLA. Almost overnight the total strength shot up to 12,000 or more, and by the end of the year Fedayeen fighters must have numbered over 20,000.

The main Fedayeen organizations were now Fatah, the PLA, the Front for the Liberation of Palestine, the PFLP, and the Saiqa, but there were about eight or nine smaller ones, such as the Syrian Popular Liberation Force, a splinter from the old PLA. At least half-a-dozen other small guerilla bodies appeared during the course of the year, but for the small fry the going was hard as they were overshadowed by the larger organizations that wanted to gobble them up or eliminate them, there being considerable rivalry between the groups. Not all the small ones survived.

After the battle of Karameh, Fatah moved its headquarters from Damascus to Amman, where Arafat concentrated upon creating a large politically inspired military force. Asifa for a while retained its old organization, operating in groups of 40 to 50 fighters, although smaller formations had to be used to infiltrate into Israel. Now able to attract a better type of individual, the hired thug was dispensed with, and Asifa was soon composed of a large proportion, perhaps half, of intellectuals, teachers, professional men, graduates and students, all of whom were idealists, and who included a number of girls. The remainder were enthusiastic young men from the refugee camps, selected for physical fitness, intelligence and political dedication. After a basic course of instruction, they had carried out short periods of active duty on a rotary basis, usually a month at a time, with Asifa in the field, and then returned to their civilian occupations, which had been a convenient system, economically necessary, while Fatah was short of funds and arms. New-found affluence changed this, and by the end of 1968 most Asifa fighters were full-time members. The removal of the restricting financial disadvantage enabled a large 'regular force' to be formed and trained, and for the reserve, the Fedayeen militia, also to be developed. Many of the confusing discrepancies in Fatah strength estimates were due to the blurring of the demarcation between the regular Asifa and the Fedayeen militia.

Secrecy had been an essential part of the Fatah movement, especially when host Arab countries were suspicious of its political motives, and also for the safety of the leadership from the thug element within. Hostility and fear of other guerilla groups were other reasons for secrecy, but after the battle of Karameh this was relaxed among the leadership to a degree, interviews were given to the Press, leaders appeared on television and prominent figures appeared in public with their Fedayeen bodyguards. Partial secrecy was retained as to the movements and locations of leaders and units, in case governments arrested any of them or wanted to curb them; junior leaders and rank-and-file were discouraged from seeking individual publicity. For example, Fatah contained former members of the Muslim Brotherhood and its sympathisers, and so was regarded with suspicion by President Nasser,[1] and also by the Syrian Baathist Government.

The PLA brigade in Egypt, about 4,000 strong, was kept static under Nasser's firm hand. A few of its personnel were used in sabotage operations in the Suez Canal region in the Sinai, but they were given little scope or publicity. The PLA brigade in Syria, under Syrian officers, was also static, as was the smaller formation in Iraq, all of which were nominally under the control of the PLO, but in fact were rigidly restricted by the governments of the countries they were in.

Syria remained the main host country for Palestinian guerillas, giving some arms and money and plenty of encouragement to raid into Israel through Jordan. Until the battle of Karameh it had been largely able to call the tune, as Fatah was almost completely dependent upon it in so many ways. But restraints irked Fatah and were contrary to its declared policy of not being tied to any Arab country or its policies[2] and it had been restless for some time. Sensing the independent spirit that was heightened by popularity, and realizing that Fatah was no longer a servile suitor but had to be humoured, the Syrian Baathist Government formed a Fedayeen organization of its own as a counter-balance. This became known as the Saiqa (the Storm), and Palestinian Baathists were recruited from refugee camps, armed and trained by the regular army. Saiqa was led by regular officers, and by mid-1968 had about 400 men in the field, with twice as many in training. Syria also controlled the small Popular Liberation Force, but it was deliberately kept ineffective. Soon detachments of Saiqa were sent into the Jordan Valley, ostensibly to raid into Israel, but also to be an embarrassment to King Hussein, who was in dispute with the Syrian Government.

The other principal organization was the Popular Front for

---

[1] When he came to power in Egypt in 1954 Nasser arrested some 18,000 members of the Muslim Brotherhood, and later, in 1965, made another 6,000 arrests of members of this movement.

[2] Then defined as being to 'create a democratic Palestinian and Jewish state in which Arabs and Jews would enjoy equal rights'.

the Liberation of Palestine, the PFLP, which was quite small but extremely virile and determined. It was formed in 1967 by George Habash, a Christian Palestinian Arab and a veteran Marxist. Habash had been involved in political subversion since the 1948 War, after which he moved to the Lebanon to found the Arab Nationalist Movement, the ANM, sometimes known as the 'Haraka', from its full title of Haraka al-Quamiy-yin al-Arab. This was a nationalist, pro-Nasser organization, reputedly financed by Egypt and alleged to have contacts with Egyptian intelligence sources. Through it Habash worked to help President Nasser achieve Arab unity, but although its leadership was in general accord with this policy, the ANM had tended to become somewhat Marxist in character. Habash was disliked and distrusted by both the Syrian and Iraqi Baathists, and had indeed been imprisoned by the Iraqis for alleged involvement in an attempted coup by Aref Abdul Razzak against President Aref in Baghdad in July 1966.

Moving into Jordan after the June War, Habash formed the PFLP as the guerilla arm to his ANM, setting up its head-quarters in Amman, but it made a slow start as Habash and two of his principal lieutenants were arrested while on a visit to Damascus. Later they were rescued by PFLP personnel who attacked their escort when Habash was being taken from the prison to visit a dentist. Largely for this reason the PFLP did not expand as rapidly as did its main rival, Fatah.

Arafat worked and schemed to unite all the diverse guerilla organizations under his leadership, and was able to persuade 13 of them to come to a meeting chaired by himself in Cairo on the 20th January 1968. Some of these groups were small, others were splinters and most were mainly political, with negligible guerilla forces. The PLO was not represented as it was going through a soul-searching time under the temporary leadership of Yahya Hamouda, after having jettisoned Shu-kairy. A representative of the PFLP did attend, but soon withdrew from the meeting, loudly expressing the view that Fatah was too nationalistic and parochial. As it was largely supported by nationalists and sympathizers of the Muslim Brotherhood, Fatah was naturally in conflict and disagreement with the Marxist PFLP and other left-wing Arab political organizations. This left Arafat with his strong Fatah support in a dominant position, and under his encouragement those who remained at the conference agreed that they were not interested in merely avenging the June War but in regaining the whole of Palestine, expressing the belief that this could be done only 'with guns'.

Despite deep political differences, Arafat continued to work to bring the guerilla groups together. On the 20th March he succeeded in getting the leaders of the PLO and the PFLP to meet him, and he was on the point of persuading them to take steps to unify political and military activity when he was overtaken by events—the battle of Karameh occurred the following day. In its aftermath of guerilla glory each of the major organizations saw an opportunity for individual expansion, and in this mad rush for power, none had any time or quarter for the other.

Arafat then began to move in to take over the shattered remnants of the PLO. His men seized by force its offices, not only in the Middle East but also in Europe and elsewhere, but continued to operate them in the name of the PLO. By sheer political acumen, energy and initiative Arafat's men infiltrated into the PLO framework and soon were occupying key positions, the virtually leaderless and aimless organization being unable to put up any effective individual resistance. Arafat and his nominees stepped in to provide the motivation that brought the PLO to life again as a political force in the Arab world. It was due to his efforts that in July the Palestinian National Council, a kind of impromptu governing body without executive powers, was formed. It had 115 seats,[1] of which Fatah took 40.

The Palestinian National Council, the PNC, met in Cairo from the 10th to the 17th July, after which it issued what became known as the Palestine National Covenant. This stated that the only way to liberate Palestine was by means of an armed struggle, and that Fedayeen action formed the basis of this struggle. The slogan adopted for the Palestinian people was that of 'national unity, mobilization and liberation'.[2]

[1] The number of seats varied in the ensuing years, but sometimes 'observers' were included in the total quoted.

[2] The *New Middle East* of March 1970.

54

There was discussion on whether an 'Arab Palestine' should be altered to a 'Democratic Palestine', and some argument as to the future status of the Jews. This meeting revealed many shades of political opinion within Fatah. It was fairly broadly based, and some elements would not accept the Palestine National Covenant in its entirety. The PNC announced that it would set up a Co-ordinating Council, to be comprised of military representatives from each guerilla group, but this was still a dream of the future, as each wilfully went its own way. Arafat had gained much influence, but sought more. Especially did he covet the PLO seat on the Arab League and the subsidy the Arab League had given the PLO before the June War, but as yet the suspicious Arab heads of state, who still called the financial tune, would allow him neither.

The PLA formation in Syria (the Kadesiyeh Brigade, as it became known), strictly under government control under regular seconded Syrian officers, was starved of weapons, equipment and money, and kept inactive, which displeased many younger officers who were anxious to make their names in battle. There were also other dissensions within this PLA brigade as some officers looked to the Baathist government, some to Arafat and others to President Nasser for inspiration and guidance. Discontent came to a head in August (1968) when a group of young officers arrested Colonel Abdul Razzak Yahya, the commander of the brigade, who had recently been appointed Chief of Staff of the PLA by the PLO, its sponsor organization. There were frequent differences between the PLO and the Syrian Government over senior appointments. This time, although the Syrian Government had some sympathy with the rebels, it had to back down, when Yahya was reinstated and a few junior officers were removed.

Arafat made a further unsuccessful attempt to establish a Co-ordinating Council within the PNC to bring the various guerilla organizations together in November. During the same month a Cairo announcement stated that a new guerilla organization was to be formed in the Sinai, to be sponsored by the Government, it being claimed that it was the first Arab government to sponsor officially a Fedayeen group. At this stage Syria still had not admitted its sponsorship of Saiqa. The

Egyptian group was to be called the Association of Arabs in the Sinai, the AAS, and it was no doubt hoped that they would be able to penetrate the Israeli Bar Lev Line along the Suez Canal and carry out sabotage operations behind the Israeli lines, but little came of this, it being merely an attempt by President Nasser to outshine the Syrian Saiqa, which as yet had done little. On the 20th November Asifa revealed that one of its leaders, Subhi Mohammed Yassin, had been murdered by his own men. He was the founder of the Fatah 'Commando Vanguards', an early name for part of the regular guerilla element. Details were not revealed but it was assumed that Fatah still contained an unreliable thug element.

Realizing Islamic antipathy to communism, the Soviet Union coldly ignored the several Arab communist parties, all of which were illegal in their own countries, and dealt directly with Arab governments in its quest for influence in the Middle East, but despite periodic bursts of generosity with money, aid and weapons, the Russians had yet to discover that Arab states would not devolve into complacent satellites, as had some East European countries. The Soviet view was that a four power agreement between the Soviet Union, America, Britain and France on the Middle East problem should be mediated by the United Nations, but none were interested. The approach of the other protagonist in the cold war was the opposite; America was committed to peace in the Middle East and held that Israel had a right to exist, but at the same time wanted better relations with the Arabs. Uneasiness was felt by the big powers that the Fedayeen, while owing allegiance to no Arab government, had the power to sting Israel into savage reprisals which could escalate. In December (1968) the Soviet Union urged a political settlement and stated for the first time that it would not permit a resumption of war in the Middle East.

As regards strategy, the Soviet Union thought that while small guerilla groups raiding into Israel might cause the Israelis some inconvenience, they would not force them to withdraw from the occupied territories but, on the contrary, might provoke another Arab-Israeli War, for which the Arabs were by no means ready. The Soviet General Staff silently disapproved of guerilla warfare, feeling that the main effort should always be to support regular forces. It noted that while Arab regular forces were under national control and susceptible to conventional pressures, the guerilla groups were not. The Russians wanted the guerillas to unite under some central form of control, preferably that of Egypt, so that President Nasser could reap a full harvest of the wave of Fedayeen popularity; but other Arab states disagreed, and Syria, for example, was determined to retain as much control over the guerillas as possible, thereby indirectly wielding a degree of supra-national influence.

Fatah had no direct contact with the Soviet Union, and through Arab governments had requested aid and recognition, but the Soviet riposte had always been to ask if any future Fatah state or government would veer towards the Soviet Union. Fatah would not commit itself. Also, the Soviet Government asked if Fatah contained any members of the Muslim Brotherhood, as that organization was in conflict with President Nasser, to which Fatah always diplomatically replied that its object was to freeze all ideological differences. The suspicious Soviet Union was not convinced or impressed, and gave no support or recognition, demanding that the Arabs place restrictions on 'undisciplined groups'. Fatah could not openly ask for Chinese aid for fear of alienating Kuwait and Saudi Arabia, which provided much of its funds.

After the battle of Karameh in March 1968 most of the Fedayeen camps were hastily drawn back from the east bank of the River Jordan to be more secure from Israeli commando raids. This now meant at least a two-night operation for guerillas to penetrate into Israel, and so they became more difficult to mount and carry out. As a counter the Israelis set ambushes on the frontier paths, and plotted the course of Arab intruders so as to be able to trap them on their return journey. The Israelis also erected a 40-mile electronic and wire fence barrier along the west bank of the river, its outer fence being 8 feet high and its inner one, some 11 yards back from it, 5 feet high, the space between them being mined. Sensory detection devices were placed at intervals, which turned on searchlights and warned detachments of soldiers, who could quickly be taken by helicopters to any point the Arabs were trying to penetrate. Gaps were deliberately left at certain places. Israeli successes were such that penetration into the West Bank was considered to be a form of 'guerilla suicide', but despite failures and heavy casualties Fedayeen raids continued. The bulk of such activities that occurred in 1968 were undertaken by Fatah fighters, but a few were carried out by members of the Syrian Saiqa, now established in the Jordan Valley, which was becoming more active.

The Fedayeen view was that its policy was not to conquer Israel by force of arms but by using guerilla and terrorist tactics to induce the Israeli leaders to acknowledge that there would be no real peace until Arab demands were met. The Fedayeen thought that their war of attrition, to grind and bleed Israel to death, had begun, that time was on their side, and that the Israelis could not last out but must capitulate sooner or later. Many Arabs also felt that the western powers, especially America, would not let Israel be destroyed in open war, so destruction from within by terrorism and guerilla warfare was the only means left to them.

The small but virile PFLP sent its members into the main cities and towns of Israel and the occupied territories. Early in June (1968) an explosion in the Gaza Strip killed two Israelis and wounded five others. The PFLP claimed responsibility. This incident resulted in one of the first serious demonstrations, by over 200 Arab women, in protest at some 2,000 suspects being arrested by the Israelis and held overnight. The PFLP was succeeding in arousing the antagonism of the people in that area. Other demonstrations followed, some by students and others by schoolgirls. Another incident was a battle between the security forces and 900 students in a high school at Gaza. In one demonstration Israeli troops had to open fire, wounding five Arab girls. In August over ten people were injured by grenade explosions on the West Bank, provoking the Israelis to attack with aircraft a small cluster of PFLP camps near Salt in Jordan. In September an explosion in a Tel Aviv bus station killed one person and injured several others, and in October a grenade attack at the Tomb of the Patriarchs in Hebron injured 48 Israelis, while on the 22nd November a vehicle packed with explosive went off in a Jerusalem market, killing 12 and injuring 55.[1]

The Israeli General Staff appreciation by mid-1968 was that Fedayeen operations were badly planned, badly executed or not executed at all, and then inflated into major actions for propaganda purposes. It noted that there were no deliberate attacks on the Israeli armed forces, only on civilians and civilian targets, and that the majority of the military casualties were caused by mines. In fact, by July the guerillas had been largely reduced to fire-fights across the River Jordan, firing rockets and sneak raids at night to lay mines on the edge of the occupied territories. Summarizing later, the Israelis said that during 1968 they killed or captured 2,650 Fedayeen, while on the other hand in that period the guerillas claimed to have caused over 1,000 incidents, killing or wounding 900 Israelis.

After rapid expansion during the latter part of 1968, the Fedayeen went through a phase of consolidation and development, in which they concentrated on propaganda, recruitment and communications. In the propaganda field Fatah was allowed by President Nasser to use a Cairo radio station for a short period every day, which beamed out threats and boastful communiqués, gaining an extremely wide audience that reached into Jordan, Syria and the Lebanon. These broadcasts, by the Voice of Fatah (Saut al-Fatah), appealed to the Arabs because they were listening to what they wanted to hear, and were frequently and dramatically punctuated with code words and mysterious phrases. The signature song of the Voice of Fatah[2] was eagerly awaited. As they were the only Arabs believed to be carrying the war into Israel and were seen to be doing something while Arab governments only talked, Fatah in particular, and the Fedayeen in general gained a fascinating hold on Arab opinion. The Fatah credibility gap was wide, but the Arabs did

---

[1] Fatah also claimed responsibility for the Jerusalem explosion, and was given a 'credit' for it by the PNC, which tried to adjudicate on such competing claims.

[2] The Fatah signature song was usually translated as:
'The Revolution of Fatah exists,
It exists here, there and everywhere.
It is a storm, a storm in every house and village.'

not know that. Apart from being false, several of the claims were ridiculous, such as that to having destroyed the Israeli Chief of Staff's garage (he did not have one) at his home, to being responsible for killing Premier Eshkol (who died in February 1968), or to having wounded Moshe Dayan in March (he was in fact involved in an archaeological accident), to having attacked the Israeli Independence Day parade (the world press saw nothing) and to having started a fire at Lydda airport (which had begun accidentally).

After rising to a certain strength, recruitment slowed down and Fatah became far more selective, taking only Palestinians, who were given strict medical examinations, and, later, psychiatric tests. The whole Fedayeen movement might have had between 20,000 and 25,000 members, the majority of whom were Fatah. A string of bases and staging camps was set up in the mountainous strip of Jordan adjacent to the River Jordan reaching down into the Negev, which were estimated by the end of the year to number about 50, in addition to which there were at least a dozen field hospitals. In these camps, in theory at least, were about 10,000 guerillas poised to strike into Israel; there were as many again in the Palestinian refugee camps in Jordan, or in Amman and other population centres, either in training or involved in fund-raising, recruiting or political jockeying for position.

Fatah and the PFLP, and other groups to a lesser extent, either took over existing youth organizations in the refugee camps, or began them, to indoctrinate and harness to their cause the youngsters, who became known as Ashbals.[1] At the age of eight boys could become Ashbals. They were initially organized and trained by Fatah in the Jebel Wahdat refugee camp, near Amman, and later at other places too. At the age of 13 both boys and girls were eligible to join the normal youth organizations, when further training was given by Fatah. In practice the designation of Ashbal was retained until the age of 17, when they were able to become Fedayeen fighters if selected. The PFLP ran a similar scheme for the youngsters in the Bakaa refugee camp near Amman, its stronghold base, which made great progress.

[1] Variously translated as 'tiger cubs' or 'lion cubs'.

Fund raising was carried out by all the Fedayeen groups on an individual basis, to the point of blackmail and terrorism. For instance, Fatah issued propaganda stamps, which were forced on unwilling buyers. These stamps, without which letters could not be accepted for posting, depicted guerilla fighters in various heroic poses with suitable slogans, one of which showed a child with burns, and the slogan 'Shalom and Napalm'—which gave an indication of the standard of efficiency their propaganda department was achieving. General sympathy for the Fedayeen greased many wheels; thus goods entering Arab ports or airports marked 'For the Palestine Nation', or bearing some similar designation, passed through the customs with the barest of formalities, if any.

Wealth enabled Fatah to improve its Martyr Families Welfare Service, which looked after the dependants of any Fedayeen fighters who were killed or wounded. Pensions were paid, cash grants given and young orphan children were cared for and educated in special schools. Raids into Israel caused heavy casualties, and many guerillas did not return, but they immediately became heroes and martyrs. Their photographs were publicly displayed and their deeds and character extolled. Emphasis on the Islamic belief that any Muslim killed in battle goes immediately to Paradise completed the picture.

Communications within the Fatah framework were still poor, despite equipment donated or brought. Apart from code words given over the Cairo radio station by the Voice of Fatah, most other instructions had to be sent by letter by couriers because the field radios and the telephone service were so unreliable.

After the battle of Karameh, King Hussein progressively lost authority over the guerillas in Jordan, as the major groups openly established headquarters in Amman and settled on one or the other of the several refugee camps to use as a power base, and as other guerilla organizations appeared in his country. By early summer armed guerillas began to appear on the streets of Amman and other towns, at first timidly, and then more boldly as they gained confidence. By autumn they were strutting about arrogantly jostling Jordanian soldiers and police who were mainly desert Bedu out of sympathy with the town-bred sophisticated revolutionary Fedayeen fighter. Amman had become an overcrowded city, its population having risen from about 130,000 in June 1967 to over 450,000 some twelve months later. Scuffles and incidents became more frequent as the Jordanian authorities sought to curb the guerillas. In mid-October Fedayeen leaders complained about road-blocks and vehicle searches, alleging that they hampered them in their operations against the Israelis. They also complained that the Fedayeen were barred from certain towns and villages, that their operational plans had to be first submitted to the Jordanian army, and that Jordanian soldiers press-ganged youths from the streets and took them to remote desert camps to prevent them being recruited by the Fedayeen. Friction increased, but despite rising strength and more arms, the guerillas hesitated to confront King Hussein openly, feeling they were not yet strong enough to take on the Jordanian army in a pitched battle.

The view of the Fedayeen leaders was that time was on their side, and that the situation was veering in their favour, as the people's admiration for the guerillas increased, and even elements within the Jordanian Government and army were sympathetic to their cause. Thus encouraged, early in November (1968) Fatah came out into the open and held its first-ever press conference at which Arafat, amongst other things, rejected the idea of any Middle East settlement.

Despite the caution of the main Fedayeen groups, on the 4th November a spark was ignited. Fighting broke out on the streets of Amman between the Jordanian army and a small guerilla group known as the Legion of Victory (Kataib al-Nasr), the military arm of the Syrian-backed Popular Organization for the Liberation of Palestine (the POLP), which was dedicated to the overthrow of King Hussein. Although extremely small, having only about 30 fighters, the Legion of Victory had already been responsible among other incidents for an attack on a police station in Amman on the 28th May, so a clash with the Jordanian Security Force was inevitable sooner or later. Any disturbance in the capital caused tension and excitement, and immediately brought thousands of the curious, idle and mischievous on to the streets in thousands. Mobs hovered in the background as Bedu soldiers moved against this guerilla

organization, heavily and mercilessly. The PLO openly dis-
associated itself from the Legion of Victory, while Fatah and
most other Fedayeen groups urged their members to remain
passive. On the second day Bedu soldiers attacked a Fatah
camp in their action against the Legion of Victory, killing nine
and causing Fatah to alert its '7,000 members',[1] but a major
confrontation did not occur, and the Jordanian army crushed
the Legion of Victory within 48 hours. At a press conference
on the 6th, King Hussein said that 24 civilians, four soldiers and
one policeman had been killed in the fighting, and that 89
civilians, eight soldiers and three policemen had been injured.
In this action he had been tacitly supported by President
Nasser, who privately deplored the 'wild-cat' activities of the
guerillas.

Seeing how quickly this small group had been eliminated and
realizing that other groups might be picked off individually, to
preserve themselves as they were not ready for a head-on clash
the Fedayeen leaders appealed to King Hussein to end the
fighting, which he did. He was subjected to conflicting advice
and pressures. The Jordanian army wanted to be able to deal
in a similar manner with any guerilla organization that became
openly troublesome, but many of the junior and the Palestinian
officers were in sympathy with Fedayeen ideals and King
Hussein was uncertain of their loyalty in such an event. Also,
he was uncertain of his political backing; for example, Wasfi
Tal, a former Premier, wanted him to adopt the Fedayeen
cause, take it over and so overshadow and dominate the present
guerilla leaders.

Once the Jordanian troops ceased firing, the Fedayeen
leaders raised a clamour, alleging that deliberate attempts were
being made to stir up feeling against the Palestinians in Jordan,
and that Prince Hassan, King Hussein's brother and heir to
the throne, was associated with this movement. They also
alleged that the incident had been engineered as a trial of
strength, and that King Hussein used it as a exercise pre-
liminary to crushing the Fedayeen in Jordan completely.
Feeling in the Arab world was whipped up against him, armed
guerillas once again walked the streets of Amman, tension

[1] *The Times* of 22nd November 1968.

mounted and trigger fingers became itchy. Many urged prompt action to bring the guerillas to heel, but others advised a working arrangement with them. King Hussein hesitated. Then Saudi Arabia, fearing for its oil deliveries, pressed for an agreement with the Fedayeen. He also had to consider what action, if any, the Iraqi division stationed in northern Jordan might take if his army moved against the guerillas. He came to a decision when one of his main supporters, Sheikh Akif al-Faiz, his Minister of Communications, threatened to resign if the army moved against the Fedayeen. This was an unusual attitude, coming as it did from the leader of a large Bedu tribe, and it caused King Hussein to become anxious about the solidarity of his Bedu support.

King Hussein met guerilla leaders, who demanded freedom of movement, the lifting of all curfew restrictions and the release of all guerillas detained. After some discussion he came to an arrangement on future relations with them, which became known as the November Agreement. On the Fedayeen side the November Agreement had been negotiated mainly by Arafat, and in the course of the negotiations much of the secrecy surrounding the guerilla leadership fell away. Under its terms the guerillas agreed to carry identity cards, conform to certain rules when operating against the Israelis, and not to wear uniform or carry arms in the towns. In return King Hussein had to withdraw his demand that guerillas in refugee camps be disarmed and that high-level co-ordination take place with the Jordanian army and the Fedayeen before operating into Israel. Neither gave more than they had to, but the basic unspoken agreement was that Arafat would not rouse the guerillas to move against King Hussein if he on his part would not restrict Fedayeen movement. Arafat had some difficulty in persuading the majority of the groups to approve the November Agreement, and in fact two would not sign it. They were the PFLP and a small organization consisting mainly of Palestinian ex-officers who had served in the Jordanian army, many having been dismissed from it.

The guerillas took full advantage of their now officially recognized freedom to run their own show without hindrance in the refugee camps. While Jordan was now the main staging area for the Fedayeen, Syria remained its principal backer, influence and instigator.

The November Agreement caused discontent within Jordanian Government circles, the hard-liners feeling that King Hussein had been too soft and had paid over-much regard to opinion in other Arab countries. The army, smarting from its 1967 defeat, in particular felt a sense of chagrin and frustration as it did not doubt its ability to smash the guerillas. Even the younger officers who felt the Fedayeen should be harnessed in some way to the common cause rather than eliminated or chastened resented the arrogant attitude of the guerillas and their behaviour in the streets of Amman.

The November press conference held by Arafat, at which he poured scorn on the idea of a Middle East settlement on any of the various lines proposed, caused President Nasser, who may have secretly toyed with such an alternative, to shy away from it. As Fatah had swung the weight of Arab public opinion so heavily against it, he was forced on the 5th December to announce that Egypt rejected the reported US peace plan to allow each Arab state to settle its own problems directly with Israel. Accusing Arab eyes then turned to Jordan. To allay suspicions, Premier Bahjat Talhouni stated on the 7th that his country was not prepared to take a separate line of action in any Middle East solution either. The Fedayeen had won their point.

Mutterings in governmental circles caused King Hussein to reshuffle his cabinet on the 26th December, to include a few who favoured stronger action against the guerillas. Talhouni remained as Premier, but handed over the portfolio of Defence to the Deputy Premier, Ahmed Toukan. Brought into the cabinet was Field Marshal Habes al-Majali, a former Minister of Defence, who had been Commander-in-Chief of the Jordanian army from 1957, when he had been instrumental in saving the life of King Hussein in an assassination attempt, until 1967, when having been largely blamed for the Jordanian defeat by the Israelis, he had been removed from that position, but retained by the King as his Military Adviser. Appointed Minister of the Interior was Major-General Mohammed Rasoul Kailani, a former Chief of Intelligence, who had been one of the

E

first to recommend that steps be taken to curtail Fedayeen activities in Jordan. There were three or four government intelligence services in Jordan, which had tended to act independently, and on occasions representing conflicting interests they had clashed to such an extent that at one stage they nearly brought the Government down. Kailani's task was to weed and weld, and a combined intelligence and secret police organization developed known as the 'Mahabrat', which was constantly criticized by the Fedayeen, for obvious reasons, as its efficiency increased.

Meanwhile, across the border in Syria a power struggle within the Baathist ruling clique was taking place, where three men jointly held power. A shift in this tussle occurred on the 29th October 1968, when the head of state, Nureddin al-Atassi, became Premier and formed a new government. Although differences remained, he still shared some power with Hafez al-Assad, the Defence Minister, and Salah Jadid, the Secretary-General of the Baathist Party. The three 'strong men' continued to govern Syria, but the emphasis veered a little towards greater friendliness with the neighbouring Iraqi Baathist Government.

The lesson of the battle of Karameh had not been lost on the Israelis, who confined retaliation to aerial attacks on known guerilla camps in Jordan and directing artillery fire to counter Arab shelling of Israeli territory, a policy that continued until December, when there was a sudden increase in both guerilla terrorist activity and Arab shelling. On the 3rd the Israeli air force struck at the village of Kafr Assad, 10 miles inside Jordan, the Jordanians claiming that ten civilians were killed, and the next day (4th) it made heavy air attacks on Iraqi guns, positions and ammunition dumps in the area to the west of Irbid, after which Iraqi guns were silent for about three weeks.

This increase in guerilla activity was attributed by the Israelis to King Hussein's November Agreement, which brought about a change of Israeli reprisal policy. On the 20th December Israeli aircraft bombed the Jordanian police station at Adasiya, south of the Sea of Galilee, which had been used by guerillas after making bazooka raids on Israeli patrols. Previously, Jordanian police posts and installations had been left alone.

The Israelis alleged that between the 16th November and the 20th December over 50 guerilla incidents occurred. On the 20th Iraqi guns again opened fire on Israeli territory, provoking the first Israeli reprisal raids for months, when on the following day helicopter-borne troops demolished a road-bridge and a rail-bridge, some 40 miles east of the southern tip of the Dead Sea, killing two civilians and wounding four. The Israelis withdrew before Jordanian troops could reach the spot. This commando raid drew the caustic comment from Cairo that Egypt would not be drawn into another war to serve Israel's purpose. On the 20th Israeli artillery opened fire on the Iraqi guns and an artillery duel ensued, lasting over five hours, which was only terminated when Israeli aircraft came into action and silenced the Arab guns.

The some 160,000 Palestinian refugees in the Lebanon were kept as firmly under control as possible. As they were refused work permits, many were forced to emigrate to Saudi Arabia, Qatar, Kuwait or elsewhere to earn a living. Within the camps the refugees remained grouped under their original leaders, the mukhtars, who retained a traditional and restraining influence over their followers, particularly the young, so that by the end of 1967 a steady stream of young men (and a few girls as well) had begun to leave the camps for Syria to join Fatah or one of the other guerilla organizations. The Lebanese Government forbade the Fedayeen to operate from its territory, and for many months the small Lebanese army was able to enforce this, few guerillas crossing into Israel from the Lebanon. This decision was influenced partly by political and partly by economic considerations. Traditionally half Muslim and half Christian, the Lebanese Government had to maintain a delicate balance by giving lip-service to Arab ideals to please the Muslims and by doing nothing about them to please the Christians. Much of the prosperity of the country, which rested largely upon business, banking and tourism, was dependent upon stability, which the Fedayeen was out to upset.

The Lebanese Government tended to regard itself complacently as secure from attacks from Israel, and no particular anxiety had been felt when after the June War Moshe Dayan had said that now all Israel's boundaries were natural except

67

that with the Lebanon. This seemed to indicate that the Litani River might be a more defensible frontier for the Israelis, and the hint was that this section of the Lebanon could be in danger if it was used by the Fedayeen. Part of the Lebanese army was moved to the south of the country, and there was talk of giving people in the region military training, which was not compulsory in the Lebanon. It did mean that army units were already in position near the border and so able to deter the Fedayeen from crossing into Israel. However, guerilla organizations were allowed to operate openly as regards propaganda and recruiting. Some had offices and agents in Beirut and elsewhere in the Lebanon, there being frequent contact between the Fedayeen in the Lebanon and those in Syria. Because of a comparatively quiet frontier, so far no Israeli air strikes or reprisal raids had been necessary, as had been the case in Jordan.

The lone wolf of the Fedayeen, the PFLP, decided to attract world attention to the Palestine cause, and began a policy of attacking Israeli airlines. It moved dramatically into this international field on the 23rd July 1968 when three PFLP members hijacked an El Al airliner in flight between Rome and Israel and forced the pilot to fly to Algiers. The Algerian Government held 12 Israelis and the aircraft while it bargained for the release of certain Palestinian guerillas held in Israel. Eventually the aircraft and hostages were released on the 1st September, and on the 3rd the Israelis released 16 detained guerillas as a 'gesture of gratitude to the Italian Government', which had mediated.

Violence was always a characteristic of the PFLP, as was demonstrated on the 26th December when two of its members[1] attacked an El Al airliner on the ground at Athens airport with automatic fire and grenades, killing one passenger and wounding an air hostess. The two men, who were arrested by the Greek police, had flown from Beirut to Athens for this purpose.

The Israeli riposte was swift, savage and surprising. Two days later, on the 28th, a small group of Israeli soldiers in four helicopters raided Beirut airport, the busiest in the Middle East, and destroyed 13 airliners belonging to three Arab

[1] The two men were not brought to trial until February 1970, when both boasted of being PFLP members.

68

airlines found on the ground, as well as damaging installations and runways. Foreign aircraft were ignored, and there was no loss of life in this raid. After being on the ground only 45 minutes, the Israelis flew away, having caused damage estimated at nearly £40 million. The Lebanese were slow to react. No aircraft took off to intercept the Israeli helicopters until far too late, the one spark of action occurring when a squad of Lebanese soldiers approached one of the Israeli blocking positions, only to withdraw when fired upon. Fortune had favoured the Israelis, who had expected only six Arab airliners to be at the Beirut airport at this time. The Israelis stated that this raid was a punitive one. They accused the Lebanese Government of harbouring Fedayeen, and pointed out that the two PFLP members concerned in the Athens airport incident had come from the Lebanon.

This dramatic raid and its results momentarily stunned the Arab world. The UN Security Council met on the 30th and the 31st to condemn the Israeli action. On the 7th January 1969 President de Gaulle, incensed that French helicopters had been used, decreed a total embargo on all French arms to Israel, and the French stated that they would 'give full support' to the Lebanon, in the hope that this ponderous threat might be interpreted as implying that French troops could be available if Israel attacked the Lebanon; but the days of 'gunboat diplomacy' were over and the Israelis were neither over-awed nor impressed, although they sorely missed the spares for their French aircraft. However, instead of having the anticipated effect of warning guerillas to keep out of the Lebanon, the raid had the converse one of attracting Fedayeen attention in considerable volume to that country.

# 4. Fedayeen Crescendo

During 1969 the Fedayeen movement gathered momentum, which grew into a crescendo as it expanded its base in Jordan almost to become a 'state within a state' and attempted to do the same in the Lebanon, while keeping up the incidence of terrorist attacks, with the smaller PFLP ever seeking dramatic, world eye-catching activities. During this year Arafat became an influential political leader in the Middle East, causing President Nasser to treat him with more respect.

On the 3rd January (1969) an election was held in the Palestine National Council. Fatah obtained 33 seats, with the PFLP and the VPLW (Vanguards of the Popular Liberation War) as runners up with 12 seats each, closely followed by the PLO, which gained 11 seats, to which should be added another five won by the PLA. Of the others, the Student, Trade Union and Women's Federation gained three, and the Palestine National Fund (an office established to handle funds granted by the Arab League to the PLO) one. The remaining seats went individually to independent guerilla organizations. Seeing which way the wind was blowing, President Nasser in his inaugural address to a newly elected Egyptian National Assembly lavished praise on the Fedayeen for the first time. He planned to persuade them to use Cairo for their high-level meetings, so that he might have more chance to gain influence over them.

Accordingly, the newly elected PNC met in Cairo during the first week in February. On the 4th Arafat was elected chairman of an 11-man central committee[1] which in fact made him *de*

---

[1] Sometimes referred to as the executive committee.

*facto* chairman of the PLO. That body was not sufficiently organized and so was not represented at this meeting, thereby enabling Arafat neatly to assume the vacant seat of power to which he was later formally elected. This meeting was also boycotted by the PFLP, because it did not think that 12 seats were sufficient. Also, the PLA, which had five seats, stayed away because its recently appointed Commander, Brigadier Midhat Budeiry, was feuding with Arafat, as Arafat had openly criticized it for inactivity. The central committee now consisted of Arafat as chairman, three Fatah, two Saiqa, two PLO and three independent members. The following day (5th) Nasser publicly approved of this decision. So Arafat emerged as one of the most influential leaders in the Middle East, having direct contact with the Arab League and all Arab governments, and under his control, nominally or otherwise, were agencies for all guerilla groups. Arafat could now claim to speak for the whole Fedayeen movement, as he virtually controlled the PLO, as well as his own Fatah.

Back in Amman frictions and dissensions arose within George Habash's PFLP. They reached such a pitch that fighting broke out between the factions and erupted on to the streets in February. It led to a formal split on the 23rd, when a small extremely left-wing group, led by Nayef Hawatmeh, a Marxist, splintered from the PFLP, to become the Democratic Popular Front for the Struggle for Palestine, the DPF, with a platform calling for Palestine to be a bi-national state for both Jews and Arabs. The DPF remained small and poor, as it received no money or arms from the PLO. Most other groups received a distribution shrewdly designed to keep them in line as much as possible. Hawatmeh, a Christian Arab, who had visited both Hungary and the Soviet Union (but not China), called for greater passive and active resistance in the occupied territories. The change of emphasis from the pre-June War days when the Fedayeen aim was to 'drive the Jews into the sea' was now clearly noticeable. Palestinians of all shades of political opinion, even the extreme PFLP and DPF, now seemed to accept and visualize a Palestine that was a multi-national state in which Muslims, Jews and Christians would live together, vaguely on the pattern of the Lebanon.

Later in the year two other small factions splintered from the PFLP, again largely for ideological reasons, but also because they differed with Habash over the degree of loyalty that should be accorded to President Nasser. One became the Front for the Popular Palestine Struggle, the FPPS, led by Ahmed Jabril, and the other the Arab Movement for the Liberation of Palestine, the AMLP, led by Ahmed Zahrur. Both remained small and poor, making little real contribution to the Fedayeen effort, but they were fiercely independent and idealistic.

Concerned at the large number of PLA in the Suez Canal Zone, firmly under Nasser's thumb, and anxious to give them a more active role and bring them under his thumb instead, Arafat announced on the 10th February a proposal to transfer all 4,000 of them to Jordan. Nasser presumably had agreed as he would have been only too pleased to be rid of his PLA brigade, but King Hussein had not been consulted; also Arab opinion was suspicious of the project. Arafat's star was rising, so much so that on the 14th, Moshe Dayan, the Israeli Defence Minister, had to deny publicly that he had attempted to make contact with him. On the 16th, Arafat was negotiating on equal terms with King Hussein, but he was unable to persuade him to accept the 4,000-strong PLA brigade in his country. Two days later, on the 18th, both Arafat and King Hussein were publicly seen together visiting Fatah camps near Amman. Reports of the projected PLA move to Jordan were denied by its sponsor, the PLO.

Fatah still favoured commando tactics. It claimed that in January (1969) it carried out 90 raids into Israel against road bridges, railway lines and military camps, in which, it alleged, it inflicted 650 Israeli casualties for only nine guerillas killed or wounded. The smaller PFLP, intense, selective and constantly looking towards the international stage, carried out its third attack on Israeli airliners on the 18th February, when four of its members assaulted an aircraft with small arms fire and explosives at the Zurich airport, wounding two Israelis. One of the four was killed by the aircraft's security guard, and the other three, one of whom was a woman, were arrested by the police, as was the Israeli security guard.[1] The dead guerilla became an instant hero, but King Hussein would not permit his body to be brought back to Jordan for burial. Instead, he was given a gigantic symbolic funeral on the 14th March in Amman, which caused the Jordanian authorities some anxiety. Three days later an explosion in a Jerusalem supermarket killed two and injured nine, and the PFLP claimed responsibility, as it did for a bomb explosion later that wounded 29 people in a cafeteria in the Hebrew University at Jerusalem.

Despite the Syrian ban on Fedayeen operating into the occupied territories from Syria, a number of incursions were made. After 12 such raids into the Golan Plateau during the first three weeks of February, the Israelis hit back on the 24th, striking with aircraft into Syria for the first time since the June War, attacking two Fedayeen camps. One camp, at Maisaloun, was a main Fatah centre, and the other, at El Hamma,[2] was a large Saiqa camp. The element of surpise was gained, and the Israelis claimed to have killed about 80 guerillas and shot down two Syrian MiG-17s. On their side the Syrians claimed to have brought down three Israeli planes, but admitted losing 15 dead, while the Fedayeen only admitted to two guerillas wounded and five civilians killed.

The Israeli air raid into Syria indirectly brought to a head the continuing power tussle between the three generals ruling the country, one of whom, Hafez al-Assad, the Defence Minister, had long been dissatisfied with existing policy, feeling that the Syrian armed forces were not getting fair treatment. He had objected to the best brigades being withdrawn to Damascus during the June War, instead of staying on the Syrian Heights and fighting back at the Israelis, and the recent loss of the two aircraft rankled, as did the non-arrival of expected Soviet arms. On the 1st March a bloodless coup brought about a shift in the power set-up, when Assad pushed aside the régime of President Nureddin al-Atassi and took over

---

[1] On the 22nd December 1969 a Swiss court sentenced the three PFLP members to terms of imprisonment, but acquitted the Israeli security guard.

[2] Not to be confused with Hamma, which was on the Golan Plateau in the occupied territories.

the Government. He adopted a more aggressive military policy towards Israel, and one of his first acts was to reinstate some 500 officers who had been dismissed. In a complicated way all three men, Assad, Atassi and Salah Jadid, remained uneasily sharing power between them.

For months Syria and Iraq had been involved in an ideological dispute which marred co-operation and prevented the implementation of the much discussed eastern front against Israel. Assad immediately took steps to lessen tension. On the 15th March, under an agreement between Assad, who retained the defence portfolio, and the Iraqi Chief of Staff, a brigade of Iraqi troops entered Syria. The following day King Hussein flew to Cairo to meet Nasser to see if more teeth could be put into the eastern front.

On the 20th, Syrian leaders and politicians gathered in Damascus for the fourth Baathist Party Regional Congress. While it was in progress Assad deployed troops in strategic places around the capital to prevent any attempt at a counter-coup, but all passed off peacefully. The Congress re-elected Nuraddin Atassi, who was still President of Syria, as Chairman of the Party, and Saleh Jadid remained as Secretary-General. At the Congress Assad called for a federal union between Syria, Iraq and Egypt, and a reunification of the Baathist parties of Syria and Iraq (all old political cries), and he also encouraged support for the eastern front project.

By mid-April some progress had been made on the eastern front. In addition to the Iraqi division in Jordan, which had risen in strength to 17,000 men—an extra brigade having been temporarily dispatched—there were two brigades of Saudi Arabian troops, about 6,000 men, and two Syrian brigades, of 5,000 men, which had just moved over the border, as well as an Iraqi brigade in Syria, all of which, in theory at least, together with the Jordanian army were the regular Arab formations earmarked for the eastern front. On the 28th April, a nine-man politburo was formed to govern until a people's assembly was elected, on which day there were demonstrations in Damascus in support of freedom of movement for guerillas in the Lebanon. A month later, on the 29th May, there was another power shift, when President Atassi formed a government with a Baathist majority, in which Assad retained the portfolio of defence, so still the three Syrian generals shared power between them.

Iraq also had its small share of guerillas owing allegiance to no one, notably detachments of the Syrian-backed Saiqa, and a unit of the Egyptian-orientated PLA, but being involved in the Kurdish Revolt,[1] although irked by their presence, the Government took no action, until in April it decided to form its own Fadayeen group, largely as a counter to the Syrian Saiqa. This became known as the Arab Liberation Front, the ALF. On the 17th of that month the Iraqi left-wing newspaper, *Al Nida*, reporting this event, said that the Government objected to the presence of Palestinian guerillas and that all who wanted to stay on Iraqi territory should join the ALF—the only Fedayeen group to be permitted. The ALF never amounted to much—it was not intended to—but it enabled the authorities to lean heavily on all other guerillas, gradually to freeze most of them out of the country, and to restrict severely the movement of those remaining. Iraq was well on the way to solving its Fedayeen problem.

Arafat's position as chairman of the central committee of the PNC made it easier for him to achieve his ambition, which was to unite all guerillas under his leadership. On the 2nd April he succeeded in forming the Palestine Armed Struggle Command, the PASC, which embraced most, but not all, Fedayeen organizations and presented a façade of unity to the world. In view of the diverse ideologies, feuds and personal ambitions, this was perhaps Arafat's greatest achievement so far. Neither the PFLP nor the DPF were in the PASC, which aimed at co-ordinating guerilla operations, dictating strategy, controlling propaganda and clearing press statements and releases. The PASC tended to favour the larger and stronger organizations, disregarding the smaller ones as much as it could, in the hope that they might merge or wither away. To a degree this did happen, but only slowly. Most small groups existed, or were allowed to exist, to enable their host country to exert influence on them so as to exclude others, each host country wanting to have the least number of guerillas possible, and for them to be amenable or subject to conventional pressures. The several small groups,

[1] See *The Kurdish Revolt* by Edgar O'Ballance.

which must have exceeded 15, made plenty of noise, but achieved little as they naturally concentrated predominantly upon survival. Even at this stage there was still a tendency for guerilla leaders to live on past Arab glories and victories, many imaginary, rather than realistically plan for the future. Arafat, Habash and their colleagues were exceptions.

The guerilla groups had varying relationships with each other and with certain Arab states, which it is well to appreciate. For example, the Iraqi Government was abrasive towards the Syrian Saiqa, as was also its ALF as it developed. Syria and Iraq seemed to have an alternate love-hate relationship with each other. Fatah, the largest, most powerful and most popular with the Arab masses, was viewed with secret envy by President Nasser, who feared it might eclipse him, and other countries and groups were jealous of its success. The PFLP was particularly antagonistic towards Fatah, although it was careful to maintain contact with it and the PLO, but it had good relations with both Saiqa and the Syrian Government, despite previous differences. All Arab states took what steps they could to control the guerillas in their territory, and both Syria and Iraq had far more success than the Lebanon and Jordan. The Fedayeen continually declared that they had no conflict with national authority as long as they could raid into Israel or the occupied territories freely, which was all very well for Iraq, which had no common frontier, but was far more difficult for the Lebanon and Jordan, which had only small armies and a growing number of independent Fedayeen fighters to deal with. In Egypt Nasser kept the guerillas on a very tight rein indeed.

The Soviet Union tried to persuade the Syrians to restrain its guerillas from operating in the Lebanon, but on the other hand wanted the Lebanese Communist Party, still illegal, to support them—a tactic aimed at further dividing the country. In Jordan the active, but also illegal, underground Communist Party supported guerilla resistance in the occupied territories, but deplored such slogans as 'Liquidate Israel', of which many were in evidence, and condemned many Fedayeen exploits as unfortunate adventures that drove away progressive Palestinian elements.

The Soviet Union still had no direct contact with Arafat,

and would not respond to hints to invite him or other PLO members to Moscow, or give him any material aid; but this policy had to be modified, as by this time the Soviet Union and China were competing for influence with guerillas of the Middle East and Africa. The great cultural revolution was drawing to a close, China was beginning to look outwards again, and weapons of Chinese origin were finding their way into Fedayeen hands. In April 1969 a consignment of Chinese arms arrived at an Iraqi port, and the Soviet Union told the Iraqis that they must not let them be unloaded, and that if they did all Soviet aid would cease. The popularity of the Fedayeen was such that the arms were unloaded and distributed to guerillas, but Iraq promised not to let this happen again. By May 1969 China had supplied arms worth about £1·5 million to the Fedayeen.

Guerilla attacks against Israel continued as the year dragged on, and these were carried out mainly, but not entirely, by Fatah. Activities had been restricted during the first weeks of the year by bad weather and heavy rain, which caused the River Jordan to run very high, making crossing difficult. Raiders were compelled to cross into Israel much farther south in the desert, but despite such handicaps Fatah claims averaged three operations daily, which the Israelis to a degree confirmed. Precise details are vague, the Fatah being over-boastful, while the Israelis used quiet, and selective, censorship. Fatah made further attempts to establish cells on the West Bank, with less than moderate success; the Arabs there had no wish to become involved in guerilla war and a continual Fedayeen weakness was that, unlike the Viet Cong and the FLN, they had no bases inside enemy territory. There were a few demonstrations in Jerusalem, Ramallah, Nablus and other towns at times, but they never posed a serious security problem to the Israelis. Giving figures (on the 19th February 1969) Moshe Dayan said that 'Arab terrorist organizations' had killed 144 people in the past four years, including 37 civilians, and wounded 634, of whom half were civilians, and that 34 'undesirables had been deported across the River Jordan' in this period.

On the 2nd May Fatah launched another phase in its campaign against Israel, when an Asifa group infiltrated on to the Golan Plateau to seize the village of Hamma, and held it against

Israeli counter-attacks for three hours, during which time the Palestine flag was raised on Israeli occupied territory. Fatah claimed much destruction; while the Israelis admitted some, they kept as quiet as they could over this incident. The Hamma incident marked the first major change of policy in six months, and showed that Fatah was stronger, better trained and becoming bolder. Almost daily the guerillas moved to the border, fired a few rockets, and then quickly withdrew before Israeli artillery could be brought down on them. On the 26th the Israelis reported nine such incidents in one night. The 16th May was celebrated in the Arab world as Palestine Day, but it passed off quietly, except for grenade incidents in Jersalem and Gaza.

The Saiqa also tried commando tactics. On the 17th May three of their guerillas were killed in an attack on El Al, on the Golan Plateau, and on the same day a Fatah group assaulted an Israeli military post near the River Jordan, but was driven off leaving 12 dead behind, for the cost of one Israeli soldier killed. It was unusual for the Fedayeen to attack military positions. In Jerusalem, on the 20th June, three explosions near the Wailing Wall injured two Israelis and three Arabs, but led to the seizure by Israeli authorities of nearby buildings and the removal of Arab families that lived in them. But as the Israelis took counter-measures the impetus of this Fedayeen phase ran down, and on the 19th July seven guerillas were killed during a night raid on the Golan Plateau, and another five in the Jordan Valley, for no Israeli losses.

The PFLP was not to be left out, and on the 30th May it claimed responsibility for blowing up a section of TAPLINE oil pipeline on the Golan Plateau, thus stopping the flow of oil from Saudi Arabia to the terminal at Sidon in the Lebanon. The ironic fact was that about 30 miles of this pipeline passed through Israeli-occupied territory, and so far the Israelis had tacitly let the Arab oil flow. This made the Fedayeen extremely unpopular with King Feisal, who threatened to suspend all payment to the PLO for the guerillas, which was about £1·4 million annually. It appeared that the PFLP, desperately short of cash and not being allocated any funds by the PLO, as it was not a member, had approached King Feisal direct for aid and been refused. In revenge the PFLP had stopped the flow of his oil. Jordan, Syria and the Lebanon each received large transit fees for the oil passing through the pipeline in their countries, and Egypt too relied on a large subsidy from the oil-rich states to offset the losses of the June War and the closure of the Suez Canal, so this caused general anxiety. Israel now became obstructive and refused to allow repairs to be carried out, but was eventually persuaded to change its mind and agreed on the 10th July, on the condition that if the pipeline was again sabotaged the overflow of oil would not foul the waters leading into the Israeli National Water Carrier system.

Commencing in February (1969) Israeli air attacks into Jordan caused guerilla camps to scatter widely and move often, as the rising spate of Fedayeen commando activities was countered by strikes on known guerilla bases. On the 16th March Israeli aircraft attacked Yahuda, between Amman and Akaba, Dhibin, five miles from Jerash, and Shaubak in southern Jordan—all Fatah camps. On the 26th an Israeli plane was brought down in Jordan when assaulting a Fedayeen base, and another one was lost on the 22nd April while on a similar mission, when the Israelis claimed to have killed 18 Fatah and PFLP members and wounded another 25 near Salt. On the 19th May Israeli aircraft attacked more Fedayeen bases just north of the Dead Sea, after which the size of the camps, and the groups engaged in commando operations, was reduced. Land operations were resumed by the Israelis, who on the 9th May carried out their largest raid into Jordan since the battle of Karameh, blowing up several houses in the deserted village of Yabis, one mile from the River Jordan. On the 21st Israeli tanks and motorized infantry attacked the villages of Safi and Feifa, south of the Dead Sea; from there guerillas sniped at Israeli patrols and potash workers, a four-hour battle ensued and houses were demolished.

In January (1969) the Israeli Government approved the Alon Plan in principle, which was to establish fortified settlements on the outer edges of the occupied territories. In July it was announced that the eighteenth kibbutz had been established, there being eleven on the Golan Plateau, three in Sinai and three in the Jordan Valley. In the occupied territories there were waves of demonstrations in February and March, especially in Nablus and Gaza, by students and others. Sabotage incidents continued; indeed, 1969 began with an Israeli claim to have captured 20 saboteurs and 38 collaborators three days previously. On the 2nd March the Israelis arrested 50 PFLP suspects, and on the 11th another 100, on which day they blew up four houses in Ramallah, three in Hebron and two in Nablus, all suspected PFLP meeting places. On the 11th May a large Fatah group was arrested in Hebron—and so the pattern went on throughout the year.

As Fedayeen operations continued to be launched primarily from Jordan, more air strikes were made on the 18th June, while on the 23rd an Israeli night air attack damaged the Jordanian East Ghor Canal. The following day the PFLP blew up a section of oil pipeline running from the Haifa refineries to Krishon Port, causing a five-hour blaze.

Until Assad took over the direction of the Government on the 1st March 1969, Syrian policy had been the almost rigid one of a closed frontier with Israel for the Fedayeen, who were encouraged to raid from Jordan and the Lebanon but not from Syria, although the authorities had never been able to enforce this rule. Under his direction the Syrian army had recovered from the June War defeat, shattered formations had been reformed, many dismissed officers had been reinstated and morale was rising. Formations were progressively moved away from Damascus back to the frontier region until a couple of months later at least five out of the nine regular brigades were again facing the Israelis on the Golan Plateau. Behind strengthening defences the Syrians became bolder and Assad permitted the Fedayeen to use Syria as a springboard into the occupied territories, hoping to terrorize the Israelis on the Golan Plateau and compel them to evacuate. Both Fatah and Saiqa guerillas began to raid from Syria against the Israelis.

The Syrian air force had lost about 60 of its some 120 aircraft in the June War, and was left with about 30 combat aircraft, mainly MiGs. On the 8th July the Syrians lost 7 MiGs shot down in dog-fights with Israeli planes, for no loss to the Israelis, and on the 30th of that month the Israelis attacked Syrian territory, striking at a staging area, allegedly used by 400 guerillas, on the slopes of Mount Hermon, wounding 11 men. The following day the Syrians carried out their first air raid on Israeli territory since the June War, when two Sukhoi-7s bombed an Israeli military post in the same border region. On the 13th August two Syrian MiGs lost their way and landed in Israel; the Syrian air force was not making a happy or successful comeback on to the Middle East battle scene.

It would be an understatement to say that the Syrians were dissatisfied with the supply of Soviet arms. The Soviet attitude remained cool, and on the 23rd May a projected visit by President Atassi to Moscow was suddenly cancelled. The Syrian reaction was to send its Chief of Staff, Major-General Mustafa Talas, to Peking to ask for military help, where he met Premier Chou En-lai, but was unsuccessful. Still smarting from his recent Soviet rebuff in Algiers, when President Podgorny refused to allow any member of the Soviet delegation to speak to him, Arafat had asked Talas to seek arms and help for Fatah while he was in Peking, but in this Talas was also unsuccessful.

During the year President Nasser's policy towards the Fedayeen fluctuated. On the 13th May he adopted a slightly harder line, calling for more co-operation and co-ordination between the guerillas and the Arab states they used as their bases. The Fedayeen were dismayed, fearing that this might be but a first step to a general restriction of their activities. Nasser was still the most influential leader in the Middle East, and the guerillas thought that he would not speak out against them. The Fedayeen were also disappointed by lack of support from the Soviet Union, which distrusted the non-communist and independent character of the guerillas and continued to withhold aid. However, Nasser thought fit to modify his policy against the popular Fedayeen and in July said, perhaps without any great sincerity, that: 'We on our part are giving them everything we have in the military, political and technical spheres. We shall continue doing so without any reservations or restraint', which was not quite accurate, but it mollified the guerillas, as it was intended to do.

The Israelis estimated that there were about 7,500 armed and trained guerilla fighters along the borders of Jordan, Syria and the Lebanon facing Israel. The Fedayeen boasted strength was about 50,000; they had claimed 27,000 the previous year but these figures were considered to be inflated by double-counting owing to movement, false strengths given by the smaller organizations and the inclusion of the Fedayeen militia. As yet no official figures have ever been issued. After a comparative lull during the summer, Fatah launched an all-out commando and terrorist campaign in August 1969, and for some time blow and counter-blow were struck alternately by Arab and Israeli. On the first days of that month there were rocket attacks on the Israeli town of Kiryat Shimona, a frontier town in Upper Galilee with a population of about 15,000, in which two Israelis were killed. On the 7th Fatah claimed to have launched its biggest operation so far, when it attacked three settlements and three army posts south of the Sea of Galilee, and there was a three-hour battle in which the Fedayeen used mortars and rockets near the village of Tardena. On the same day a bus carrying Israeli soldiers was blown up between Samakh and Hamma on the Golan Plateau, two being killed and twelve wounded. In reply Israeli aircraft struck at guerilla camps around Irbid. On the 10th Israeli planes again raided the East Ghor Canal, claiming that there had been 38 Fedayeen attacks from Jordanian territory in ten days. They breached it at Adasiya, near the cease-fire line, after which Israeli snipers stopped Jordanians working to repair it until Jordan agreed to restrain the guerillas.[1] The next day Israeli aircraft raided guerilla camps in the Mount Hermon foothills following over 20 incidents from Lebanese territory within that month. In the third week in August three Israeli soldiers were killed on the Jordanian border, and again Israeli planes hit at Fedayeen bases in Jordan.

In Arab Jerusalem[2] there were riots after an Australian set fire to the Aksa Mosque (on the 21st August), and on the 26th a number of rockets, still on their launchers, were found near

---

[1] As the result of American intervention it was repaired on the 22nd September 1969, the Israelis allowing the work to proceed on the understanding that there would be no more incursions from that area.

[2] The expression includes the old city and environs formerly held by Jordan prior to the June War, also known as East Jerusalem.

Bethlehem, after three had been fired by Fedayeen. In the Hebron area Fatah tried to use Viet Cong tactics and to terrorize the population into compliance. On the 25th August five Arabs from the village of Hilhul, which had a population of about 6,000, were murdered by guerillas. One Arab was allowed to return to tell the tale. Moshe Dayan assembled the villagers and offered them arms with which to defend themselves, saying that they could have either 'normalization or Israeli counter-action'. The villagers were afraid to accept arms, and so Hilhul, with its long-standing contacts with Bedu and smugglers, remained a guerilla centre and haven, with Fatah busily establishing underground cells. On the 26th October, after an Israeli had been killed and two others wounded, a block of some eighteen houses was demolished in the village by the Israelis, the first occasion this type of reprisal had been undertaken on such a scale. Previously, on the 6th October, the Arab mayor of Ramallah was expelled to the East Bank.

During the last two months of the year the Jordanian border was alive with incidents. On the 16th November, for example, Israeli aircraft attacked Jordanian army positions near the frontier, after an Israeli post near Adhot Yacov had been mortared. On the 26th the Israeli air force carried out its longest and most intense air assault since the June War on Iraqi artillery positions around Irbid; Baghdad radio claimed that two Israeli aircraft were brought down, but the Israelis denied this. On the 28th December, after alleging that they had suffered over 120 acts of aggression from Jordanian territory against Israeli settlements in three months, Israeli aircraft destroyed the Ajlun radar station.

Meanwhile, on the Arab side little had materialized in relation to the eastern front, despite periodic meetings of chiefs of staff of the several countries. By May 1969 the only troops still assembled there were the Iraqi division in Jordan and a single Saudi Arabian brigade in southern Jordan—the rest had been withdrawn. In August President Atassi of Syria, and Hafez Assad, the Defence Minister, went to Cairo to discuss reviving old joint defence agreements, when Assad invited Iraqi units to join those of Syria near the Israeli-Syrian border. An Iraqi brigade moved to Dera, in Syria. In September Hardan Takriti, the Iraqi Defence Minister, visited Amman to co-ordinate the actions of the Iraqis and the Jordanians along the eastern front, and several meetings of defence ministers and others followed, but the eastern front remained shadowy and weak.

During 1969, in Jordan, as the Fedayeen strove to become a state-within-a-state, so did the Government become more uneasy and divided amongst itself as to what line of action, or inaction, it should take against the guerillas. On the 23rd March Bahjat Talhouni, who had been Premier since 1967, resigned and was succeeded by Abdul Moneim Rifai.[1] But it was a game of musical chairs, as on the 12th August Talhouni again became Premier, while on the 27th General Amer Khamash, who had been the Jordanian Chief of Staff during the June War, was replaced as Defence Minister by Ahmed Toukan, the changes being due to the dilemma as to how to deal with the Fedayeen.

On the 10th April rockets were fired at Eilat from Akaba, for which belatedly Fatah claimed responsibility, and the Jordanians arrested several guerillas. This was a breach of the secret agreement between King Hussein, who was in America at the time of the incident, and the Fedayeen, that no guerilla attacks should take place from Akaba because it was so vulnerable to reprisal. Jordanian police surrounded refugee camps near Amman, and Fatah and other groups were placed on 'emergency alert', but gradually the tension relaxed a little. On his return King Hussein flew off to Cairo to seek Nasser's support, but he drew a blank. Nasser had not yet changed his policy towards the Fedayeen (as he was about to do the following month) of urging them to collaborate with their host countries. There were reports that Haj Amin al-Husseini had been appointed leader of a new Palestine movement, which was backed by both King Hussein and King Feisal, but this never seemed to get off the ground. Hussein had to continue to praise the guerillas, but he did tell a congress of Palestinian students in Amman that while the Arabs must be prepared for battle,

[1] Not to be confused with Samir Rifai, his brother, who had previously been Jordanian Premier on several occasions, the last time being in 1963.

the regular Arab armies would play the major part and that the guerillas would only 'strike at the enemy to weaken him'. This was not well received; the Fedayeen wanted to be the main offensive force, with the Jordanian army providing the defence in depth for the eastern front.

A troublesome organization in Jordan was the Islamic Liberation Party (Tahrir), the ILP, which had clashed with the authorities on several occasions and had in September fired shots at the Amman radio station.[1] The ILP had been founded in the 1930s by Sheikh Takieddin Nabhani, and it advocated a return to the Caliphate and government based on Koranic law. Generally unpopular, it was banned in all Arab countries. The ILP had about 100 members in Jordan. Their plan was to assassinate King Hussein and his ministers, an attempt being made on the 6th October. The following day Mohammed Rasoul al-Kailani, Minister of the Interior, stated that foreign elements had been involved in a plot by right-wing Muslim fanatics, which had been crushed. Most of the ILP members in Jordan were arrested. On the 12th November nine members of the Legion of Victory were sentenced to death in Amman, and others, including the leader, Taher Dablan,[2] were given prison sentences for their part in the November 1968 riots.

On the 30th June 1969 Sherif Nasser ben Jamil, uncle of King Hussein, was appointed Commander-in-Chief of the Jordanian forces, and Major-General Ali al-Hayari, became the Chief of Staff. Sherif Nasser at once forbade the firing of rockets and mortars from Jordanian territory into Israel, but only Jordanian soldiers obeyed him; he had no control over the Fedayeen. Being a strong hard-liner against the Fedayeen in Jordan, he formed a brigade of special troops, later to be known as the Saiqa (Storm) Brigade, which consisted of carefully vetted officers and mainly Bedu soldiers, many being recalled reservists. This formation, which was given special training, was stationed near the Basman Palace, King Hussein's official residence in Amman. In November the Jordanian Government found an excuse to refuse admission to Arabs expelled by the

[1] This was considered by many Jordanians to be the act that started the civil war.

[2] Dablan died in prison on the 23rd March 1972.

Israelis from the West Bank, thus thwarting, it thought, a suspected Israeli scheme to Judeaize the West Bank. On the 22nd November a Soviet military attaché was appointed to Amman, the first since diplomatic relations had been established with the Soviet Union in 1964. This was 'one upmanship' for King Hussein, as the Fedayeen had been eagerly courting the Soviet Union without success for some time.

During 1969 many Fedayeen frictions came to the surface. On the 24th April the Iraqi Government had given all guerillas in its territory an ultimatum that they must either subject themselves to its control and join the ALF, or leave, which caused bitter comment that swelled as the Iraqis were able effectively to restrain guerilla freedom of movement. Static and unhappy about its role, the PLA, commanded by Brigadier Midhat Budiery, a regular officer, remained with its larger element in Syria under Syrian control. Suddenly, on the 5th June, Budiery was dismissed and replaced by another Syrian officer, Colonel Fathi Saad a-Din, but he shared the power with Colonel Yahya, who remained as Chief of Staff. These moves reflected the underlying tussle between the Syrian Government and the PLO. Although taking no apparent commando action against Israel, an interesting sidelight was revealed on the 26th May, at the Swedish trial of two Arabs charged with planning to assassinate Ben Gurion, a former Israeli Premier, while on a tour of South America, when both the accused claimed to be members of the PLA.

A particular source of friction in guerilla circles was the constant competing and identical claims for responsibility for incidents by several organizations. Especially was there rivalry between Fatah and the PFLP in this 'war of communiqués'. Many claims were false and fanciful as, for example, when two Israeli ships in Eilat harbour were damaged by an underwater explosion; Fatah said it had been caused by its members, although far more probably it had been done by Egyptian frogmen operating from Akaba. The PASC was supposed to examine and co-ordinate claims and vet press statements, but the PFLP was never a member of the PASC and so could not be controlled in this respect. The smaller DPF was now in the PASC, but it ran a solitary course in an independent way. As yet the DPF had done little of a warlike nature, concentrating still upon raising money, recruiting and preparing for the future. On the 23rd July 1969 yet another splinter group broke away from Fatah, to become known as the Action Committee for the Liberation of Palestine, the ACLP. The ACLP claimed responsibility for the explosion in a Tel Aviv bus station and other incidents, which caused a toll of one Israeli killed and 22 wounded, as well as six Arabs injured.

In August Shukairy, former leader of the PLO, emerged briefly to address a press conference in Beirut, at which he demanded, amongst other things, that Arab governments subscribe £50 million for guerilla action against Israel and £5 million for guerilla propaganda and arms for Palestinian Arabs living under Israeli rule. He also stated that the Arab regular armies were not capable of liberating Palestine. Little notice was taken of him, and he sank back into obscurity for a while.

Personalities clashed, breeding personal hatreds. The first sweet taste of individual publicity for the Fedayeen leaders had faded, becoming soured by fear of assassination. On the 7th July a Fatah spokesman in Amman said that a parcel bomb attempt on Arafat's life had been foiled; on the 7th September the Syrians accused the PLO of exploding a grenade in a Damascus park the previous day, which had injured many people; and on the 15th October the Beirut headquarters of the PLO was hit by four rockets from an adjacent house. Shunning the limelight, Fedayeen leaders went in fear of their lives, not only from their rivals but from the Israelis, who had an extremely effective intelligence service. They moved incognito from camp to camp keeping their whereabouts and future movements secret, as they were afraid that either Arab or Israeli agents would infiltrate their organizations.

One of the main features of the year was the development and partial arming of the Fedayeen militia, which was conservatively estimated by the end of 1969 to be at least 15,000 strong, the majority belonging to Fatah. The bulk of the Fedayeen militia had been given some military and political training, and was utilized in a supporting role, to collect information, provide labour, to obtain supplies, to raise money, and to produce an 'instant mob' whenever one was required. The regular Fedayeen themselves were generally armed with the now familiar Soviet AK-47, the Kalesnikov automatic rifle, which was more modern than many of the weapons carried by regular soldiers in some Arab armies. The Fedayeen had Katyusha rockets, grenades and ammunition, and also plenty of transport and communication equipment, although the latter was never used properly. Becoming well known was the Fatah badge, consisting of crossed rifles and a grenade. During the year the Ashbals and youth organizations in the refugee camps developed and became regularized. On the political side one of the main gains was on the 23rd September, when a PLO delegation was admitted as observers to an Islamic summit, held for the first time outside an Arab capital, at Rabat. The summit turned out to be rather a shambles, as both Syria and Iraq boycotted it, but Saudi Arabia, Kuwait and Libya agreed to pay some £110 million annually to the PLO. The Fedayeen constantly sought communist support, which was warily withheld. On the 14th December 1969 an Italian communist delegation arrived in Amman to be taken on a tour of inspection of Fatah bases and refugee camps, but it departed a few days later without commenting or helping.

In their efforts to obtain widespread international support, especially from among the youth of the world, Fatah organized a party of about 145 people, mainly students, from several countries, including 48 from Britain, to visit and live in Fatah camps in Jordan for a month in July and August. This had unexpected results, as the visitors were badly behaved, would not conform to Fatah camp routine, drank alcohol, praised the PFLP and criticized Fatah tactics. This public relations exercise was not repeated, although later there were other visits, but the personnel were carefully vetted, briefed and controlled.

The psychological factor became evident in the three-sided struggle between the Fedayeen, their host countries and the Israelis. The 'propaganda war' over the radio and in the press, as well as the 'war of communiqués' have been mentioned; during 1969 yet another aspect peeped through—that of brainwashing. On the 16th September the PFLP complained that some of its Ashbals were undergoing psychiatric treatment to eradicate the effects of alleged Israeli brain-washing, the PFLP saying that the boys had been captured when they had been sent into the occupied territories on missions. The number of PFLP Ashbals was said to be ten only, but it was believed that the larger organizations, such as Fatah, had a similar problem on a larger scale. The Israelis were silent on this matter.

Briefly summarizing the Fedayeen fortunes for the year, it can be said that throughout 1969 the guerillas had been hoping and waiting for the Arab masses in the occupied territories to rise at their instigation on the Viet Cong pattern, or at least to respond in some way to overtures, but this had not happened. The Fedayeen had also hoped that people living under old, traditional régimes, such as in Saudi Arabia, Kuwait, Qatar and even Jordan, would revolt, cast out their rulers and spontaneously join the guerilla movement. This did not happen either. Fatah apologetically claimed that the failure of large-scale resistance in the occupied territories was not the result of an incapacity but of national pressures. While on the whole the Fedayeen had ample small arms, mines, rockets and small mortars, they were disappointed because Arab states would not accede to their request for heavy arms such as tanks, guns and even aircraft. The PLA detachment in Syria had been given a few old T-34 tanks but that was all. The Arab states had no intention of allowing the Fedayeen to build up strong conventional forces on their territory which would have attracted Israeli reprisals and been an internal danger to themselves. However, what did happen was that Fatah produced an ideal of Palestinian unity, which gave a measure of hope to the thousands of refugees who felt lost and abandoned. Fatah also became popular with many left-wing West Bankers, who had never really accepted King Hussein's rule, and more recently had become disillusioned with his inability to protect them.

Throughout the year the Fedayeen attempted to penetrate into Israeli-held territory, but were met by strong countermeasures. In particular the guerillas suffered in ambushes. The Fedayeen fighter infiltrated to plant mines and to set up ambushes, but usually he quickly withdrew again. Internal terrorism continued spasmodically, and caused fear amongst the Arabs in the occupied territories as terror squads eliminated a few who would not help. The Israelis threatened that when terrorist incidents occurred not only would the individuals concerned be punished, but others also for non-co-operation. It was a slow escalation of fear, but even though the Israelis only demolished houses and imprisoned terrorists, while guerillas murdered some who would not support them, the Israelis generally kept the situation under control. Moshe Dayan stated on the 12th November that as reprisals against Arabs aiding the Fedayeen, 140 houses had been demolished since the 1st April, and that since the June War 71 people had been expelled to Jordan. A notable Israeli success occurred on the 28th October when, despite threats and warnings from the Fedayeen not to co-operate, thousands of Arabs in east Jerusalem voted in municipal elections, many for the first time, as under Jordanian rule only property-owning men over 23 years of age were eligible to vote.

The PASC also reviewed its activities for 1969 and came to rather pessimistic conclusions, admitting that its operations in the occupied territories remained at a low level, that it had lost 'several hundred fighters', that several guerilla underground networks had been exposed, and that Israeli counter-measures were becoming increasingly effective. However, it also expressed general satisfaction on how the guerilla 'war of attrition' was going, claiming to have inflicted huge losses on the Israeli armed forces. Later (on the 4th March 1970) in the Knesset, Moshe Dayan said that 2,600 suspects were detained during the year (1969), including 100 Israeli Arabs, that during clashes 586 Arabs were killed, and that 10 Arabs had been killed on the West Bank and 57 wounded, while arms captured included '100 bazookas and mortars, 1,000 mines, large quantities of explosives and grenades and 1,000 light arms'.

# 5. *Fatahland*

The sudden Israeli commando raid on Beirut airport on the 28th December 1968 brought about a new guerilla phase, which escalated. In the Lebanon, usually quoted as being the second country to make a peace settlement with Israel, and whose 63-mile border with that country had been the quietest of all Israel's frontiers, reaction from the guerillas there was quick. On the night of the 30th December nine rocket attacks from mobile launchers were made on the border town of Kiryat Shimona, the Fedayeen claiming to have killed two Israelis. This was followed by a similar rocket attack on the same town on the evening of the 2nd January 1969, when in reply Israeli artillery shelled a Lebanese village. Lebanese guns joined in and a short artillery duel broke out, signalling that a fourth Israeli war front had opened.

This caused Premier Abdullah al-Yafi to state that while he gave support to the Palestine cause, there were no Fedayeen bases in the Lebanon. This was not strictly true, as the first guerilla fighters, mainly Fatah and Saiqa, moved into the Lebanon about October 1968. It is usually alleged that General Chehab[1] had tacitly allowed them to enter, to recruit in the refugee camps of which there were at least sixteen,[2] to open offices in Beirut and to put out propaganda. They were not supposed to train in, or operate from Lebanese territory, and while they were in such small numbers, perhaps hardly 100, the Lebanese Government was able to enforce these restrictions. Why Chehab allowed the guerillas to enter his country is not

[1] Former President and Commander-in-Chief.
[2] Some sources say more.

quite clear, but there was a great deal of sympathy amongst the Muslims in the Lebanon for Fedayeen ideals, and perhaps he did not anticipate that they would attempt to become the cuckoo in the nest. It was suspected that Chehab, who was still a political power in the land, retained contacts with the guerillas.

The Israelis insistence that the Fedayeen had camps in the Lebanon was true only to a minor degree until January 1969, when the raid on Beirut airport spotlighted that country, making it suddenly attractive to the Fedayeen, and especially to adjacent Syria, wanting to exploit its Saiqa and inclined to be jealous of Arafat who was independently doing rather well in Jordan, where his Fatah was outshining the Syrian Saiqa. During January Fatah and Saiqa mmebers moved over the border and infiltrated into southern Lebanon, establishing themselves in the Arkoub area, in the broken country of the Mount Hermon foothills, to the east of the Hasbani River, where they began to organize themselves. This area, varying at times from 20–50 square miles, became known generally as Fatahland, and it remained under guerilla domination. The Lebanese Army warily stayed on the west bank of the Hasbani River and Lebanese police and officials gradually disappeared from the Arkoub sector as the guerillas became stronger.

Internal security was handed over to the Lebanese army, which moved into positions around Beirut airport, the Defence Minister trying to absolve it from any blame by saying that airport security had been a police responsibility. On the 8th January Yafi's Government fell, to be replaced by one led by Rashid Karame,[1] who formed a coalition and promised to introduce conscription, to strengthen the army, to fortify the southern villages and to further the Palestine cause—all controversial subjects in the Lebanon.

The Israeli Government declared that it would not tolerate

[1] Rashid Karame, who had led the Nasser-inspired rebellion in the Lebanon (which had largely rested on the basis of Christian and Muslim rivalry) in 1958, when US troops were landed to restore order, had been Premier five times already, the last occasion being during the June War when he had ordered the Lebanese armed forces into action against the Israelis—but they had refused to march.

guerilla activity across its northern border, and the Lebanon became apprehensive in case the Israelis took serious reprisals, so steps were taken to contain the guerillas, which included arresting several of them. The Syrian Government then accused the Lebanese of preventing the Fedayeen from operating into Israel, which brought the retort from Premier Karame that his country would not give any pretext to the Israelis to attack it.

Lebanon and Syria

Arafat, with his growing prestige and power, decided that he would like to establish Fatah in the Lebanon on the same lines as in Jordan, and on the 14th February he met Premier Karame for talks. He offered to fortify the frontier villages and

93

defend them with his guerillas in return for freedom of movement within the country, but the Lebanese Government would not agree to this noting that the Fedayeen, not being responsible to any Arab government, were not subject to normal diplomatic and international pressures. By the end of February there were about 300 armed guerillas in the Lebanon, with more arriving daily, which brought about a degree of tension as the Lebanese army tried to contain them to the east of the Hasbani River and limit their activities.

The guerillas in Fatahland carried out a few terrorist and commando operations, but mainly this was a period of establishment, preparation and expansion for them in the Lebanon. They became active in the refugee camps, recruiting, arming and training, and they set up a number of small camps in the Arkoub area. Fatahland was germinating. In an effort to maintain control the Lebanese authorities arrested some guerillas, but protests at their detention by the Fedayeen and their sympathizers mounted and culminated in two days of violent rioting in Beirut and elsewhere, on the 22rd and 24th April, in which 16 people were killed and 62 injured. There was a wave of demonstrations demanding freedom of movement within the Lebanon for the guerillas, stones were thrown at the police in certain refugee camps, riots occurred in some camps in the south of the country, and Palestinian refugees stormed Tyre and tore down the national flag.

The Government imposed a state of emergency and a five-day curfew was clamped on the trouble spots. On the 25th Premier Karame resigned, but continued as a caretaker and on the following day more violence erupted. Not yet ready for a head-on clash with the Lebanese Government, Arafat tried to calm the situation. Urging the Palestinian refugees to co-operate with the security forces, he cancelled a demonstration planned to be held for guerillas killed on the 23rd. The Syrian Government loudly criticized the actions of the Lebanese Government, and there were demonstrations in Damascus in favour of the Fedayeen. Then followed days of indecision on the part of the Lebanese authorities, of which the guerillas took full advantage to increase their hold on the refugee camps, smuggling in more arms and explosives. The police were driven from one refugee camp near Tripoli, and in others they were only tolerated provided they remained passive.

The Lebanese attitude to the Fedayeen in their midst was divided; the Christian element wanted the guerillas to be ejected, while the Muslim element demanded that they be supported. After a period of hesitation President Helou compromised and ordered the Lebanese army to contain them. In Fatahland the guerillas were anxious to clear all police posts from this area, and in April (1969) a detachment of Saiqa captured a police post at the foot of Mount Hermon. There had been incidents of guerillas firing on military patrols around Hasbaya, a village with a population of about 2,000, and the waiting Lebanese army moved into action and retook the police post, in the process killing five guerillas, wounding ten and capturing forty. In the fighting a Lebanese army unit was ambushed and one soldier killed. The Lebanese authorities claimed that the prisoners were Syrians and not Palestinians, but the Syrian Government denied this—the unspoken responsibility was assigned to the Syrian Saiqa. The guerillas had been somewhat surprised by the resolute action of the deprecated Lebanese army.

Something of a stalemate now set in, with the Lebanese army surrounding the refugee camps and blocking guerilla moves in Fatahland, and the Fatah leadership refusing to talk to the Lebanese authorities until all arrested men were released and the siege of the camps lifted. On the 9th May Arafat came to the Lebanon and for three days unsuccessfully tried to negotiate, demanding the right to establish bases facing Israel and freedom of action within the country. The Lebanese Government might at this stage have agreed to allow the guerillas to set up camps in certain areas in southern Lebanon, provided all Fedayeen movement from Syria would be through a fixed 'corridor' controlled by the Lebanese army, but Arafat would not accept this, and the smouldering tension continued. On the 24th May it was reported that the Lebanese army had blocked a Saiqa attempt to move some 400 guerillas into Fatahland, where it was now estimated that there were between 500 and 800 armed fighters, part Fatah and part Saiqa, being contained on the east side of the Hasbani River. From Fatahland the guerillas could only raid through the foothills of the Mount Hermon range on to the Golan Plateau, their sole lifeline back to Syria being by mountain tracks over the range.

The population of the Lebanon, which had an area of about 4,300 square miles, was about 2·7 million, of whom roughly half were Christian and half Muslim, the precise proportions being blurred to avoid rivalry. Traditionally political power was apportioned in the ratio of six Christians to five Muslims, power being shared; the President, for example, was always a Christian and the Premier a Muslim. Each was studiously tolerant of the other, and there had been comparatively few inter-racial or inter-religious disturbances, that in 1958 being somewhat an exception in recent years, although a strong current of antipathy ran deep beneath the surface. The Lebanese army, a voluntary service one, had a recruiting problem, having difficulty in attracting sufficient men to maintain its establishment of just under 14,000—the total establishment of the armed forces being just over 15,000. In fact, its actual numbers were down to nearly 11,000. Having become a political instrument to some extent, the army was not held in very high esteem. It consisted of two armoured units, one having some 40 Centurions and the other 40 AMX-13s, with some light armoured vehicles, and eight infantry battalions, while the small artillery element possessed about 40 guns of various types. The Lebanese air force, having about 1,000 men, had 12 Hawker Hunters, 6 Vampires and 12 Alouette helicopters, while the first Mirages (of 12 just bought from France) had begun to arrive.

With only a caretaker government in charge, the Lebanese crisis dragged on. Its handling of the Fedayeen brought mounting criticism from Arab states, even the distant régimes of Libya and the Sudan condemning the Government and praising the guerillas. Despite the official policy of support for the Palestinian cause, on the 24th June President Helou said that 'persuasion or pressure' might be necessary to remove Fedayeen bases that had become established in the Lebanon. Anxious how Israel might react to the situation, on the 2nd July he stated that the Lebanese National Assembly had unanimously agreed that 'Arab armies be permitted to enter the Lebanon should the need arise', but he also warned guerillas against giving the Israelis any excuse for invading southern Lebanon.

The Lebanese army continued to show unexpected resolution in containing the guerillas in the few square miles of Fatahland, even laying mines to hamper their movement, but despite this they managed at times to penetrate the Lebanese military cordon and slip to the Israeli border (instead of to the Golan Plateau ceasefire line which was open to them), to fire rockets and mortar bombs and lay mines, sometimes firing over the heads of the Lebanese soldiers. This provoked an Israeli reprisal raid on the 16th July (the first since the raid on Beirut airport), when the Israelis attacked the border village of Maji Miyyeh, demolishing three houses that had been used by guerillas.

Although devoting most of their energies to resisting Lebanese army pressure and consolidating their base, the guerillas in Fatahland undertook a series of raids into the Golan Plateau. Following twenty such incidents within the month, on the 11th August Israeli aircraft raided Fatahland camps. In an effort to inspire terror amongst the inhabitants, the majority of whom were Druze,[1] on the 15th the guerillas executed three Druze, allegedly for passing information to the Israelis. The Druze in Israel had completely thrown in their lot with the Israelis, and formed a majority in the Israeli border police units. They were also allowed to volunteer for service with the Israeli defence forces; they had collaborated, too, with the Israelis on the Golan Plateau, practically the whole of the 6,400 inhabitants remaining after the June War being Druze.

Guerilla commando raids continued. Five Fedayeen were killed on the Golan Plateau during the third week in August, which provoked an Israeli air attack on Fatahland, and on the 28th seven Israelis were wounded in a border incident, which brought further reprisal air raids on to the Arkoub area. Guerilla raids and reprisals followed, and on the 3rd September there was a large Israeli air assault on camps in Fatahland.

[1] The Druze are a sect mainly inhabiting mountainous parts of northern Syria and adjacent areas, whose religion is based on both the Koran and the Bible and whose prophets include Adam, Noah, Abraham, Moses, Jesus and Mohammed.

Fedayeen also managed to penetrate Upper Galilee, and on the 5th an Israeli commando force, supported by aircraft, crossed the Lebanese frontier and attacked the village of Halta, killing 15 guerillas and demolishing 12 houses. Again, on the 3rd October, after more incidents, a similar Israeli assault was made on the border villages of Miza, Dahujat and Itrun, all used by the Fedayeen. On the 9th a still larger Israeli ground force struck in the same region, penetrating a distance of nine miles, in reprisal for Fedayeen attacks on an Israeli hotel and bus.

During the summer the guerillas had been busy gaining influence in the refugee camps, smuggling in arms and issuing propaganda. The PLO, and some other organizations, opened offices in towns near the Israeli border, operating them quite openly. Their efforts had gained a volume of sympathy for their cause from the radical parties and the students, as well as from the Muslim masses, as might be expected, but there was also deep opposition, especially from the right-wing Christian political organizations. The Lebanese army, roughly half Christian and half Muslim in composition, had remained loyal to the caretaker government, and did much to restrict guerilla activity by being close to the refugee camps, putting down road-blocks and carrying out searches. On the 7th September Lebanese soldiers seized a consignment of over 100 rifles from an UNRWA truck, just north of Beirut. In Fatahland about 800 armed guerillas were penned in by Lebanese army units positioned firmly on the west bank of the Hasbani River, forcing the guerillas mainly to penetrate into the Golan Plateau, a much more dangerous project than slipping into Upper Galilee. However, the Fedayeen succeeded to a minor degree in penetrating the Lebanese army screen to carry out acts of terrorism which, they anticipated, would provoke Israeli reprisal raids that would attract support in the Lebanon, as they were by a common enemy and would thus weaken the resolve of the army, especially the Muslim part of it.

An interesting incident occurred on the 29th September, when two Soviet diplomats were arrested in Beirut after a gun-battle with the police, in which one was wounded. The Lebanese Government alleged that they were in a plot to bribe a Lebanese pilot to fly his Mirage plane to Baku. The Soviet

Government denied any implication. After this the Lebanon, which from a Press point of view at least was the most liberal of all Middle East countries, on the 2nd October imposed censorship.

The unyielding stand of the Lebanese army, which was becoming irritated by the arrogance of the Fedayeen, was stifling the expansion of Fatahland. With the approach of winter the guerillas became anxious about supplies from Syria when the donkey tracks over the Mount Hermon range would be made impassable by snow, as the Lebanese army blocked the natural route to Syria along the Bakaa Valley on the west side of the Hasbani River to the main Damascus-Beirut highway. In mid-October the guerillas began to probe and press with larger patrols to see if the cordon would give way at any point—it did not, but instead began to react to this pressure aggressively, and on the 17th October armed clashes occurred which lasted several days.

On the 20th, apparently without orders, as the caretaker government remained indecisive, the Lebanese army opened up with artillery fire on a 200-strong Fedayeen unit which had penetrated as far as the village of Majdal Selim, in southern Lebanon, when it refused to withdraw. This was followed by the shelling of two more villages in the area of Bint Jebeil, near the Israeli border, and also Shukra, which killed several guerillas, especially at the latter place. The following day Lebanese troops advanced on Majdal Selim, surrounded it and killed some ten guerillas. On the 22nd there were further clashes in this region as a group of about 120 guerillas tried to settle in the villages of Shukra and Majdal al-Fil, both of which were well outside the Arkoub area, for their winter quarters, and were shelled by the Lebanese soldiers. A government communiqué stated that during these six days of skirmishing in southern Lebanon there had been eight Lebanese and 11 Fedayeen casualties, but the guerillas claimed that they had lost 14 killed and that 40 had been arrested. Caretaker Premier Karame, and two of his ministers, resigned in protest, and at this critical moment the country was left without a government.

Encouraged by the Syrian Government, the guerilla leaders decided to make a push in strength against the Lebanese army to force and hold a route from the Syrian border to Fatahland, and beyond to the northern Israeli frontier if possible, and coincident with this there was to be an internal dissident campaign in the cities, towns and refugee camps in support. On the 22nd there was a meeting at the PLO headquarters in Beirut, attended by Brigadier Yahya, now commander of the PLA, and others, which pledged support for the projected Fedayeen offensive; Syria closed its frontier with the Lebanon; Arafat ordered Fatah to 'fight against Lebanese intervention to the last bullet', and the Iraqi Government threatened to place its troops in Syria and Jordan under Fedayeen command. Syrian regular units were moved right to the Lebanese frontier to protect the assembling guerillas and to deter Lebanese troops from crossing into Syria to take action against the Fedayeen in the heat of battle.

Fatah and Saiqa units, numbering about 200 men in all, were selected for the assault, and on the 23rd, after mortar and rocket fire, they attacked three Lebanese customs posts. At those of Arida and Bukeiha, which they quickly occupied, they captured 24 police and customs personnel,[1] but at the third, that of Masnaa, the customs staff had hastily evacuated. On the following day, the 24th, this body of Fedayeen moved forward in Syrian trucks, to occupy without opposition the larger village of Yanta, which was near the northern tip of the Mount Hermon range, and make it their base in preparation for an assault on the crusader fortress near the village of Rashaya, another ten miles or so to the southwest. Rashaya commanded the vital road junction, and barred their route southwards through the Bakaa Valley to Fatahland. The guerillas stayed at Yanta for five days, contenting themselves with spasmodic mortar firing, the only tactical move of any note being to establish about 50 men in the village of Aiya, about four miles across the Valley from Rashaya on a wooded hillock.

While the attacking body of Fedayeen hesitated at Yanta, guerillas inside the Lebanon stirred up trouble whenever they could, but a curfew was clamped down on most cities and towns on the 23rd for the daylight hours, and this was successful in preventing many strikes and demonstrations. On the

[1] On the 24th they were exchanged for the body of a guerilla.

24th guerillas took control of the district in Beirut inhabited by Palestinian refugees, but the curfew prevented barricades being erected. It seemed as though the Lebanese Muslims were not yet ready or willing to act against the army in the capital. In Tripoli the guerillas were encouraged by Farouk Mokaddem, a Baathist leader and rival to Karame, who was also a native of that city, and they took over the citadel and old city centre, ejecting both the army and the police. Guerillas took up positions and there were exchanges of firing, in which the government forces admitted killing four and wounding five; but the Fedayeen claimed that their casualties were far heavier. There were more clashes in Tripoli on the 26th and the following day, until by the 28th the death roll had crept up to 18, but the violence was largely confined to the citadel area. In Sidon, on the 26th, the local Fatah commander had been arrested, but elsewhere in cities and towns, although the shops were closed, there were few demonstrations and little sign of mass spontaneous support for the guerillas.

On the 24th President Nasser urged President Helou to come to some settlement with the guerillas. On the following day (25th) Arafat held his first open press conference at Damascus, at which he both boasted and complained. His boasts were the usual platitudinous ones, while his complaints were that as the Lebanese had used Palestinian soil for their fight for freedom against the French, so the Palestinians should have the same right to use Lebanese soil. He also alleged that he had reached a 15-point agreement with General Emile Bustanti, the army commander after the April crisis, that guaranteed freedom of movement for the guerillas in the Lebanon, but he complained that it had been nullified by higher authority. It was denied over Radio Damascus that the Syrians were helping the guerillas, as the Lebanese were alleging.

On the 26th Nasser sent an envoy to Beirut to mediate between President Helou and Arafat. On the 28th General Bustanti went to Cairo for talks on the Lebanese situation. Arafat refused to attend at either capital, and from Damascus called on all Arabs to oppose the 'Lebanese plot against the Fedayeen'. He was hoping for more military gains before he was prepared to negotiate. Pierre Gemayel, leader of the Falangist

Party, Raymond Edde, leader of the National Bloc Party, and Camille Chamoun, leader of the National Liberal Party, all prominent Christian politicians, expressed anxiety over the Cairo talks, and accused Lebanese army leaders of having failed to liquidate the Fedayeen in the country in January (1969) when they 'numbered only 140 men', while now they 'numbered between 1,500 and 2,000 armed men'.

The three-day battle for the fortress at Rashaya began on the 28th October, when about 50 guerillas moved out from the village of Aiya to attack this Lebanese post, blocking the route southwards through the Bakaa Valley, which was held by only 17 soldiers. The assault was halted by the Lebanese, who killed five guerillas and captured another five, after which the remainder withdrew across to the wooded slopes on the east side of the valley, where they remained for another day until they were reinforced. The Lebanese garrison was also quickly strengthened on the 29th, until it consisted of about 150 soldiers with guns and mortars, and a small armoured unit began moving towards Rashaya.

At dawn on the 30th the guerillas opened mortar fire from Aiya on the Rashaya fortress, and Syrian artillery fire also came down in this area. The guerillas were just about to launch another assault on the Lebanese position when they were caught in the flank by Lebanese tanks which had arrived the previous evening and had started a dawn sweep to clear the valley. By noon Aiya had been cleared of Fedayeen, who withdrew to Yanta, leaving five dead on the field. Firing continued for the remainder of the day, but the battle for Rashaya was over. The guerillas had failed. The Lebanese Government admitted only to seven soldiers wounded.

On the 31st Arafat arrived at Yanta, the forward guerilla post, just after the Fedayeen had been defeated. Although a large number of them, estimated to be at least 400, were massed near the frontier village of Masnaa, he could not persuade them to advance again to force their way down the valley, which western newsmen were now referring to as the 'Arafat Trail'. Winter was approaching and already there was snow on the Mount Hermon range, but the Lebanese army had stood fast, and Arafat had to accept defeat on the field of battle.

102

The Fedayeen tried to organize a flurry of incidents and attacks inside the Lebanon in support of the Rashaya assault, and also to influence the talks in progress in Cairo, but they did not have a great deal of success. The main efforts were a series of four attacks in five days on the police post at Mashta Hassan in northern Lebanon, each of which was driven off with the aid of armoured vehicles; an assault on the 30th on the Kleyat airfield just two miles south of the Syrian border, where Lebanese Mirages were positioned, in which a soldier was killed, but which was repulsed with artillery fire; and another assault on the same day on a military road block near Sidon, in which a soldier was wounded.

After his failure at conventional military operations, Arafat went to Cairo on the 1st November and joined in the talks there with President Nasser and others. A number of Arabs, who had been on the side of the guerillas in the initial stages of the turmoil in the Lebanon, had changed their views when they saw the resolute stand of the army. Saleh Mahdi Ammash, Vice-Premier of Iraq, who had consulted both Nasser and President Helou, completely changed his attitude from the one he had adopted the previous week, when his Government was threatening to place its troops under Fedayeen command, to urging the protagonists to come to a settlement. He now rejected guerilla claims for permanent bases in the Lebanon, saying that 'corridors' for guerillas to filter along were sufficient. Ammash reasserted the Arab states' right to determine the course of the war against the Israelis, and insisted that guerillas must act within the framework of the overall Arab plan. The Fedayeen demanded not only bases and freedom of movement within the Lebanon, but the release of all guerillas arrested and the punishment of those responsible for the arrests.

Personal mediation by President Nasser brought about a cease-fire at midnight on the 2nd, and a written pact between Arafat and General Bustanti, which became known as the (Lebanese) Cairo Agreement[1] was signed. This agreement was a secret one and no details were published, the joint communiqué

[1] It was known simply as the Cairo Agreement, but is referred to in the text as the (Lebanese) Cairo Agreement to differentiate it from the later Cairo Agreement that concerned Jordan.

merely saying that the Lebanon's relations with the Palestine Revolution must be based on 'confidence, frankness and positive co-operation', while guaranteeing 'Lebanese sovereignty'. Neither the Lebanese nor the guerillas had obtained what they wanted, but both were partially satisfied, the Lebanese feeling that they had checked guerilla power, and the Fedayeen that they had gained recognition of the right to be in the Lebanon. Although the clauses were secret, it became obvious as the weeks passed that the main ones included allowing the guerillas to have influence in the refugee camps, to have small, mobile bases in Fatahland, and to be able to move along the Arafat Trail; they were not to fire into Israeli territory from Lebanese soil, but were to penetrate deeply before striking, and to inform the Lebanese army of all projected operations. The guerillas were to evacuate the dozen or so villages they had occupied in the Bakaa Valley along the Arafat Trail.

A co-ordinating body was set up, which became known as the Higher Committee for Palestine Affairs, consisting of both Lebanese and guerilla members. The Fedayeen had little intention of accepting any of the conditions, but were momentarily content to be allowed to remain in the Lebanon. Their object was to bring down the Lebanese régime by provoking Israeli reprisal raids that would render large numbers of people homeless, jobless, hungry and discontented. The Lebanese insisted that their 'sovereignty' had been secured, but they were unhappy. Especially was the army, which had done so well and surprised many in the Middle East, discontented with the (Lebanese) Cairo Agreement, as it wanted to move in and finish off the guerillas. Its morale was high, perhaps at its highest ever, but its operations should be kept in perspective as all its actions had been on platoon, or at the highest, company level—there had been no battles of any size or engagements of any magnitude. On the 4th Raymond Edde protested that the Lebanese constitution did not allow for secret agreements and demanded a debate in the National Assembly.

Arafat's attempt to match his guerillas against the Lebanese army had been abortive, denting the Fedayeen image and lessening its influence in the Lebanon. Despite over-confident and arrogant boasts it was seen that they had neither the morale,

training nor combat ability to undertake conventional operations, and had been repulsed by the tiny army they held in
contempt. The guerillas found no mass support in the Lebanon,
not even from the lukewarm Muslims, and none at all from the
Muslim element in the armed forces. The guerillas had been
too closely associated with the Syrian Baathists, who were
hated by the Lebanese Christians and mistrusted by the
Lebanese Muslims. The army used psychological warfare to the
extent of spreading rumours that the attacking guerillas were
all part of a Syrian plot against the country. The guerilla
strength and actions alarmed all in the Lebanon who, whatever
their political persuasion, tended to draw unconsciously together against them. Concerned with their continuing rivalry
with the Syrian Baathists for influence in the Lebanon, when
they saw the guerillas were incapable of winning in the field the
Iraqi Baathists changed their attitude and supported their own
Government's view. Arafat had been forced to appeal to pan-
Arabism, which he professed to be independent of, and aloof
from, to bring pressure to bear on the Lebanese to cease fire
before his men were eliminated in the Lebanon.

President Atassi of Syria had long wanted the moderate
régime in the Lebanon to be replaced by a communist or revolutionary one, and the Syrian army had provided the guerillas
with trucks, equipment and communications, and a strongly-
held frontier to operate from. There is no firm evidence that
any Syrian troops entered the Lebanon during this fortnight
although, of course, numbers of the Syrian-sponsored Saiqa
had done so, but they had fired shells and mortar bombs in
support of the guerillas.

On the 13th November Syria reopened its frontier with the
Lebanon; on the 14th the guerillas evacuated the Tripoli
citadel area which they had occupied since the 24th October,
and on the 16th, after three weeks, the curfew was lifted
throughout the Lebanon. On the 25th Karame formed a
government, which included all political factions except
Raymond Edde's National Bloc Party, thus ending the seven-
month long political crisis in the country.

Feeling between the Lebanese Security Forces and the
guerillas still ran high. On the 20th November they clashed at

a refugee camp near Sidon, when the army objected to the guerillas in the camp leaving it wearing uniform and carrying arms. When a body of guerillas attacked an army post there was a four-hour battle, but they were beaten off as the Lebanese brought up armoured vehicles and shelled the attackers and also positions inside the refugee camp. The Lebanese reported that six soldiers and 43 guerillas had been wounded.

The fifth Arab summit met at Rabat from the 19th to the 23rd December. It was attended by 14 members of the Arab League and also a PLO delegation led by Arafat, but it broke up without issuing a communiqué. It had been a demonstration of Arab disunity, differences being highlighted between the 'traditional bloc' led by Saudi Arabia, which had wealth, and the 'progressive bloc' led by Egypt, which had little or none. President Nasser's plan for the distribution of money from the richer Arab states was unpopular. Boumedienne, of Algeria, scarcely concealed his low opinion of some Arab countries and their achievements, or lack of them, for the Palestine revolution. Arafat, able to speak at a summit for the first time, demanded money, and was promised £26 million, almost as much as he had asked for, but the amount was later denied and disputed. King Hassan, of Morocco, was reported to have said that he would give Fatah £20 million. There was eventually a wide credibility gap between promises and payment.

The guerillas continued to raid into the Golan Plateau. On the 3rd December, in reprisal, an Israeli commando detachment attacked a Fedayeen camp near Fatahland, and in the fighting, that lasted for two hours, one Israeli officer was killed, but the Israelis claimed to have killed 12 guerillas. On the 13th two Israelis were killed in a rocket attack on Metulla, causing Israel to warn that further such incidents from Lebanese territory would bring grave consequences. On the 31st December guerillas kidnapped an Israeli home guard from Netulla, presumably in the hope of trading him for the release of Fatah members detained in Israel—the first instance of their taking such a prisoner. Rockets were again fired at Kiryat Shimona.

This kidnapping provoked an Israeli reprisal two-pronged raid, one prong of which hit at a Lebanese frontier post, and the other at Kafr Kala. Few shots were fired, but the Israelis returned with 21 prisoners (11 soldiers and 10 civilians). The Lebanese claimed that in the fighting three Israelis were killed, which in turn was denied by the Israelis. So far Israeli ground raids had been mainly in the hilly, arid north-eastern sector of the Lebanese frontier, and this marked a new phase as Kafr Kala was more to the centre of Israel's northern frontier. There were other similar raids in January and in February, as well as aircraft strikes on Fatahland and on the Arafat Trail, along which, the Israelis alleged, over 1,000 guerillas had filtered during the past twelve months.

Criticism mounted in southern Lebanon against the Government, and also the army, owing to lack of protection against both the Israelis and the Fedayeen. On the 4th January (1970) Pierre Gemayel and others called for an end to the (Lebanese) Cairo Agreement and the expulsion of all guerillas from the Lebanon. After a stormy secret session in the National Assembly General Bustanti, the Commander-in-Chief, was dismissed and replaced by Brigadier Jean Njeim, who was promoted Major-General. No official explanation was given.

After conferring with guerilla leaders in Beirut, Kamal Jumblatt, Minister of the Interior, stated that the Government was committed to the (Lebanese) Cairo Agreement, but that the guerillas had undertaken to restrict their activities on Lebanese soil, not to put their men nearer than 'one kilometre' to any village, to cease training in the refugee camps and to move deeper into Israel to strike. It was doubtful whether they meant what they said, or even if they had actually agreed to these conditions, as they carried on as before. A joint statement was issued in Amman on the 11th by guerilla organizations accusing the Lebanon of breaking the conditions of the (Lebanese) Cairo Agreement and threatening to 'explode anew the October crisis' unless the guerillas were allowed to train in refugee camps and operate from the Lebanon. On the 13th the Government decided to spend an extra £13 million on defence to buy more arms, strengthen the defences of southern Lebanon, to train and arm the civilian population there and to build bomb-proof shelters. But this project was slow to start, being limited in fact to purchases of extra arms for the regular army, which still had difficulty in attracting enough recruits to bring it up to its establishment.

Local inhabitants protested that the PLO offices in Hasbaya and Nabatiyah would attract Israeli reprisals, and after a conference between Kamal Jumblatt and General Njeim the Government ordered them to be closed. Further meetings with the Fedayeen resulted in a statement on the 4th February that Lebanese security forces would resume policing the refugee camps. But this was countered on the 26th by the joint Lebanese-Fedayeen Higher Committee for Palestine Affairs, which said the responsibility for protecting the Palestine revolution in the camps belonged to the guerillas, and that they would be allowed training facilities outside the camps as well. On the same day the Government announced a new agreement with the Fedayeen, and banned their carrying or using firearms in populated areas. The security forces and the guerillas were to share check points on the Syrian frontier, and in return the guerillas were to be allowed to operate from the Lebanon. The Government was desperately trying to control the guerilla influx, but these statements were mainly empty ones, as neither gave an inch unless jostled back by the other.

On the 6th March, following 37 alleged incidents from Lebanese territory since the 1st January, Israeli commandos launched a reprisal raid on the village of Aita e-Shaab (population about 3,000), in which one guerilla was killed and two others captured. On the following day five Fedayeen were killed in an incident near the Lebanese border. The Lebanese authorities were now faced with a growing internal refugee problem of their own as people fled from the dangerous southern region to Beirut and other cities, and on the 10th March, in clashes with the police, one refugee was killed and ten injured. Friction between the army and the Fedayeen was never far below the surface, and on the 18th the Fatah commander at Bint Jebeil, a guerilla-controlled area, was killed in a skirmish with soldiers.

On the 24th March there occurred in Beirut a demonstration of arrogant disregard for the civil power by the guerillas, when a gun battle broke out between a group of five smugglers, who had sought refuge in a house in the city, and some guerillas.

During the incident guerillas took over the control of traffic while the police stood helplessly aside. The smugglers had been based on nearby refugee camps and been mainly concerned with smuggling cigarettes from Kuwait and Saudi Arabia, where tax on them was negligible, to the Lebanon, where it was heavy and for some reason they had fallen out with the Fedayeen, who killed them. The smugglers also probably dealt in hashish, and had been used by the guerillas to bring arms in and explosives. The Fedayeen were frequently accused of smuggling for personal profit, but had always denied this.

This blatant incident caused the Government anxiety, and particularly upset the right-wing Christian Falangist Party, which had an armed militia, generally estimated to be about 10,000 strong. On the following day, the 25th, a body of Fedayeen was attacked by the Falangist militia as the funeral procession of one of the guerillas, killed the previous day, passed through the Christian village of Kahale, near Beirut. In the fighting the Fedayeen lost eight killed and suffered 25 wounded. This sparked off four days of clashes between the Fedayeen and the Falangist militia, in which 42 people were killed and 80 wounded. The Lebanese army stood aside, the only incident being on the 28th, when guerillas captured a Lebanese customs post in retaliation for an alleged army ambush, and also shot up a military truck, wounding three soldiers.

The Falangist militia seemed to get the better of the tussles. On the 30th the Fedayeen admitted that 80 per cent of its fighting strength was involved in protecting their camps, and backed away. The guerillas had been fought to a standstill by the Falangists, and thwarted in their attempt to spread and openly operate in the cities. In their chagrin the Fedayeen turned their attention to firing rockets at some American buildings in Beirut, on the score that America had tried to stir up civil war. This outburst of fighting alarmed the Government—all ministers, except perhaps Kamal Jumblatt, being against the guerillas. After talks with the Fedayeen, Premier Karame announced that he had reached a four-point agreement with them, which reaffirmed the (Lebanese) Cairo Agreement, but in fact meant little. The Fedayeen remained uneasily quiet as they licked their wounds, before turning their attention again to raiding into Israel. At this period, the Lebanese Government estimated, there were about 1,500 armed guerillas in the country—about 800 in Fatahland, about 400 on the coastal strip, and another 300 on the rocky ridge between.

Anxious about the safety of Upper Galilee, which contained sources of the Israelis' water supply, and where about 40 per cent of the population was Arab, Israel commenced putting up wire fences of various types at common crossing points, but despite them the Fedayeen continued to raid across the Lebanese frontier. On the 7th May four guerillas were killed on the Golan Plateau, and the Israelis put down artillery fire on guerilla camps just across the border. When another attack on the same day killed two Israelis, Moshe Dayan warned that he would hit back. On the 8th six Israeli soldiers were wounded when their patrol came under fire from Lebanese territory near Metulla, making a total of five Israelis killed and 14 wounded in 48 hours. On the following day, the 9th, Israeli aircraft pounded Fatahland for 90 minutes, but more minor guerilla attacks followed until, the Israelis estimated, there had been 61 in six weeks, which had killed eight Israelis and wounded 30.

On the 12th May an Israeli commando force, nearly 2,000 strong, with armour and artillery, in nearly 100 vehicles, swarmed across the border into the Lebanon opposite Kiryat Shimona, to occupy about 45 square miles of territory and to hold it for about 34 hours. The main body moved towards a cross-roads at Khraibe, about four miles from the border, and Israeli aircraft interdicted a Lebanese armoured force moving from its camp at Marjayoun. With good air and ground support the Israelis surrounded and occupied six villages, screening all present, and then became involved in close fighting with the guerillas in another half-dozen. The Fedayeen admitted losing 20 killed in the opening stages of the fighting. The only Israeli clash with the Lebanese army was at long range, near Mebariyeh where Fedayeen control ended, and was mainly confined to artillery exchanges, although Israeli aircraft came into action too.

On the second morning, when the Israelis had penetrated deeply, the Syrian air force intervened, which caused Israeli planes to be diverted from ground support. Guerilla reinforce-

ments also began to arrive, causing the Israelis, who admitted
that some guerillas fought well and that they had run into
stiffer opposition than had been anticipated, to have difficulty
in withdrawing. Arafat had rushed to the scene of the battle
to direct its final stages, which indicated that he was still
elbowing for sole leadership and wished to win a reputation as
a successful field general.

The Israelis, who held a victory parade with prisoners and
booty through the streets of Kiryat Shimona, which had suffered so many guerilla attacks, claimed to have killed between
30 and 100 guerillas, captured 15 and demolished 39 houses
for only 11 wounded. In the air, the Israelis claimed to have shot
down three Syrian planes, which was admitted by the Syrians,
who in turn claimed to have downed three Israeli aircraft, which
the Israelis denied. On this raid Israeli soldiers handed out
propaganda leaflets.[1] The Lebanese army said that its casualties
were six killed and 15 wounded, and its losses were six tanks,
three guns, and four trucks; it claimed that the Israelis had
lost seven tanks, seven half-tracks and one truck—but the
Israelis would not comment upon this estimate. The Fedayeen
claimed that this two-pronged attack was aimed at trapping
the guerillas in Fatahland. Denying this, the Israelis said that
the raid had four aims: to punish the guerillas, to persuade the
villagers not to co-operate with them, to teach the Government
that it must control the Fedayeen, and to bolster Israeli morale
along the border region. There were doubts in Israel as to the
success and value of this excursion.

The guerillas swiftly reacted. Less than 12 hours after the
Israelis had withdrawn from Lebanese territory they were back
in their former positions near the frontier, once again firing
rockets and mortars on to Israeli soil. On the 14th a detachment
of the Syrian army entered the Lebanon, along a route they
had constructed across the northern end of the Mount Hermon
range, to recover a MiG of theirs that had been brought down in
the battle near Deir al-Asayir, together with its pilot who had
landed safely, but they left the following day. On the 16th

[1] One pamphlet contained a proverbial Arab poem that began:
    He who sows thorns will not harvest grapes,
    And he who lights a fire may be burnt.

General Njeim reported that 2,000 Syrian troops had moved into Fatahland, but this was not so; it was the arrival of about 650 Saiqa in Syrian army trucks, which brought the number of armed guerillas there up to the 1,500 mark.

The Lebanese Government hastily authorized the increase in its armed forces from 15,000 to 25,000, but this was merely symbolic as volunteers were not forthcoming, and the issue of conscription was a thorny one. On the 17th Premier Karame rushed to Damascus, anxious in case Syrian troops entered the Lebanon without permission, and full of concern over the number of men and volume of supplies moving southwards down the Arafat Trail, now that the route over the Mount Hermon range had been completed and Lebanese troops were no longer in a position to prevent them. On the 22nd fears arose over the lack of a Lebanese army presence in the Bint Jebeil area in case the Fedayeen tried to turn it into another Fatahland. The Government was under pressure from the Arab League and Arab states to admit contingents of national Arab armies to protect southern Lebanon from Israeli attacks, but it was reluctant to allow this, and had already (on the 14th) refused an Iraqi offer. In addition, the internal refugee problem was a growing anxiety, it being calculated that at least 30,000 people from the southern border regions had descended penniless and homeless on Beirut, Tyre, Sidon and other population centres.

On the 24th May an Israeli bus carrying school children was ambushed on the frontier road near Avivim by PFLP members who fired rockets at it, killing eight children and four adults, and injuring 20 children. The Israelis unleashed a heavy artillery barrage on the adjacent villages around Bint Jebeil, which lay opposite Avivim, the Lebanese alleging that it killed 13 civilians, wounded 32, hit 83 houses and created another 17,000 refugees. Moshe Dayan rushed to Avivim and declared that 'if the Government of the Lebanon proclaims it is not its job to police its territory against terrorists, we will do it'. Then followed a policy of large Israeli patrols moving just inside the Lebanese border, which went well for a few days but soon ran into trouble as such tactics were susceptible to ambushes, and so had to be abandoned.

The guerillas in the Lebanon went through a period of internal dispute over the school bus incident, Fatah saying that it was not Fedayeen policy to attack civilian targets, and that the local PFLP commander at Bint Jebeil was at fault. This irked the PFLP, as did criticism that the PFLP, which dominated the majority of the Palestinian refugee camps in the Lebanon, had taken care not to clash with the Lebanese security forces in the recent fighting, and had left all the action to Fatah and Saiqa. The Fedayeen was generally unpopular in the Lebanon, especially amongst the Christians, whose villages were often interspersed with those of the Arabs and Druze in the south. On the 28th Christians clashed with guerillas at the frontier village of Ramaish, and at another village opposite Avivim guerillas were stoned when they attempted to enter.

Kamal Jumblatt, Minister of the Interior, again tried to persuade the guerillas to exercise restraint and to abide by the conditions of the (Lebanese) Cairo Agreement; he publicly forbade them to fire into Israel or to lay mines near the border. He also demanded that guerillas committing offences be tried by Lebanese courts, instead of being handed over to PASC representatives, and also said that carrying firearms without a licence would be an offence as from the 15th June; as, however, he exempted members of the PASC, which really only left the PFLP, this meant very little. The PLO representative in Beirut gave verbal, but no practical, support to Jumblatt's remarks—but the guerilla struggle in the Lebanon was being overshadowed by fighting breaking out in Jordan.

Syria had been putting increased pressure against the Golan Plateau since its change of policy in the spring of 1969. There had throughout that year been a gradual stepping up of aggressive activity, both by the army and the Fedayeen, although the Government still preferred the guerillas to operate into Israel from either Jordan or the Lebanon. By the end of the year there were periodic tank and artillery duels across the Golan Plateau ceasefire line. On the 10th December, for the second time in a week, Syrian tanks shelled Israeli tractors working on the Plateau, but when Israeli artillery was brought into action they withdrew. The Syrian air force also became active against the Israelis and was involved in dog-fights on occasions. On the 11th December (1969) three Syrian MiGs[1] were shot down by the Israelis in reprisal, according to the Israeli Chief of Staff, for the imprisoning by the Syrians of two Israeli civilians from a hijacked airliner. Guerillas, especially Saiqa, were given a free hand to raid into the Golan Plateau as they wished.

The new year of 1970 brought fresh Syrian aggressiveness. During January the Government decided to increase its pressure on the Golan front to relieve that on the Suez Canal front. This was partly a response to pleas from President Nasser, and partly because there arose a spontaneous feeling in Syria that something should be done to help the Palestine cause. The Syrian Government had been hesitant so far, as it wanted more arms before it did anything to provoke the Israelis into serious retaliation. The Soviet Union wanted Syria to reach a settlement, but Syria was reluctant to do so, and this attitude affected the supply of Soviet weapons; for example, Syria was still waiting for the promised SAM-3s.

Becoming bolder, on the 29th January a Syrian plane 'buzzed' Haifa. The Israelis retaliated the following day by 'buzzing' Damascus, Aleppo, Latakia, Homs and El Hamma. On the 29th a four-day battle began involving tanks, artillery and aircraft. When it died down the Syrians had lost three killed and had five wounded, but they claimed to have inflicted 30 Israeli casualties and destroyed five Israeli tanks. The Israelis admitted losing one plane from ground fire but denied any casualties or vehicle losses.

On the 12th March a body of regular Syrian troops crossed into the Golan Plateau, penetrating 22 miles and ambushing several Israeli patrols, killing one Israeli and wounding 13, before withdrawing. These figures were admitted by the Israelis, and only one Syrian body was left on the battlefield. This was the most serious and best organized Syrian raid so far. It caused anxiety because it posed a different problem from that of small groups of guerillas making hasty incursions for purposes of terrorism and then hurrying back to safety. In

[1] Making, according to Israeli estimates, the seventeenth Syrian plane to be lost since the June War.

reprisal, on the 15th, lifted by helicopters, Israeli commandos landed north of Damascus to demolish a power pylon on the Damascus-Homs road. That day Israeli artillery shelled a Syrian army camp, about ten miles over the cease-fire line along the road to Damascus. On the 22nd the Syrians admitted the loss of six soldiers in an action on the Golan Plateau, but claimed to have killed five Israelis. On the 27th, in a large raid, again on the Plateau, the Syrians claimed to have destroyed '21 Israeli fortified positions' for the loss of only one soldier missing and three wounded, while the Israelis claimed that a force of about 20 Syrians had been repulsed when it attacked Israeli positions in the Hisfin area.

The fighting was escalating. On the 2nd April occurred the biggest clash on the Golan front since the June War, when Israeli troops with tanks, guns and aircraft attacked Syrian positions in reprisal, it was claimed, for 185 alleged incidents across that border so far in the year. Heavy firing, with aerial fights overhead, continued until dusk, when the battle subsided. Both sides claimed success. The Syrians said that they had shot down seven Israeli planes and taken some of the aircrews prisoner, destroyed 25 armoured vehicles and damaged extensively a military farming settlement. They admitted the loss of two planes, as well as 16 killed and 35 wounded, but boasted that they had inflicted over 120 casualties on the Israelis. Certainly Syrian anti-aircraft guns had been active and had worried the Israeli pilots, who admitted losing one aircraft but claimed to have shot down three Syrian ones. Syrian aggression was rising.

During April 1970 fighting on the Suez Canal front dominated the Arab-Israeli struggle, and frictions in the Lebanon and Syria with Israel were overshadowed, while even deeper shadow was cast on them by the activities of the PFLP and the approaching civil war in Jordan. Even on such a darkening scene Arab rivalries continually bubbled to the surface. In May 1970, for example, the Syrian Government was still refusing to allow the TAPLINE oil pipeline that had been accidentally damaged by a tractor near Dera, near the Jordanian border, to be repaired, despite urgent requests from Saudi Arabia. It was noted that when the same pipeline had

115

been sabotaged the previous year, also by the PFLP, Syria had not condemned the action. Its patience exhausted, on the 11th May the Saudi Arabian Government broke diplomatic silence and threatened that its subsidies to the Arabs and the PLO would be terminated if oil did not soon flow again through the pipeline. Tension between these two Arab countries continued, and the pipeline was not repaired until the 25th November that year.

# 6. Prelude to Civil War

During 1969, under the leadership of George Habash, the PFLP strove to make an impact on the international scene to provoke Israeli reprisals and attract world attention, caring little of the effect its activities had on host countries and ignoring disapproval and protests when it attacked airliners and disrupted the TAPLINE oil pipeline. Like the other guerilla organizations it bragged repeatedly and made its full share of false claims. On the 27th August the PFLP put on show to the press an allegedly captured Israeli soldier, but the Israelis said he was merely an ex-soldier who, after serving a term of imprisonment for desertion, had been discharged as mentally unfit.

After a comparatively quiet summer the PFLP turned its attention again to the international airlines. On the 29th August two of its members hijacked a US TWA Boeing, with 116 personnel on board, *en route* to Athens, and forced it to land at Damascus, in reprisal, it said, for the American agreement to send Phantom aircraft to Israel. On the following day the crew and passengers were released, except for four women, who were later freed on the 1st September, and two men, both Israelis, who despite strong diplomatic protests were held by the Syrians until they were eventually exchanged on the 5th December for 13 Syrians held by the Israelis. The two PFLP members were also detained, but were allowed to go free on the 12th October.

Next, on the 8th September, four members of the PFLP Ashbals attacked the El Al offices in Brussels with grenades, and other Ashbals attacked the Israeli embassies in Bonn and the Hague in a similar manner. Most reports at this stage indicated that the PFLP had up to 2,000 Ashbals, mainly orphans between the ages of 12 and 16 years, in various stages of training, mostly at the Bakaa refugee camp near Amman. On the 28th November a grenade was thrown by a member of the PFLP into a crowded El Al reception hall at the Athens airport, killing a child and injuring 14 people. The two concerned were arrested by the police.

PFLP action against international airliners continued on into 1970. On the 9th February a bus carrying El Al passengers was attacked with grenades and pistols at the Munich airport just as they were about to board an El Al plane for London. One passenger was killed and 11 were injured: the police arrested three PFLP assailants. On the 21st February an explosion occurred on board an Austrian airliner carrying mail for Israel, but it managed to land safely at Frankfurt airport. Some two hours later, on the same day, a few minutes after it had taken off from Zurich, a Swiss airliner bound for Tel Aviv exploded in mid-air and crashed, killing all 47 people on board, of whom 13 were Israelis. It was established that both these explosions were caused by altimeter-detonators in parcels, the new-styled 'General Command' of the PFLP claiming responsibility. Both King Hussein of Jordan and the Lebanese Government condemned the acts as being 'un-Arab'; other Arab countries were silent.

On the 23rd the Soviet paper *Izvestia* accused both America and Israel of using a forged document to blame Arab governments for the destruction of the Austrian airliner. On the following day the German police named two Arabs thought to be responsible for posting the 'parcel bombs'. On the 25th Arafat spoke out against the PFLP, saying that 'The Palestine revolution is against killing civilians wherever they may be. The Unified Command [newly formed on the 18th] is making an urgent fundamental study of the whole question of attacking aircraft'. On the 27th the German police arrested two Arabs suspected of being involved with the two airliner incidents. The following day the 'General Command' of the PFLP retracted its claim to responsibility, claimed that it had carried out ten operations outside the Middle East, including hijackings, but insisted that no Europeans had been injured in them. The PFLP was having to bend slightly with the wind of Arab

118

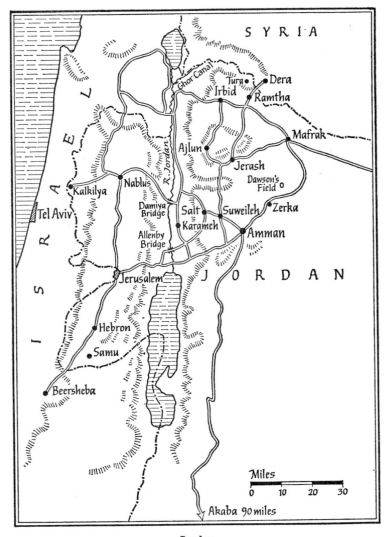

Jordan

reprobation, but only slightly—it was not repentant, and neither did it intend to change its policy.

On the 15th March an explosion occurred on an Egyptian Anatov airliner just out from Alexandria, on the regular Cairo to Athens run, which blew off its undercarriage. Only one person was injured. Although the PFLP eagerly claimed responsibility, this was never satisfactorily explained,[1] and it was doubtful whether the PFLP had been involved. On the 25th April a member of the PFLP threw a bomb into the El Al office at Istanbul, but no one was hurt. Farther afield, on the 4th May, two Arabs burst into the Israeli Embassy at Asunción, in Paraguay, wounding one official and killing the wife of another. Again the PFLP claimed responsibility.

After the Rabat conference, on the 8th January 1970, King Hussein stated that Jordan would never seek a separate peace, but the distrustful guerillas were not so sure. In the succeeding weeks they became more arrogant, openly carrying arms on the streets and jostling the Jordanian security forces, who bridled at the restraints placed on them by the Government. The situation was rapidly deteriorating, so on the 10th February King Hussein issued an 11-point decree designed to control Fedayeen activities within Jordan, that included a ban on carrying, using or storing firearms, demonstrations, party political activities and political publications, and orders that guerillas must carry identity cards and license their vehicles. This caused a storm of protest. The Fedayeen denounced the decree as likely to provoke civil war. They demanded that Hussein cancel it, withdraw army units from the cities and towns, end military operations against the guerillas, give them freedom of action and movement, and restore former 'normal relations' between them and the Jordanian Government. Exempted from the decree was the Jordanian militia. Reputed to be about 45,000-strong (but more likely less than half that number), this semi-clandestine, part-time force had been raised by Sherif Nasser ben Jamil, the Commander-in-Chief, in the previous year, to combat subversion. This caused a further

[1] In October 1968 an Egyptian Anatov airliner had similarly exploded over the Mediterranean, with the loss of 68 lives, also without a satisfactory explanation.

protest from the Fedayeen, who in their turn demanded that King Hussein disband his Saiqa Brigade.

The guerillas alerted their militia in the refugee camps, distributed arms and allowed the militiamen to roam the streets of Amman. On the 10th street fighting broke out between the guerillas and the police, there was much random firing, and the 3rd Armoured Brigade, commanded by Brigadier Said Ibn Shaker, a cousin of the King, was moved into the centre of the city. This formation, sometimes referred to as the Royal Brigade, consisted mainly of Bedu personnel, considered loyal to the King and who had been given some psychological warfare training. Few regular guerillas were involved in this fighting. Arafat was absent on a visit to Moscow and there was no central direction, but the Fedayeen militia seemed to have been given free rein to riot as they pleased. One of the principal incidents was a raid by a party of regular Fedayeen from the Jebel Wahdat refugee camp, a Fatah stronghold, on a Bedu police station, which they attempted to take over. In the ensuing ten-hour battle, it was admitted, one Jordanian was killed and five others wounded, but the Fedayeen claimed to have killed six and wounded over 20. Precise casualty figures were impossible to assess, but probably up to 80 people were killed in four days of disturbances in the capital, during which time the guerillas were in control of over half the city.

Neither the guerillas nor King Hussein wanted a head-on clash. The Fedayeen knew that if Hussein were toppled there would be a struggle between them for dominance which would decimate their ranks. For the moment they were content with the situation as it was, with the Jordanian army as their shield against the Israeli defence forces for their commando operations across the River Jordan, and which they anticipated would come to their aid should Israeli troops enter Jordan to attack them. For his part King Hussein was not over-sure of the loyalties of some of his younger Palestinian officers should they be put to the test, suspecting that many might be more than a little in sympathy with Fedayeen ideals, so he restrained his army and entered into talks with the guerillas.

On the 13th, in a radio speech, King Hussein suspended his recent decree and so backed away from the problem, insisting that he had no intention of trying to liquidate the Palestinian Resistance Movement, and uttering his famous declaration 'We are all Fedayeen now'. He agreed to dismiss the unpopular (with the guerillas) Minister of the Interior, Mohammed Rasoul Kailani, to allow the guerillas to retain their own travel documents which were to be honoured by the Jordanian authorities, and to allow them to continue to run their own affairs in the refugee camps. Fatah had in fact achieved a high degree of organization and administration, and had its own hospitals[1] to look after its wounded and sick, as well as schemes and pensions to help widows, orphans and the disabled. By the 15th Jordanian troops had withdrawn from the centre of Amman to its outskirts.

Both the Bedu, and the army, especially its Bedu element, were dissatisfied with the result of this confrontation between King Hussein and the guerillas, and were even more chagrined as the army continued to be held on a tight leash when guerillas moved in and took over the town of Zerka. The King was asked to meet Bedu leaders, and on the 20th February some 200 sheikhs, representing over 25,000 Bedu, the bedrock of his support in Jordan, gathered in the desert a few miles from Amman. The head of the Beni Shaker tribe, one of the largest, voiced disquiet at the way the Palestinian guerillas were operating in Jordan, and asked that measures be taken to restrain them.

These few violent days of crisis had thrown the guerilla organizations together and they reviewed their lack of positive action. After discussion they decided to form a field command in Amman to co-ordinate their activities. On the 18th February they announced that it was to be called the Unified Command, which was to be controlled by a political committee headed by George Habash. Arafat was still absent in the Soviet Union. It was to be independent of, and separate from the Cairo-based PASC, although it would be in close liaison with it. One of the primary objects of the Unified Command was to enforce a code of discipline on all guerilla organizations in Jordan and their

[1] Fatah at this time had four 'blood banks', while the Government of Jordan could boast only one, and its wounded were sent to recuperate in Bulgaria and Yugoslavia.

members, some of whom tended to become a law unto themselves.

At this time there were probably 14 political organizations each with a guerilla arm, ostensibly dedicated to the Palestinian cause. Of these only ten operated in Jordan,[1] all of which, with the exception of the PFLP, were in PASC. They all came into the new Unified Command and, indeed, the PFLP took a prominent part in its decision-making. Fatah remained by far the largest organization and was the most moderate in its political views and activities. Both King Hussein and President Nasser would have preferred to deal with it alone, rather than the multiplicity of groups that existed, and would have liked Fatah to have absorbed them all. The new Unified Command, with its guiding political committee, worked to turn the temporary arrangement with the King, which was so advantageous to them, into a more permanent one, and a secret agreement was signed on the 22nd February on behalf of King Hussein and the PLO.

So far Arafat had received no help from the Soviet Union despite his appeals, so on the 10th February he went to Moscow on a visit that lasted ten days to try to win support and supplies. He failed as the Soviet Government refused to give him direct aid, and he was shocked and disappointed to be accorded such a low-level reception. He had become accustomed to receiving the 'red carpet' treatment when he visited foreign countries. When he left Russia the official statement merely said that he had talks with the Soviet Afro-Asian Solidarity Committee. However, he did persuade the Soviet Union to add the Palestine Liberation Movement to the Soviet official list of 'Wars of Liberation'. The Soviet Union did have small second thoughts and in the ensuing weeks sent a few medical supplies, some food and relief equipment to the guerillas in Jordan and Syria, but no arms or cash. On his return, on the 22nd, Arafat had talks with King Hussein, which simply confirmed the existing understanding between the guerillas and the Jordanian Government. Back in Amman, Arafat ran into criticism from the new Unified

[1] They were almost certainly (some titles changed about this time) Fatah, PFLP, DPF, PLA, AOLP, ALF, APO, FPPS, AMLP and Saiqa.

Command for his Moscow failure and for being absent during the February crisis in Jordan, which had left the guerillas almost leaderless. His military ineptitude and lack of political effectiveness outside the Middle East were commented upon—many guerillas disliked his personality cult.

China had been sending small quantities of arms and supplies for some time to the PFLP and the DPF, both of which had connexions with the Chinese-supported Popular Front for the Liberation of the Occupied Gulf that operated in the Dhofar area of Muscat and Oman. Arafat noted that the PFLP and the DPF had Chinese small arms, grenades, mines, rockets, ammunition and money, and there were occasional unconfirmed reports of Chinese instructors as well. Neither the PLO nor Fatah had received any Chinese aid since the June War of 1967, so Arafat went off to China to try to rectify this. Again he was unsuccessful and was given a low-level reception. He went on to Hanoi, where he met General Giap, who lectured him on revolutionary guerilla warfare, but Arafat was considered to be too conservative and middle-of-the-road for either the Chinese or the Russians.

The Arab communist parties had long been on the sidelines, ignored by the Soviet Union, which preferred to deal direct with Arab governments. The Palestinian cause was too remote from the communist international platform, and so they had stood aside from the guerilla movement, but the popularity of the Fedayeen had risen to such a pitch that they were forced to reconsider their attitude as they were in danger of being out-flanked by such 'new left' organizations as the DPF. At a meeting on the 12th March of representatives of the communist parties of Syria, Jordan and Iraq, disillusioned with lack of support from Moscow, they decided to forget temporarily their principles to join the guerilla movement and form a guerilla arm to be called the Partisan Forces (al-Ansar). The Partisan Forces, the PF, which eventually had about 300 members, joined the Unified Command, as its eleventh member.

Back in Amman from his trips to the Soviet Union, China and Vietnam, Arafat worked to unify the guerillas into one group under his control, and also to assert his dominance over the

Unified Command. Supporters of the Palestinian guerillas became concerned at their lack of unity and at how few of their efforts were directed against Israel. Colonel Gaddafi, the Libyan leader, warned that if the guerillas did not close ranks he would severely reduce his financial aid to them. He accused them of spending too much time fighting each other and not enough fighting Israel. Guerilla leaders privately admitted that as many as 70 per cent of their men were engaged in 'defending the revolution'[1] in their host Arab countries.[2] On the 6th April 1970 Arafat gave out guerilla strengths for the first time, asserting that there were 32,000 regular Fedayeen in Jordan but that they had only 6,000 guns. These figures were obviously too high, but were issued to back up his claim for Soviet and Chinese aid. There were probably still between 15,000 and 20,000 regular Fedayeen in Jordan, of whom only about 1,000 were involved in operations against the Israelis.

Hebron remained a hotbed of terrorist activities, where there were frequent incidents and many casualties. A particular source of discontent was the Arab belief that the Israelis wanted to resettle the district.[3] On the 24th April 1970 the Israelis closed about 75 acres for 'military purposes', but the strong Arab rumour was that the real reason was to provide space to erect houses for 250 Jewish families. The Mayor, Sheikh Mohammed Ali Jabari, objected loudly, saying that such Israelis would become prime targets for the guerillas and so the whole population would suffer. He also protested against Jordanian restrictions on the movement of West Bank Arabs to Jordan, and called upon King Hussein to 'decide whether they are his people or not'.

Guerilla commando activity continued from Syria and Jordan, and Israeli aircraft frequently attacked guerilla camps

[1] It was 80 per cent in the Lebanon.

[2] On the 1st January 1970, on the fifth anniversary of its existence, an Asifa spokesman claimed that guerilla activity was costing the Israelis £1 million a day, that 2,442 guerilla operations had been carried out in 1969, and that 'several thousand' Israeli soldiers had been killed. He admitted that '350 guerillas had died'.

[3] Jewish settlers fled from Hebron in 1929, after 63 of them had been killed by Arabs.

and positions in those two countries. On the 16th March an Israeli force crossed into Syria to blow up pillboxes and a bridge on the road to Damascus, and in the following month in reprisal for two Israelis being killed and five wounded (on the 24th April) a heavy aerial assault was made on Syrian positions near the cease-fire line. Although most of the clashes were on a small scale, occasionally there were larger ones. For example, on the 3rd May an entire patrol of 23 guerillas was ambushed and wiped out during the night in the Jordan Valley. This was the largest death toll in this type of encounter since the June War.[1] On the 30th May an Israeli patrol was in turn ambushed by guerillas, losing two killed and four wounded, but the day previously 11 guerillas had been killed when raiding in the Jordan Valley. On the 3rd June the Israelis killed eight guerillas who had shelled a kibbutz in the eastern Negev, killing two children. The pattern continued. On the 9th June fighting flared up along the Golan cease-fire line, in which an Israeli girl soldier was killed and four other girl soldiers and five soldiers were wounded, the Syrians claiming to have inflicted 60 casualties but themselves admitting to having seven killed and 23 wounded. In the following month, on the 19th, another two days' fierce fighting broke out in the same region, in which the Syrians claimed to have brought down an Israeli Skyhawk by ground fire.

On the 31st May an Israeli spokesman stated that the security forces had killed 621 Arab guerillas and terrorists since the June War, and that they held 2,500 prisoners.[2] This statement was amended on the 3rd June, when the Israelis claimed to have killed 1,600 guerillas in that period, and said that their figure was based on body counts, obituaries in Arab newspapers and losses announced by the guerilla organizations themselves.

Meanwhile another crisis had erupted in Jordan, where

[1] On the 6th April 1970 General Bar-lev, the Israeli Chief of Staff, said: 'We have not managed to dismantle this (the Fedayeen) organization, but we have managed to keep them at a low level of activity'.

[2] On the 20th August 1970 the first two Arabs were sentenced to death for acts of terrorism, both being members of Fatah, but later their sentences were commuted to imprisonment.

relations, which had been creaking along for a while between the Fedayeen and the Government, suddenly deteriorated early in April, when Fatah alleged that the Jordanian army had let it down badly over a small operation against the Israelis south of the Dead Sea. This was a new trend, as so far Fatah could have been regarded as being the most moderate of all the guerilla organizations. At the same time a wave of intense anti-American feeling swelled up amongst the Fedayeen, mainly because the USA was sending aircraft and weapons to Israel. When it was learnt that Joseph Sisco, the Assistant Secretary of State, was to visit Jordan on the 15th April, there were demonstrations in protest; a huge procession through the streets of Amman consisted mainly of students, but it did include a party of Fedayeen militia. The demonstration degenerated into a riot and the mob rampaged through the city, burnt down the American cultural centre and attacked the US Embassy. No particularly strong preventive action was taken by the security forces at the time, and it was thought that King Hussein, who only a few days before had firmly vetoed a guerilla plan to fire rockets into Eilat, was treading carefully as his relations with the guerillas were extremely delicate. In fact, it had been the military police element of Fatah that had dispersed the rioters from the US cultural centre. The anti-American bias was stronger among the people than with the Fedayeen. The proposed Sisco visit was cancelled and on the 18th, at the Jordanian request, the American Ambassador to Jordan was recalled because of this. On the 19th April Premier Bahjat al-Talhouni reshuffled his cabinet after its formal resignation over the affair.

On the 30th April the PFLP held a Press conference at Bakaa refugee camp near Amman, alleging a plot between the American CIA and Sherif Nasser ben Jamil to assassinate guerilla leaders, including Arafat and Habash. There were some disturbances in Amman, and scuffles broke out in Zerka. After a brief truce on the 3rd May, fighting was resumed at Zerka between the army and both the Fatah and the PFLP, which developed into a ten-hour battle before it died down. Fatah alleged that the Jordanians, using tanks and armoured cars, wounded ten guerillas, took two prisoners and blew up three houses, while the PFLP said that 14 guerillas had been killed and 24 wounded.

On the 30th May the Palestine National Council met in Cairo and, being concerned with retaining and more firmly establishing its authority over the Fedayeen movement, was particularly anxious about the impromptu Unified Command that was functioning in Amman. It wanted to set up a central committee vested with power over all the organizations, to consist of a chairman, the Commander of the PLA[1] and representatives of the main guerilla groups, but it failed entirely to agree on this matter, and indeed on other points raised, political and military. The PNC dispersed on the 4th June, having failed to unite the guerillas under one command, its only positive achievement being an agreement to establish a Jordanian-Palestine higher committee to work for greater co-operation.

On the 5th June, the third anniversary of the commencement of the Six Day War, the Fedayeen called for strikes and demonstrations throughout the Israeli occupied territories, to which there was a poor response, although there were a few incidents of terrorism, mainly in Nablus, in which one Israeli officer and two guerillas were killed and 15 others injured.

On the 7th June fighting lasting for some hours broke out again at Zerka, mainly between the PFLP and the Jordanian Saiqa Brigade; the guerillas admitted nine killed and 15 wounded, but claimed to have killed ten Jordanians. Situated about 12 miles north-east of Amman on the only good north-south road in the country, Zerka was the Aldershot of Jordan, having a large military camp complex and being the headquarters of the army. Apart from the town, which had a large influx of Palestinians, there was also a large refugee camp[2] close by which had become a Fatah stronghold. After a lull on the 9th, fighting spread to Amman, being sparked off when a party of guerillas attacked the prison with the intention of freeing some Fedayeen. The 3rd Armoured Brigade and other units moved into Amman, with their tanks and guns, and as road blocks manned by guerillas sprang up, commenced shelling

---

[1] The PLA claimed to have 12,000 members at this time.

[2] Known as Gaza refugee camp, but to avoid confusion it will not be referred to by that name.

the refugee camps. The guerillas took to the streets in large numbers, and firing became general. Hurrying back to Amman, King Hussein's motorcade came under fire near Suweileh. The King was not hurt, but one of his escort was killed and five others were wounded. Fatah radio continually incited Jordanian officers and men to change sides and desert their Government. On the 10th, on which day the American assistant military attaché was killed when guerillas broke into his house, King Hussein and Arafat met and agreed to a cease-fire, but this was difficult to put into effect and firing continued on both sides. During the fighting, in which the guerillas failed to capture the radio station, there was considerable anti-American looting and damage.

Both the PFLP and the DPF rejected Arafat's cease-fire agreement with King Hussein. On the 11th they moved in and took over the Intercontinental Hotel to hold hostage the resident 33 Americans, British and West Germans, and the Philadelphia Hotel, where they held hostage another 35 people, who were all kept for 48 hours. The guerillas threatened to blow up the two hotels with the hostages unless the Jordanians stopped shelling the refugee camps. The two organizations accused Crown Prince Hassan of trying to overthrow King Hussein at the instigation of the American CIA, and both demanded that Sherif Nasser ben Jamil, the Commander-in-Chief, Brigadier Said Ibn Shaker, Commander of the 3rd Armoured Brigade, Mohammed Rassoul Kailani, Minister of the Interior, and others be removed. Then Fatah demanded over its radio that King Hussein should either dismiss the three persons mentioned or lose his throne—in other words, face civil war. The King gave in and dismissed Jamil and Shaker, saying that Kailani had already left for London. The following day the fighting died down, the guerillas returned to their camps and the soldiers left the centre of Amman. A further Fedayeen demand that the Jordanian Saiqa Brigade be disbanded was deferred for the time being.

On the 13th Moshe Dayan warned that 'Israel cannot remain indifferent to events in Jordan'. At a press conference on the following day Arafat claimed that his Fatah had been responsible for bringing order to the streets of Amman, as

I                                129

mostly his men had been passive, and when his guerillas with-drew the others were too small and weak to stand against the Jordanian army on their own, and so withdrew with them. There was some truth in this as the extremist organizations, although the smallest and weakest, were the most violent and less controllable. The Jordanians stated that in the course of the four days' fighting, mainly in Amman but also in Zerka, about 400 people had been killed and 750 wounded. During this crisis the US 82 Airborne Division in the United States had been alerted for possible employment in the Middle East.

The dismissals of Jamil and Shaker had been unpopular with the Jordanian army. On the 13th some elements of the 3rd Armoured Brigade commenced to move back into Amman to resume fighting the Fedayeen, and were only halted and per-suaded to return by the personal intervention of Major-General Haditha, the Chief-of-Staff, who was wounded in the incident.[1] Once the 3rd Armoured Brigade was brought under control, the turmoil subsided a little. Haditha was regarded as a moderate who had some sympathy for the Fedayeen ideals and who was something of a buffer between them and the Bedu element in the army. Admitting that the removals had become unpopular and had caused anger, King Hussein personally took direct control of his army.

The Jordanian-Palestinian higher committee came to life to liaise with King Hussein, its guerilla members being Arafat, Habash, Hawatmeh, Dafi Jamani, leader of the Syrian Saiqa in Jordan, and Kamal Nasser, PLO representative in Jordan. The main achievement was a system of joint patrols and joint road blocks in Amman, in which the guerillas worked with the Jordanian soldiers. After functioning for a few days, mainly because the Jordanians were carefully picked and the Bedu element largely excluded, it broke down. The June crisis brought about a change of government. On the 28th June Abdul Moneim al-Rifai became Premier, signing an agreement with Arafat on the 10th July which virtually gave the guerillas the freedom of the Palestinian refugee camps provided they stayed out of the centre of the city.

[1] Some reports indicate that it may have been an assassination attempt.

On the 25th June US Secretary of State William Rogers announced a new American peace initiative in the Middle East, but declined to give precise details. Basically he called for the Israelis to withdraw from the occupied territories, for the Arab states to recognize Israel, and for both to enter into discussions for peace. Under cover of vague words there was much behind-the-scenes pressuring and lobbying, which went on for a month, until suddenly and unexpectedly President Nasser, on the 25th July 1970, announced that he accepted the Rogers peace initiative. This immediately made him unpopular with the Fedayeen organizations, and on the same day George Habash, of the PFLP, held a Press conference at Beirut, at which he condemned both the peace initiative and President Nasser for accepting it. Most guerillas were both puzzled and disappointed, but most adopted a wait-and-see attitude; the main exceptions were the PFLP and the DPF, which on the 28th organized demonstrations in Amman that openly denounced Nasser. Rising to the challenge, on the same day (28th) President Nasser abruptly withdrew the broadcasting facilities in Cairo which he had allowed Fatah[1] and the PLO[2] to use. This was the first direct action he had taken against the Fedayeen since the June War. It was a heavy blow to Fatah, whose communications were notably poor, as it had relied upon its programme beamed out from Cairo to send messages and signals in code to its fighters in the field, which were picked up on transistor sets and acted upon.

On the 29th the Lebanon, the Sudan, Libya and Jordan approved President Nasser's action, and the Sudan also closed down the one Fedayeen radio station it allowed to operate on its territory. That day both Syria and Iraq came out openly criticizing Egypt for having accepted the Rogers Peace Initiative—once again there was disarray in the Arab world. Both countries afforded the guerillas certain radio transmission facilities, to try to make good those they had just been deprived of, but the signals were much weaker and could not reach all guerillas in the field. At this time there were noticeably fewer terrorist acts, which formely had followed code words broadcast

[1] Saut al-Asifa—Voice of the Storm.
[2] Saut al-Falastin—Voice of Palestine.

from Radio Cairo, so the Fedayeen attempt to step up activities against Israel to foil the Rogers Peace Initiative was hardly successful. On the 30th July Israel had accepted the initiative in principle. The Arab disarray was such that the proposed seven nation Arab conference of foreign and defence ministers, scheduled to meet in Tripoli, had to be cancelled as Iraq and Algeria refused to attend.

The PFLP again hit the world headlines and at a time when an Athens court was trying two of its members for the grenade attack made in November 1969. On the 22nd July six PFLP guerillas hijacked a Greek airliner on a run between Beirut and Athens and held the 53 passengers hostage at Athens airport for eight hours, until the Greek Government promised to release seven Arabs held for similar offences. The hostages were released and the aircraft allowed to fly with the hijackers to Cairo. There they were given a heroes' welcome, which tended to embarrass President Nasser, who was negotiating a cease-fire at the moment, but he had to take advantage of the mood of his people. The Athens court formally sentenced the two Arabs to terms of imprisonment on the 26th, but all seven (including one woman) were eventually released on the 13th August.[1]

On the 5th August fighting had broken out in Amman between the PFLP, which was firmly against the Rogers peace initiative, and the pro-Nasser Action Organization for the Liberation of Palestine, the AOLP. After a pause it was resumed on the 7th, and in clashes the PFLP took 23 prisoners from the AOLP and killed at least five others, but lost at least three killed themselves and suffered three wounded. In this fighting the Iraqi-backed Arab Liberation Front, the ALF, joined with the PFLP to attack the AOLP.

At midnight (local time) on the 9th August 1970 a cease-fire across the Suez Canal between the Israelis and the Egyptians came into effect. It proved to be an additional shock to the Fedayeen organizations, which were preparing to step up activities against Israel and to move into Jordan to try to topple

[1] Two El Al passengers on a BOAC flight from Tokyo were detained by the Israelis on the 14th August, when the plane stopped at Lydda, one of whom was reputed to be a senior officer in the Algerian intelligence service.

King Hussein. Fatah refrained from openly criticizing President
Nasser, but the extremists became bitter, and were not mollified by Nasser's explanation that the cease-fire was meant only
to cover the Suez Canal front and not the others. Encouraged
and emboldened, King Hussein brought back the dismissed
Brigadier Said Ibn Shaker as Deputy Chief of Staff, which
caused the guerillas to call for a second Vietnam in Jordan.
There was difficulty in persuading the guerillas to stop hostilities
in Jordan. Libya indicated that it would only continue to
support Fatah provided that organization was able to remain
in the ascendant and could control the extremists, such as the
PFLP and the DPF. On the 13th the Jordanian Foreign
Minister stated that the Government had no intention of using
force 'to restrain guerilla action against the Israelis'. But these
soothing words fell on deaf ears. On the 17th Iraq came to the
fore, making an attempt to wean Fatah completely away from
Syria and to take that country's place as its sponsor, but
Arafat played for time.

The Arab disarray over Egypt's acceptance of the Rogers
Peace Initiative, and the cease-fire with Israel, caused a split in
the command of the eastern front, which in theory consisted of
all regular Arab troops facing Israel in Jordan and Syria but
was in practice a fiction. In March the Iraqis had sent another
small brigade into northern Jordan, bringing their forces in
that country again up to the 15,000 mark, and additionally
there were 50,000 Jordanian troops, about 6,000 Syrians, who
were recalling reservists to fill formations, and about 3,000
Saudi Arabians.[1] Co-ordinated by the Arab Defence Council,
all fronts were nominally commanded by Lieut-General
Mohammed Fawzi, an Egyptian. The eastern front in turn was
commanded by Major-General Mohammed al-Nouri, an Iraqi
officer whose staff was also mainly composed of Iraqis, but
neither the Syrians, Jordanians nor the Saudi Arabians would
obey his orders. Iraq's strong line against President Nasser's

[1] On the 16th March it had been admitted by King Hussein that there
was also a detachment of Pakistani troops in Jordan, who when asked
if they amounted to 2,000 had replied: 'Not quite so many'. Their
probable strength was about 800, they remained inconspicuous, and
guarded King Hussein's palace in Amman during the February crisis.

action, which was approved by King Hussein, made the position of the Iraqi commander of the eastern front impossible; on the 15th August he was withdrawn and the eastern front was nominally divided between King Hussein, who now officially commanded all Arab troops in Jordan, and President Atassi, who now commanded all those in Syria. As far as Jordan was concerned it was just another fiction, as neither the Iraqis nor the Saudi Arabians would take orders from the King. The small Syrian brigade, which had moved over the border into Jordan on the 13th August, was withdrawn to Syria.

At a graduation ceremony of Fatah recruits at the Jebel Wahdat refugee camp on the 16th August Arafat alleged that King Hussein was moving four brigades to surround Amman as a prelude to crushing the Fedayeen movement, and boasted: 'We shall turn Jordan into a graveyard for plotters'. The following day the Egyptian Government admitted that it had expelled 140 Palestinians, all students and all members of Fatah, the PFLP or the DPF, back to Jordan for criticizing his decisions. Anxious now that a confrontation with the Jordanian army was fast approaching, Arafat went off to Baghdad on the 19th to enlist aid. He claimed success as the Iraqi Government announced that it had placed 10,000 of its troops in Jordan at the disposal of the central committee of the PNC.

On the 24th August Arafat went to Cairo to meet President Nasser. There he was lectured and warned to take a moderate line and not to sabotage the cease-fire, or otherwise all Egyptian support and sponsorship would be withdrawn. On the 27th Arafat returned to Amman (where the previous day there had been shooting between the guerillas and Jordanian troops) to preside at an emergency meeting of the PNC at the Jebel Wahdat refugee camp, at which the whole situation was reviewed. This was the first occasion this committee had met away from Cairo, and away from Nasser's immediate shadow. The feeling was very much against President Nasser, and the opinion was that Egypt had betrayed and deserted the Fedayeen movement. The guerillas felt increasingly isolated, Nasser was turning against them, the Chinese were disappointed at the Fedayeen lack of ideological training, and Syria was also withdrawing support. In fact, since the 7th August cease-fire, Syria was merging all the Saiqa guerilla offices and establishments, which were of course supported by Syrian Baathists, into the Baathist Party organization, on the grounds that the Saiqa and the Party were one and the same, merely leaving one face-saving Saiqa office in Damascus.

The guerillas feared the ideologically trained 3rd Armoured Brigade, and were anxious in case King Hussein recalled Sherif Nasser ben Jamil; they noted that Brigadier Shaker had been brought back into the army. They decided to call more regular Fedayeen fighters into Jordan. especially to Amman and other key points such as Zerka, and to fortify certain refugee camps within the country. Worried by the amount of popular support President Nasser was gaining, the Fedayeen leaders threatened to put any guerilla supporting his views and actions on trial in Fedayeen courts as a traitor. All guerillas wanted to reject the Rogers peace initiative, and most wanted to break away from Cairo and Nasser's influence, but Arafat persuaded them not to do so, and also to desist from propaganda against Nasser and the Rogers peace initiative. On the following day, the 28th, the Fedayeen noted that King Hussein signed a trade protocol with the Soviet Union.

Meanwhile, King Hussein was also preparing for the almost inevitable confrontation. On the 20th August he had paid a three-day visit to Cairo to have talks with President Nasser.[1] On the 25th peace talks began at the United Nations between Gunnar Jarring and the ambassadors of Israel, Egypt and Jordan. Almost daily there were disturbances in the streets of Amman, and a number of shooting incidents between the guerillas and the security forces. His mind made up, and encouraged by President Nasser, King Hussein spoke to his people over television on the 29th August, telling them that he was accepting the Rogers Peace Initiative, warning the Fedayeen that he would not tolerate their challenge or their criticism of his Government or authority, and stating that the

[1] King Hussein, on the 16th August, had given an interview (to *Le Nouvel Observateur*) in which he said that he could envisage an independent state on the West Bank, but only if it came about through a plebiscite.

135

Jordanian army was exercising its absolute right to military movement throughout the country. As he spoke there was fighting in the streets of his capital, and after his speech there were clashes between the Fedayeen and his soldiers. This declaration was the last straw, and Jordan braced itself for civil war.

# 7. Civil War in Jordan

In Amman, on the 29th August 1970, street disturbances followed the King's speech. The next day the army turned its guns on Fedayeen positions in and around the Jebel Hussein area of the capital, causing the Fatah spokesman in Beirut to allege that 'the Jordanian Authorities are now launching a wholesale attack against the guerillas in Amman'. As spasmodic shelling continued at intervals, Arafat appealed to Arab heads of state for immediate intervention in Amman—but there was no practical response.

On the 1st September an unsuccessful attack was made on King Hussein's motorcade as the King was travelling to the Amman airport, the ninth attempt on his life and the second in three months. Later in the evening the central committee of the PNC announced that its headquarters on Jebel Hussein was being shelled by the Jordanian army, and by midnight fighting had extended to the airport. Next day the guerillas claimed that during the night indiscriminate firing had killed nine people, and that two shells had hit the Intercontinental Hotel. There were power cuts and the telephone service ceased, causing confusion and apprehension. The PLO alleged that King Hussein's bodyguards had shot four Fedayeen in the back, and that the Basman Palace was ringed with guns. On the 3rd Hussein declared that he would exercise authority and was setting up a ten-man council, headed by Premier Rifai, to advise him. On the following day he asked his cabinet to contact the PLO to persuade them to stop firing, but the guerillas simply demanded that the Jordanian army withdraw from its positions around the capital, and that all security forces be purged of

137

'suspected anti-guerilla elements' before they would enter peace talks. Spasmodic firing continued in and around Amman. However, on the 5th the two sides came to some agreement. King Hussein ordered his soldiers to withdraw to the outskirts of the city, and the Fedayeen leaders told their men to stop firing. Colonel Gaddafi, of Libya, announced that he had stopped financial aid to Jordan until the dispute was settled, and that he would also withhold money from the guerillas if they used it to publish periodicals or leaflets attacking President Nasser.

On the 1st the Jordanian Ambassador in Baghdad had been summoned and warned that unless all Jordanian attacks on guerillas in Amman ceased, the Iraqi Government and Iraqi troops in Jordan would take all measures to protect them. The following day saw movement of troops from Syria into Jordan, and it was suspected that the Iraqis were sending in another brigade. Although this was not so, it caused alarm in Amman. On the 4th King Hussein asked Britain, America, France and the Soviet Union for protection against this Iraqi threat. On the 6th reports from Paris suggested that while the governments of those powers gave their moral support to Hussein in his struggle with the Fedayeen, the Soviet Union refused to use its influence to prevent Iraqi military intervention.

Before departing for a tour of China and North Korea, George Habash, of the PFLP, and his staff hatched some impressive plans for hijacking aircraft, but it was left to his deputies in Amman to implement some of them, which they did with startling success and only one failure. On the 6th September members of the PFLP hijacked a TWA Boeing 707, with 146 crew and passengers on board, on a flight from Tel Aviv to New York after a stop-over at Frankfurt, and also a Swissair DC-8, with 155 persons on board, on a flight from Zurich to New York. Both aircraft were flown to Jordan and were landed at Dawson's Field,[1] with the aid of oil flares and vehicle headlights in the late evening. The crew and passengers were kept as hostages by the PFLP and when the Jordanian soldiers approached they were warned to keep their distance, or else the planes and hostages would be blown up. Helplessly the Jordanian troops

[1] After Air Chief Marshal Sir Walter Dawson, AOC in the Levant from 1946 to 1948, as it was never officially given a name.

watched, as did the remainder of the world through the eyes of the television lens for the next six days or so. Dawson's Field, quickly renamed Revolution Airfield, was actually a flat stretch of hard sand, known locally as Ka Khanna, about 25 miles north-east of Amman, which had been used by the British just after World War II for Spitfire squadrons training with the British army and the Arab Legion in the desert on an occasional basis. There were absolutely no facilities at all, the RAF bringing with them landing equipment, tents and other essential stores, and then taking them away again when they departed, since when it had been forgotten.

On the same day yet another airliner, a Pan Am Jumbo Jet, was hijacked by PFLP members on a flight from Amsterdam to New York, with 170 on board, and first of all flown to Beirut, where the hijackers forced the airport staff to refuel it. They intended also to fly it to Dawson's Field in Jordan, but they were persuaded that the aircraft was far too large to make such a desert landing. Instead the hijackers flew the jumbo jet on to Cairo, where it was blown up immediately the passengers and crew had scrambled clear, having been wired for demolition while waiting at Beirut. The PFLP stated that it had taken this action because it disapproved of Nasser's agreement to the Rogers Peace Initiative, but in fact this one had been an impromptu hijacking, carried out entirely on the individual initiative of the hijackers and not part of Habash's master plan. Yet again on the same day (the 6th) the PFLP failed to hijack a fourth airliner, an El Al Boeing 707, on a flight from Tel Aviv to New York, after a stopover at Amsterdam, when one of the hijackers[1] was shot dead by the El Al security guard, and the other, a girl,[2] was overpowered and handed over to the authorities in London.[3]

[1] Joseph Patrick Anguello, of American-Nicaraguan parentage, which gave the PFLP the excuse to claim active international support for its cause.

[2] Leila Khaled, a Palestinian Arab school teacher, turned revolutionary, who had been involved in the hijacking on the 29th August 1969, when a TWA Boeing was flown to Damascus.

[3] Major-General Ahron Yariv, the Israeli Director of Military Intelligence, was on the aircraft, but Leila Khaled did not appear to know this. *Daily Mail*, 31st August 1971.

The PFLP later stated that the hijackings had been carried out because the Fedayeen movement in Jordan was in danger of being liquidated, and they now held hostage 301 people, British, American, Swiss, West German and Israeli. Then followed about six days of confused demands and bargaining. George Habash was absent and the other PFLP leaders, who were subjected to many pressures, some from the Fedayeen themselves, were hesitant. First of all they demanded the release of certain Arab prisoners, seven in all, in European hands in exchange for the hostages, giving a 72-hour ultimatum that they would blow up both aircraft and people if this was not agreed to. Both planes were wired ready for instant destruction. Switzerland agreed to release the Arabs serving prison sentences, and West Germany also agreed to free the three Arabs it held on charges of attacking an El Al plane in exchange for their nationals. Britain stood fast and refused to release the girl guerilla unless all hijacked aircraft and personnel were set free. Later all three governments agreed to act in unison. On the 7th the PFLP released 127 women and children, retaining 174 people, who were kept inside the two aircraft.

On the 8th a special Red Cross envoy left Geneva for Amman to negotiate on behalf of all governments concerned. During the day certain pressmen were allowed to move close to the aircraft to see the hostages and talk to the hijackers through loud-hailers. Jordanian troops formed a ring about 250 metres from the aircraft, but after General Haditha, the Chief of Staff, had talks with the guerillas, they withdrew in their armoured vehicles to a distance of about a mile, where they kept watch, as did the world's television cameras from the same distance. The pilots said that they would be able to take off if the aircraft were unloaded. Meanwhile, in almost unbearable conditions, the hostages sweated it out inside the planes.

On the 9th a further dramatic hijacking took place when PFLP members seized a BOAC VC-10 in flight from Bombay to London, just after a stop-over at Bahrein with 114 people on board. After refuelling at Beirut, where the guerillas threatened to blow the plane up if the security forces approached, it flew off and landed at Dawson's Field. Thus there were now three hijacked airliners and 288 hostages in PFLP hands. This drastic policy of the PFLP caused a split amongst the guerillas, as Arafat saw that all nations, especially Arab ones to which the Fedayeen must look for support, were becoming alarmed and alienated. The removal of the first batch of hostages to hotels in Amman had been the result of pressure by the PLO and the Unified Command, as one Arab government after another expressed reprobation. On the 10th the PFLP extended its deadline for another three days (until the 13th).

Meanwhile there were indiscriminate, and at times heavy spates of firing in Amman as the Fedayeen became bolder, where the guerillas unsuccessfully attacked the radio station and where many were arrested. Power and light had been cut off, and already there were many casualties. On the 8th, after eight consecutive days on which there had been firing and explosions in the city, a cease-fire was brought about by the Arab League, but it lasted barely hours. By the 9th, all foreigners, including pressmen, were confined to their hotels because the streets were bullet-swept and unsafe.

In the north of Jordan there were clashes between the Fedayeen and the Jordanian army, which shelled the refugee camp near Irbid on the 9th, killing some 40 people, while Bedu troops closed the frontier with Syria near Dera. There was also fighting at the mosque at Irbid, when at least seven guerillas were killed, and where they attacked the police station, killing three Jordanians, after it was rumoured that the security forces had put mutilated bodies of guerillas on show in the main square. Arafat appealed over Radio Amman for all to stop this genocide, while King Hussein instructed General Haditha to impose a cease-fire. Haditha had talks with Arafat. On the 10th the Jordanian Government and the PASC agreed upon the third truce in five days, and for a couple of days the disturbances quietened down. It will be seen that sometimes the guerillas used PASC as its authority, and at others the Unified Command, depending upon what they wanted and who was trying to call the tune, which tended to confuse.

After a long meeting of the central committee of the PNC it was decided to put all pressure on the PFLP to release hostages and aircraft, and to expel that organization (which was not in the PASC) from the PLO and the Unified Command. Arafat appreciated that the climate of Arab opinion was turning against the guerillas and this was emphasized when Iraq, which had been so vocally strong in support of the Fedayeen against King Hussein a few days before, changed its attitude and denounced the hijackings. On the 10th the PFLP released 23 Asian passengers and an English girl. On the 12th the Iraqi Defence Minister and the Chief of Staff visited the Iraqi division in Jordan. They also told a delegation from the central committee of the PNC that it was necessary to protect the Palestine revolution 'from the dangers of containment and final extermination', but the delegation could not obtain any firm commitment of active help against the Jordanian Government.

It was on the 12th that the PFLP guerillas at Dawson's Field released most of the hostages and blew up the three aircraft before dispersing, taking with them 54 hostages, who were hidden away in various refugee camps. The PFLP gave another warning to the governments of Britain, West Germany and Switzerland, but negotiations between the Red Cross representatives and the guerillas were broken off. In Amman a Red Crescent official stated that about 150 people, mostly civilians, had been killed, and 500 wounded in the capital since the 30th August. The remaining hostages were of British, West German and Swiss nationalities, and included 24 Jews, some of whom held Israeli passports. The PFLP was now demanding that some 600 Arabs imprisoned by the Israelis also be released in exchange for the hostages. On the following day the Israelis arrested about 450 Arabs in their occupied territories, but denied that they were to be counter-hostages. Most were released after a short period. On the same day 252 freed hostages were flown from Amman to Cyprus. On the 15th the PFLP gave another list of those they demanded should be released in exchange for the hostages. It included ten Lebanese soldiers captured by the Israelis and two Algerians held by them, but Britain still held out for collective bargaining with the hijackers.

The Fedayeen gained control of many areas in northern Jordan, and on the 13th had completed their occupation of Irbid and were erecting road blocks on approaches to that town. On that day the armoured brigade, with some 100 tanks, of the Iraqi division, which had been on an exercise in the Zerka area, moved northwards back to the Mafrak and Irbid region, which gave the guerillas the confidence to call a conference of 'delegates of the people' of Irbid on the 15th to determine its political future, at which the local Fatah commander, Abu Hassan,[1] declared the area to be the 'First Arab Soviet'. The population of the town would be about 100,000, but there were another 100,000 in the vicinity, mainly Palestinian refugees. Guerillas also put down road blocks near Jerash, which meant that they held a section of the main, and only good, north-south road between Jerash and Irvid, some 30 miles in all. At this stage King Hussein had difficulty in restraining his soldiers, but tried to enforce the cease-fire negotiated by General Haditha. In the south the Fedayeen had less good fortune, the local Bedu tribesmen helping the Jordanian army to attack guerillas based in the region of Maan. In the fighting some 70 guerillas were killed and their camps eliminated. In a previous clash, near Maan, Fatah had admitted 35 casualties.

On the 16th fighting flared up again when the Jordanian army tried unsuccessfully to drive guerillas from Zerka for the second time. The army surrounded the town, where the Fedayeen were well ensconced, remaining in possession of the large military installation area and the country's only oil refinery, which was the key to its mechanical mobility. During a later three-hour clash, there was shelling and mortaring by the Fedayeen.

Premier Rifai, backed by General Haditha, was in the process of coming to an agreement with the Jordanian-Palestine higher committee, when King Hussein yielded to military advice, dismissed the Rifai Government and removed Haditha from his post as Chief of Staff. In its place he appointed a military government of 12 senior officers, naming Brigadier Mohammed Daoud, a Palestinian, as Premier. He also appointed Field Marshal Habis al-Majali[2] as Military Governor of Jordan and Commander-in-Chief. The country was brought under

---

[1] One of the founders of Fatah, His real name was Hani al-Hassan.

[2] He was from the large Majali Bedu tribe.

military rule, and a governor-general named for each of the country's six military districts.

In reply the guerillas appointed Arafat 'General Commander of all the Armed Forces of the Revolution' and nominated Brigadier Yahya, of the PLA, to be his Chief of Staff. This move made Arafat the effective Fedayeen battle commander in Jordan, although all his fighters did not follow him blindly. The Fedayeen declared a general strike and demanded a national government, which was the first time they had ever called for a share in governing Jordan, governmental irresponsibility being a marked trait so far. When FM Majali ordered the Fedayeen militia to hand in their arms, Arafat told them to retain them. Premier Daoud became little more than a figurehead in the days that followed as the real power lay with FM Majali, the Military Governor. Arafat afterwards admitted he was taken by surprise at the dismissal of the civilian government and the sudden appointment of a military one, which sparked off the nine-day civil war in Jordan. The guerillas were undecided whether to go it alone, or wait for Iraqi help, but were overtaken by events, while the King's senior military advisers told him that it would be all over in 24 hours, a fact that strongly influenced his decision. The civil war was fought concurrently in two sectors, in Amman and in the north of the country, which will be described separately.

King Hussein had a mixed army and a mixed population. Of the 2·2 million people in Jordan, some two-thirds were Palestinians; of the remaining 700,000, about 250,000 were Bedu, 100,000 Christian Arabs, and the other 350,000 consisted of small groups of Circassians, Druze, Turkomans and Bahias, mainly in village communities. His army was about 56,000-strong, and consisted of about one-third desert Bedu, one-third mercenary Bedu from the adjacent deserts of Syria, Iraq and Saudi Arabia, and one-third Palestinians. There had been a much larger element of Palestinians before the June War but they had been reduced in number since the loss of the West Bank. The army consisted of three armoured brigades and seven infantry brigades basically, and possessed about 100 tanks, 200 US M-113 armoured personnel carriers, 50 British armoured cars, 150 field and anti-tank guns and ample recoilless guns. The armoured brigades were made up almost entirely of Bedu soldiers. In some infantry brigades Palestinians predominated, and so they were considered to be of doubtful loyalty to the throne. It was just over three years since the June 1967 defeat, and because of known differences between the Bedu soldiers and those with sympathies for the Palestinian cause, its morale was thought to be problematic, a factor that influenced the Fedayeen to attack.

The civil war began at about 0430 hours on the 17th September, when units of the 3rd Armoured Brigade with their armoured vehicles moved into the centre of Amman determined to flush it clear of guerillas. Artillery, tanks and aircraft were brought into play in the course of the day against the Fedayeen who, forewarned, had been able to fortify some of their strongpoints and to place snipers on roof tops. Most of the buildings in Amman were of strong concrete or stone construction, and the policy was to blast the guerillas out by sheer force of fire power and explosives. The guerillas had early rejected FM Majali's ultimatum to quit Amman.

The heaviest fighting was in the area of Jebel Amman, the Intercontinental Hotel (where some 130 pressmen had been forced to take refuge and remain because of gunfire),[1] and the British Embassy. Majali stated that any house from which a sniper fired would be destroyed, and he attempted to do this. Although by the end of the day FM Majali claimed that his soldiers were in control of most of the city and that only a few pockets of resistance remained, the guerillas denied this with some truth. The Jordanian cabinet announced that it handed over full powers to deal with this emergency to FM Majali, who ordered a complete curfew. The 600,000 inhabitants of Amman took to their houses and hid in the cellars where, short of food and water, without electric light, most remained for many hours. Numbers were killed or injured by falling rubble as buildings were blasted. With the curfew in force there were only Bedu soldiers on the streets, many with their faces blackened to avoid identification.

[1] The pressmen were confined to the Intercontinental Hotel for ten days, being unable to report on the fighting, and when released were taken straight to the airport and flown out of the country.

The bridges over the River Jordan were closed, the country was virtually cut off from the outside, and there was confusion as to what was happening. The central committee of the PNC asked for Iraqi military help, but this request was ignored, although both Iraq and Syria condemned King Hussein's actions. FM Majali announced that he would accept an Arab League proposal to stop firing if the guerillas also ceased firing and withdrew from the city, offering them a safe-conduct. Radio Amman complained that it had not been possible to make contact with Arafat, and the Damascus-based 'Voice of the Palestine Revolution' asked Arab states to move in to stop the massacre—but none moved a single soldier. On this, the first day of the civil war, the guerillas experienced difficulty in communication, being accustomed to acting on code words given over their radio—formerly an Egyptian facility—and to rehearsing and discussing their plans beforehand. The signals from the Syrian radio station were weak and barely audible. On many occasions there were no answering calls, and at times the exasperated guerillas broke into plain speech which was picked up by the Jordanian monitoring intelligence branch.

The Jordanian army's attempt to clear Amman swiftly had failed. At dawn on the second day of the civil war, after having pulled back from the centre of the city during the night, the 3rd Armoured Brigade moved back in, with all guns firing, to blast out snipers, who had returned to their strong-points and on to the house tops. Then artillery began shelling the Wahdat and Jebel Hussein refugee camps, causing the guerillas to claim that the PLO headquarters building had been hit. The Wahdat refugee camp, the headquarters of Fatah, was on one of the hills overlooking Amman, where the original tents put up some 20 years before had given way to small, box-like concrete houses. At midday FM Majali ordered a standstill in Amman to give the Fedayeen a chance to quit the city or surrender, but as they continued to fire at soldiers the bombardment was resumed, with aerial assaults on certain posts.

There were now many dead and injured on the streets of Amman. As the streets were still swept by fire, the casualties remained where they lay. Black pillars of smoke were rising in many places, and the whole situation was confused. Also there was anxiety for the safety of the 54 hijacked hostages, some of whom were thought to be hidden in the Wahdat refugee camp. Both sides claimed defections, but in fact there were hardly any, although the Jordanian army carried out psychological warfare with the aid of loud hailers, threats and promises. Libya suspended its subsidy[1] to Jordan, President Nasser warned that there could be only one winner—Israel—and General Mohammed Sadeck, the Egyptian Chief-of-Staff, flew to Amman to see King Hussein, who was at his al-Hummar Palace,[2] near Suweileh, where he remained throughout the war.

Fighting in the capital continued for the third day, the 19th, in much the same manner, the Jordanians, relying upon force of arms, bringing up guns to point-blank range to blast buildings that contained snipers. There was more shelling of the refugee camps in which there were guerilla bases. In parts of Amman the total curfew was relaxed for three hours, but few ventured out on to the streets. FM Majali issued an ultimatum demanding that the Fedayeen stop firing by 1800 hours, but this was rejected and the grinding battle continued, with the army making slow advances. The guerillas lacked heavy weapons to halt the armoured vehicles. General Sadek tried to persuade King Hussein to order a cease-fire, if only as a temporary measure. This pattern continued on the fourth day, the 20th, with the Jordanian army slowly getting the upper hand. When a short break in the curfew was announced, more people crept out from their hiding places, being desperate for food, water and medical attention. King Hussein agreed to a cease-fire, which lasted barely an hour before it was broken.

On the following day, the 21st, the Jebel Hussein refugee camp was shelled fairly heavily for two hours just after dawn, and the fighting continued. FM Majali warned that looters would be shot on sight, and enforced the ban on carrying arms and

[1] £10 million annually.
[2] During this period some considerable publicity was given to 'ham radio' conversations during the nights between King Hussein and a British 'ham', which was either designed to indicate a 'Drake playing bowls before the battle' attitude, or meant that FM Majali was doing all the day-to-day work, the King merely taking a detached nominal part and concentrating upon international or diplomatic issues.

147

driving vehicles in the major part of the capital that was under his control. Yet more people ventured out when the curfew was lifted for a while, but there was still anxiety for the hostages, somewhere in guerilla hands. Arafat met General Sadek; reports indicating that they were arranging a cease-fire were later denied. Kuwait suspended its aid to Jordan,[1] leaving Saudi Arabia as the only country to continue paying, but by this time other material aid was beginning to flow into Jordan.[2] Late in the evening the guerillas rejected King Hussein's offer of a cease-fire.

Amman airport remained closed, but Red Crescent aircraft landed at another airstrip nearby with supplies, and on the evening of the 21st the first casualties were flown out. House to house fighting continued in Amman on the sixth day, the 22nd, by the end of which the Jordanian army was in possession of substantial areas of the city, with the guerillas still holding out, mainly in the Citadel area in the centre, the Wahdat and Jebel Hussein refugee camps, around Jebel Hussein and Jebel al-Nozha, all predominantly Palestinian-inhabited areas. By evening the situation was such that FM Majali was able to send his 60th Armoured Brigade,[3] which he had held back near Amman to keep the guerilla camps on the hills on the outskirts under observation, north to take part in the battle that was developing there. The following day, the 23rd, Jordanian troops seized the Citadel area (Jebel Kala) and so were able to dominate the city itself.

The other part of the civil war, in the northern part of the Kingdom, was developing concurrently with the battle for Amman; after the guerillas had rejected FM Majali's ultimatum to quit the towns, fighting between the Fedayeen and the security forces broke out in Zerka, Irbid, Ramtha, Jerash, Karak, Bakaa and Salt. By evening the Fedayeen claimed to be in control of all Jordan above a line 15 miles north of Amman, which was more than partly true. Counter claims were made by FM Majali, who insisted, for example, that his troops

---

[1] £15 million.
[2] The British contribution, for example, consisted mainly of an army field hospital which was flown out and set up near the capital.
[3] The third one was designated the 40th Armoured Brigade.

were dominant in Zerka. There had been two batteries of Syrian guns in the northern part of the Jordan Valley since February (1970), one of anti-tank and the other of long-range field guns. They took no part in the civil war and were sent back into Syria on the 17th October.

On the second day, the 18th, guerillas attempted to set up and consolidate 'liberated areas', claiming to have done so at Irbid, Ramtha, Jerash, Ajlun and Bakaa, and to have appointed military governors for each of them. Later in the day they claimed to have occupied Mafrak, but elements of the Jordanian 40th Armoured Brigade were nearby, as were the Iraqi troops. The guerillas announced that the Jordanian Military Governor of Irbid had been sentenced to death by a revolutionary court.[1] During the day there was a movement of guerillas southwards across the Syrian border near Ramtha to reinforce the Fedayeen fighting at Irbid and Zerka, who were identified mainly as Syrian Saiqa members.

The guerilla hope was that the Iraqi troops would be on their side, and if not actually joining with them to attack the Jordanians would at least settle in the so-called 'liberated areas' to allow the guerillas to consolidate their hold by forming a protective screen for them. But the Iraqis remained passive and made no move to help, their inactivity being caused by a difference of opinion within the ruling Baath Government and Party, the military element being against intervention while the civilian element wanted Iraqi troops in Jordan to help the guerillas. An additional argument that helped the military to make their case was that they were entirely dependent upon fuel from Zerka, held firmly by the Jordanian army, and that to attack Zerka would mean a major battle which senior Iraqi officers did not think could be won without heavy casualties— if at all.

There were also divided views amongst the leadership of the ruling Baath Party in Syria as to whether Syrian troops should intervene on behalf of the guerillas. Yussef Zeayean, a former Premier, went secretly into Jordan on the first day of the civil war to assess the situation, and on his return recommended

[1] Brigadier Bahjat al-Moheisen, allegedly for allowing mutilated bodies of guerillas to be exhibited on the square.

intervention: thus in Syria the dominant civilian element decided to give general military support to the Fedayeen, on the ground only, and not to commit any aircraft. This was partly to embarrass the Iraqis and partly to try to provoke Iraqi troops to move into action. At least two Syrian brigades were moved right up against the frontier in the Dera sector. In the late afternoon, on the 18th, a small armoured unit with PLA markings on its T-55 tanks crossed the border into Jordan near Ramtha and advanced for three miles until it came up against a group of Jordanian tanks. An exchange of fire caused the Jordanian armour to withdraw back into the Irbid area, thus allowing the Syrian and PLA formations to get into positions in the hills overlooking the vital cross-roads. The PLA had a few light field guns with them. The guerillas claim to have knocked out six Jordanian tanks and captured two, which may have been accurate. The third day in the north was one of confusion, there were many hopelessly conflicting claims, and as no pressmen were with either of the combatants, there was no accurate reporting. The Jordanian Government accused Syria of moving armoured units into northern Jordan, and requested an emergency meeting of the Arab League, but this was denied in Damascus, it being alleged that the armour complained of belonged to the PLA and consisted of '40 Soviet tanks'.

The Syrian army was about 75,000 strong and consisted of four armoured or mechanized and seven motorized infantry brigades, with about 900 tanks or self-propelled guns, over 500 Soviet armoured personnel carriers and over 800 guns of various types. At dawn on the fourth day, the 20th, two Syrian brigades[1] and the Hittin Brigade[2] of the PLA were just over the edge of the border into Jordan facing the 40th Armoured Brigade, the forward elements of which had withdrawn after the previous day's skirmish. FM Majali ordered the Jordanians to stand fast, and not to give any more ground. During the course of the day Nasser, who ostensibly was playing the role of the

[1] Identified by King Hussein as the Syrian 67th and 88th Armoured Brigades, of the 5th Division, plus two infantry units and 'some guns'.

[2] The Hittin (Hattan) Brigade was named after the famous Saracen victory over the Crusaders at Hittin in 1187.

peacemaker, sent the Egyptian Brigade of the PLA, some 3,000 men, to Syria, and they were immediately sent forward to support the Hittin Brigade. This meant that there were only about 1,000 PLA members remaining in Egypt. Nasser was probably pleased at this excuse to rid himself of nearly all the PLA troops who had been stationed in the Suez Canal area, now that he had a cease-fire with the Israelis there. The Hittin Brigade had been hastily equipped with modern T-54s and T-55s from the Syrian stockpile, it being known that previously the PLA had only some old T-34s. During the course of the morning of the 20th there were two thrusts from Syria, one aimed towards Ramtha by the PLA and the other by way of Tura and Shajara, both frontier villages held by the guerillas, towards Irbid, both led by tanks with PLA markings. Perhaps 90 tanks in all ventured forward along a 20-mile wide front, but they were held by the Jordanians, now in better positions in the hills, and so after a while and some shooting they withdrew again.

King Hussein cabled Arab heads of state declaring Syria's action to be 'treacherous aggression', while William Rogers, US Secretary of State, declared it to be 'irresponsible and imprudent'. Radio Damascus claimed a victory for the PLA Hittin Brigade after a 36-hour battle, and Radio Cairo said that 5,000 people had been killed or wounded so far in the fighting in Jordan. FM Majali claimed that three guerilla leaders, two Fatah and one PFLP, had defected, to whom was later added another PFLP leader, but it is more likely that they were captured or betrayed. On the same day, the 20th, a North Korean communiqué stated that George Habash had been in North Korea since the 2nd September, studying Marshal Kim Il-sung's 'revolutionary strategy against American imperialism'. Arafat was the dominant Fedayeen personality at this critical moment, without serious rival. There was speculation whether Britain would intervene under its treaty obligations, or whether the US 6th Fleet in the Eastern Mediterranean would become involved. A Soviet warning against outside intervention in Jordan was presumably aimed at America.

In the course of the fifth day, the 21st, Syrian and PLA armour cautiously advanced, being attacked by Jordanian aircraft several times. By this time there were probably nearly

200 hostile tanks in Jordan just south of the Syrian border. In Mafrak itself, held by the guerillas, a Jordanian tank unit was surrounded and had to fight off the attackers, while at Ramtha, also held by guerillas, it was the other way round, with the Jordanians attacking. At Jerash Jordanian armoured attacks were held, while at Zerka they were driven back with loss, the Fedayeen claiming 200 Jordanian dead and 500 wounded. In Irbid the guerillas were in full control of a large sector, but not the whole town, and a second armoured attack had to be made before the Jordanians retook it. At Salt it was stalemate for a while until Jordanian armour took and held the vital cross-roads, although the guerillas claimed to have destroyed four Jordanian tanks by mines. Radio Amman claimed that the Jordanians had fought a violent battle for Irbid, but the Feda-yeen said that the PLA tanks had entered that town after 'completely liberating northern Jordan'. The guerillas were certainly in strong positions in the triangle of broken country between Irbid, Ajlun and Jerash. The Syrians denied interven-tion, but admitted that the Jordanians had captured nine of their soldiers, insisting this had happened when the Jordanians crossed into Syria. Expecting a counter attack, the Syrians were frantically preparing defences in the area of Dera.

By nightfall the Syrian and PLA tanks, positioned some 12 miles south of Ramtha and some 15 miles south of Irbid, were preparing to advance on to the capital the next morning. The Iraqi division remained absolutely passive, and when Jordanian aircraft hit Iraqi positions near Ramtha, the Iraqis hastily said that it was just a mistake. King Hussein appealed to Britain, America and the Soviet Union to take action over the Syrian aggression, and the US 6th Fleet steamed towards the Israeli coastline. Late that evening the Fedayeen rejected another cease-fire offer by King Hussein.

Beginning shortly after dawn on the sixth day, the 22nd, Syrian and PLA formations pushed on towards Amman, but were attacked by Jordanian aircraft and armour, and by afternoon had been forced to a halt. By this time the situation in Amman was more under control, and FM Majali dispatched the 60th Armoured Brigade northwards, which dominated Zerka on the way. He then ordered the two armoured brigades to make a pincer attack on the Syrian armour; the two forces made contact early, sparking off an intense 16-hour battle, in which air attacks and shelling were practically non-stop. Heavy losses were inflicted on the invaders, who were pushed back a few miles, but the fighting died down at dusk for sheer exhaustion and lack of fuel and shells. The Jordanians lost at least 19 tanks, and the Syrians at least ten. It had been good timing as the 40th Armoured Brigade had hit the Syrians head-on, while the 60th caught them in the flank, but although the Jordanians had been well supported by aircraft, they had lost twice as many tanks as the Syrians, who had hit back hard. There had also been heavy fighting for Ramtha and Tura, a few miles to the north of the tank battle.

An Arab summit was due to meet in Cairo to try to solve the Jordanian civil war, but the Syrians refused to attend. King Hussein sent his Premier, Daoud, to represent him. The summit was postponed, and instead President Numeiry of the Sudan led a small delegation to Amman where he saw both King Hussein and Arafat. FM Majali offered £5,000 reward each for the arrest of George Habash, of the PFLP, and Neyef Hawatmeh, of the DPF, but these offers were afterwards rescinded to prevent the men from going underground. Indications that a US airborne division had been alerted in the USA, as well as a US airborne unit in Germany, gave King Hussein confidence, as did the rumoured Israeli plan to move into northern Jordan should the guerillas succeed in taking over large sectors. Israeli armour had massed on the Golan Plateau, and it was said that America and Israel might collaborate against the Fedayeen, and that America might drop a paratroop unit on Amman to protect American citizens and King Hussein. The Israelis let it be known that they could reach Damascus within four hours. Their view was that Hussein could hold the southern part of his Kingdom, but they doubted whether he could hold the northern part.

On the 23rd, the seventh day, after their hard battle the Syrian and PLA armour began to pull back, enabling Jordanian armour to settle on the vital cross-roads that were the key to communications in northern Jordan, and allowing FM Majali to announce that evening that the last Syrian tanks had been driven from Jordan. Earlier King Hussein had given a Press conference at his al-Hummar Palace, at which he admitted his surprise at the preparedness of the guerillas, and said that on the previous day (the 22nd)[1] there had been a big tank battle, in which the Jordanians pushed the Syrians back five miles, and Jordanian aircraft knocked out ten tanks and assaulted other vehicles and anti-aircraft positions. He claimed that over 100 Syrian tanks had been destroyed or hit, for the loss of only ten of his own. On the other hand, the guerillas claimed that in the battle for Ramtha, perhaps the most hard-fought of the day, the Jordanians lost 20 tanks, with 50 killed and 200 wounded, but admitted that 12 Syrian soldiers had been captured. King Hussein released the four captured guerilla leaders and sent them secretly to Cairo to make contacts preparatory to an agreement, but also on that day Premier Daoud, who was still in Cairo, resigned from the Government and remained in Egypt. A Palestinian, he was frustrated by events and the fact that all the power was held by FM Majali, a Bedouin, with Bedouin sympathies. On the following day, the 24th, the eighth day of the civil war, Jordanian forces renewed their pressure upon Ramtha and Irbid, which were surrounded and constantly shelled, but they did not enter either of those two towns. Elsewhere there was a pause in the fighting while Arafat was negotiating a cease-fire.

On the 25th September, the ninth day, after a meeting between President Numeiry of the Sudan, King Hussein and Arafat, Hussein announced over the radio that he had made an agreement with Arafat for a cease-fire throughout Jordan, which recognized the PLO as the sole representative of the Fedayeen movement. Both guerillas and soldiers were to withdraw from Amman and other towns, and the Fedayeen were to move to positions near the River Jordan from where they could operate into Israel. An uneasy calm fell on Amman after this announcement, which was broken on a few occasions, particularly when Jordanian soldiers rescued 16 hostages from the Wahdat refugee camp. On the following day, the 26th, fighting flared up at the Jebel Hussein refugee camp, the headquarters of the

[1] From time to time Israeli aircraft flew over the battlefields taking reconnaissance photographs, as did US surveillance aircraft.

PLO, and there were minor eruptions in other parts of the country. That evening guerillas fired three rockets on to Amman airport, damaging one of the relief aircraft.

On the 27th, in Cairo, under the sponsorship of President Nasser, who had worked hard to bring peace to Jordan, King Hussein, Arafat and Arab heads of state signed a 14-point agreement which became known as the (Jordanian) Cairo Agreement,[1] to bring to an end the civil war. Basically it provided for the withdrawal of both troops and guerillas from the population centres, for Jordan's return to civilian rule, and for an Arab truce commission to supervise the cease-fire. That day 32 hostages were flown out from Amman. FM Majali stated that his soldiers had cleared 180 guerilla bases and posts from the capital, but admitted that a few remained. Guerillas were still holding out in Ramtha, but were surrounded, their water cut off and the roads blocked. There was also some fighting in Amman. The next day, the 28th September 1970, President Nasser, of Egypt, died of a heart attack at the age of 52 years, his last efforts being directed towards obtaining peace in Jordan. On the 29th FM Majali announced the rescue of the last six hostages who had been held in Irbid.

The nine-day civil war had been a fierce and bloody one, but it was inconclusive, there being no clear-cut winner or loser. The Jordanian army had strengthened its position and its confidence and morale had improved immensely, while the guerillas had been badly battered, losing heavily in men and material, but they had retained the right to remain and operate in Jordan. Both sides eyed each other warily, tension remained high, and clashes were frequent. The Jordanian army was full of 'hawks' who resented the cease-fire and wanted to finish the Palestinian guerillas off once and for all while they had them on their knees. The Bedu soldiers were alleged by the Fedayeen to act more as an army of occupation instead of liberators to keep the peace and distribute food and medical help.

The guerillas had been badly shaken by the Bedu soldiers' readiness to fire into the crowded refugee camps. The Bedu had, in fact, little but contempt for all Palestinians. Arafat had been

[1] Normally known as the Cairo Agreement, but I have so designated it to distinguish it from the (Lebanese) Cairo Agreement.

relying upon the Jordanian army not to fire on women and children; he felt sure that guerilla bases in the refugee camps would remain inviolate and safe. This confidence largely contributed to the guerilla defeat in and around Amman, and for them the cease-fire came only just in time as the Jordanians had begun battering their way house by house into the guerilla heart of the main camps. The hapless refugees had nearly reached the end of their tether and had to be terrorized into co-operation. Arafat was also surprised at the hostility of the Jordanian army, and was disappointed by his failure to subvert any appreciable numbers, even among the Palestinian element. The Jordanian Government was convinced that the war had been deliberately stirred up by hard-line communists, financed by China, and as proof pointed to the number of Chinese weapons found with the Fedayeen and the fact that Arafat later publicly thanked China for its help.[1]

King Hussein boasted that although his army was mixed, containing both Bedu and Palestinians, there was not a single instance of any unit refusing battle, but he had used his loyal Bedu-manned armoured brigades first, reasoning that once they broke through and dominated the guerillas, the infantry in which there was a large Palestinian element would remain loyal. In fact, the infantry were not brought into action until the latter stages, and then used only sparingly. He also said that although the Iraqi division remained passive, it allowed guerillas, arms and supplies to move freely through its areas, and that there had been a few individual Iraqi soldiers fighting with the guerillas on the streets of Amman.

Arafat, who as overall commander conducted the fighting, gained in stature and reputation as he remained throughout in Amman, except for one short, secret visit to Cairo to try to persuade President Nasser to give more active help. He had many disappointments. Although the majority of his men fought

[1] There was a Chinese military attaché accredited to Damascus, and at least 400 Chinese nationals in the Middle East, many of whom were active in the Palestinian refugee camps, often posing as pressmen or social workers. It was reported that at least three plane-loads of Chinese arms were brought into Damascus airport during the civil war and sent into northern Jordan.

well, they could not, having no heavy weapons, stand up to ruthless Jordanian fire power. The guerillas were also surprisingly short of mines and grenades. He was forced to conclude that Viet Cong tactics did not work in a Middle East setting. Arafat was sadly disappointed with the Arab states, the Soviet Union and the Western Powers. He felt that Iraq in particular had let him down, as if the Iraqi division had come out on his side, the whole of northern Jordan would have been his, but apart from Syria no other Arab country had raised a rifle to help him. Arab governments were still smarting from the arrogantly independent guerilla activities and attitude within their countries, and secretly most, if not all, would have liked to have seen the Fedayeen cut down to size. The Soviet Union regarded the guerillas coldly, and as soon as there were signs that Israel might intervene and so ignite another Arab-Israeli conflict which would affect the huge numbers of Soviet personnel in the Middle East, pressure was put on Syria and the threat used that all Soviet aid would cease unless Syrian troops were withdrawn from Jordan. This threat, and not Jordanian armour, caused the Syrian and PLA formations to retreat, and additionally President Nasser persuaded Arafat that, if he did not stop the fighting, US troops would move into the battle areas.

In turn Syria was also bitterly disappointed that the Iraqi division did not enter the war, but from the Iraqi point of view its loyalty was uncertain as it contained many politically-minded officers who had been posted there to keep them out of Iraq. The Syrian aim had been to prevent the liquidation of the Fedayeen in Jordan, and it went as far as it dared, stopping short of using its air force which could not have been concealed, while denying intervention. Nureddin Atassi resigned on the 11th October, over the war in Jordan, while the commander of one of the two brigades that entered Jordan was dismissed and the other reduced in rank. Arafat was also alarmed at the way in which he thought America might gang-up with Israel to prevent a large guerilla base being established in Jordan. Senior guerilla leaders openly admitted that it would take between three and six months to recover from this fighting, and they were glad of the respite. It was in their interests of survival for the guerillas to conform to the cease-fire, which most did for a while, many taking off their uniforms and going underground. President Nasser had master-minded the negotiations, and his supreme triumph had been to persuade Arafat and King Hussein to meet and shake hands in public. While he worked for peace, it should be noted that at the same time he sent the Egyptian Brigade of the PLA and some arms into Syria, so perhaps he also looked beyond the cease-fire to his own future interests, or perhaps it was his idea of preserving a Middle East balance favourable to Egypt.

In this short civil war a great number of people were killed and wounded, but no one knows exactly how many, as estimates varied so much. King Hussein said that his army lost 200 men, and that civilian casualties in Amman were 541. Arafat claimed that 3,490 civilians, between 2,000 and 3,000 soldiers and 900 'commandos' were killed, and that about 14,000 were wounded in all. UNRWA estimated that 20,000 had been killed or wounded, of whom 3,000 were civilian dead, while the Red Crescent arrived at the figures of 3,440 killed and 10,840 injured. The guerillas strongly insisted the Jordanian army casualties were far higher than the official estimate, and they were indeed later amended to 750 killed and 1,250 wounded. Fatah put out some figures for the Wahdat refugee camp, its main base, claiming that 50 refugees had been killed and 'hundreds wounded', and that out of 6,250 houses, 750 had been destroyed and 2,250 damaged. Twelve Syrian soldiers had been captured, who had been told that they were being sent to fight the Israelis. A concensus of estimates indicated that a continuing 15 per cent of the guerillas were non-Palestinian. The US Embassy in Amman placed the casualties at 500 killed and 3,500 wounded.

Although licking their wounds, the guerillas did not consider themselves a beaten force at all. They dragged their feet in evacuating towns, having to be jostled out by the Jordanian army, which felt it had been robbed of victory. The Fedayeen began regrouping, reorganizing and re-equipping themselves. For several days there was 'dual authority' in certain parts of northern Jordan until the Fedayeen were edged out, and they still remained firmly established in parts of Amman.

On the 1st October the Jordanian Government said that it would recognize and deal only with Fatah, and advised other guerilla organizations to co-operate with Arafat. The PFLP openly refused and declared that its aim was to bring about the downfall of King Hussein. A few days later George Habash, newly returned from his Far East travels, boasted that the Fedayeen militia in Jordan was 30,000-strong, but admitted that it possessed only 10,000 arms. Seven guerillas held by Britain, West Germany and Switzerland were flown to Cairo to be exchanged for hostages. On the 5th Israel rejected a guerilla demand for the release of 35 guerillas held by them. On the 7th the Arab truce commission gained the release of about 19,000 guerillas or Fedayeen sympathizers detained by the Jordanian authorities, and most of the remaining 1,000 or so held were released within the next few days. Life was returning to normal in the capital and many parts of the north, but not completely, and on the 11th October the guerillas declared Irbid to be the 'capital of a liberated zone'.

On the 13th, in the Tunisian Embassy in Amman, both King Hussein and Arafat signed an agreement enlarging the (Jordanian) Cairo Agreement of the 27th September, which became known as the Amman agreement, containing provisions that guerilla camps should be sited along the Israeli border and not in territory surrounding the main population centres, as Arafat had demanded. On the other hand, Hussein had to give in on his demands to control the Fedayeen militia and the right to censor all guerilla publications. On the 16th FM Majali was superseded as Military Governor of Jordan, and a civilian government, headed by Ahmed Toukan, was installed.

Arafat immediately claimed that the Jordanian army was not carrying out its part of the agreement and withdrawing from the towns. Fighting flared up in Irbid and Jerash, which developed and continued for several days, until the Arab truce commission was able to quieten the situation down. America supplied some tanks to replace losses in the Jordanian army, which came in by air from Turkey to land at Dawson's Field. The Jordanian army was unhappy that the guerillas seemed to have been given the freedom of the countryside outside the towns, and pressed as hard as it could, elbowing unwilling guerillas before it. This caused periodic clashes in Ramtha and other frontier villages, and also in Amman. Not capable of standing up in a pitched battle, the Fedayeen had to bend with the wind, and on the 27th it was announced in Amman that Fatah had agreed to notify the Jordanian army in advance of every raid launched across the River Jordan. A new government was formed by Wasfi a-Tal on the 28th October 1970, and the last guerilla reluctantly left the centre of Amman on the 7th November. While King Hussein could not have been said to have won this first major round in his fight against the Fedayeen, he certainly came off best.

# 8. Fedayeen Defeat in Jordan

The Wasfi Tal Government, which took office on the 28th October 1970, put pressure on the guerillas to evacuate the towns completely, in accordance with the Amman Agreement. The consequent jostling became increasingly rough and violent as the weeks went by, causing many spasmodic outbreaks of fighting. Wasfi Tal, a former army officer, of strong right-wing views, was firmly of the opinion that the place of the guerillas was in the occupied territories, and he worked to rid his country of them. A large Arab truce commission, consisting of over 100 officers from various Arab countries, which had descended upon Jordan, was endured rather than welcomed and helped by Wasfi Tal. Both the Jordanians and the guerillas sought to use it, and both at times sought to thwart it. The dejected Fedayeen, suspicious and uncertain, were reluctant to evacuate an inch of ground they held, or thought they held, and refused to accept that the Jordanians would quit in their turn if they did so.

All the fight had not gone out of the guerillas. In particular the PFLP caused several incidents. Although Fatah policy was temporarily to bend with the wind for survival, not all were in agreement with this line; the Fedayeen admitted that when a Jordanian patrol was fired on near Jerash on the 15th November the guerillas would not stop firing when ordered to do so by their leaders. Night-long firing on the 19th was said by the Arab truce commission to have been the work of the PFLP, and it led to a meeting between Wasfi Tal and Arafat. On the 25th the army drove guerillas out from positions near Jerash, and on the 7th December guerillas surrounded a Jordanian police station;

L                                161

in the subsequent firing one Jordanian was killed and another wounded. On the following day the army succeeded in forcing the Fedayeen from the town of Jerash. The bulk of the guerillas were now in the hills in the triangle formed by Ajlun, Jerash and Irbid, in scattered groups. Having lost the blackmailing powers they had when dominant in Amman, they were now struggling for their existence, harassed continually by the Jordanian army. Their operations across the River Jordan into Israel had practically ceased. As the Fedayeen were being pushed out from the towns one by one, and as their supply lines back to Syria became daily more precarious, the army extended its grip on the country. President Nasser's death had scarcely helped the guerillas, as he had at least supported them verbally and used his influence to prevent their liquidation. Now Arab states began to adopt a more independent policy towards them. The new government of the Lebanon warned the guerillas that it would not tolerate any threat to its authority.

Apart from being unexpected and costly, defeat in Jordan had revealed that the guerillas had no discernible strategy, a fact which so far had somehow escaped general attention, being obscured by propaganda. As with any failure there was the inevitable post-mortem, which revealed lack of unity and differing political viewpoints as the main drawbacks. Arafat also came in for criticism, and for the first three weeks in November he was absent from Amman, explaining, persuading and exhorting in the Arab capitals. On the 10th December, after signing an agreement with Wasfi Tal for both the Fedayeen militia and the Jordanian militia to hand their arms in to a central point, Arafat was shouted down by his own militia when he toured the streets of Amman with Wasfi Tal. After declaring many times that he would not return to Jordan until King Hussein dismissed Wasfi Tal, Arafat was now being photographed in his company and shaking his hand. He faced critical crowds at Jerash, where he had moved the PLO headquarters from Amman, and where it was admitted that Fedayeen militiamen had tried to kill him, but had ambushed the wrong car.

On the 15th November the Fatah newspaper reported that the guerillas were considering a plan to drop all individual group labels and merge into a single organization like the Viet Cong, to be called the Palestine Liberation Front; it was to be entirely responsible for the military and political direction of the struggle. Secret talks were held in Amman between the guerillas. On the 19th a conference of the central committee of the PNC had to be cancelled because Arafat was still absent from Amman. When he returned he ran into difficulties. Although the groups were scared by the result of the civil war in Jordan, their widely differing political ideologies were the main obstacles; but he did have some temporary success in persuading certain of the smaller organizations to come directly under the Fatah banner. The PLO announced on the 30th that the 11 groups in the Unified Command had been reduced to six. The major group, Fatah, absorbed the smaller ones, but Arafat could not persuade the extremist PFLP and DPF to come under the PLO umbrella completely. In fact, they were causing most of the trouble in Jordan. However, as boastful as ever, on the 21st December Arafat said: 'We have more recruits than we can handle'. It was estimated that there may still have been as many as 50,000 regular and militia guerillas in Jordan, the large majority semi-underground in that they did not wear uniforms or carry arms openly. Later, stating that 'We have achieved a unity of guns', Arafat said that the former 11 guerilla groups had been reduced to four, each of which was to maintain separate structures but to act jointly. He meant Fatah, Saiqa, PFLP and DPF, the others having been temporarily frightened into agreeing to come under the Fatah umbrella but he should have added the Iraqi Arab Liberation Front, the ALF.

In the first half of December there were frequent clashes, and a certain amount of looting, as the Jordanian army jostled the guerillas. The Bedu soldiers gave not an inch, and were supported by the Premier. On the 14th the Arab truce commission asked both sides not to return fire if fired upon, and stated that it was arranging for prisoners to be released. On the same day Arafat asked both Sadat of Egypt and Assad of Syria to intervene on behalf of the guerillas, but nothing came of this. On the following day the Arab Truce Commission watched the Jordanian army withdraw from Jerash, when the guerillas in turn agreed to evacuate Ajlun, one of the last remaining towns occupied by them, after which only refugee camps and hillside caves were left to them. Premier Wasfi Tal banned the carrying of arms. On the previous day, the 14th, Arafat and Wasfi Tal both said that they would collect in arms from their respective militia, and they made a start.

The culmination of recriminations over Syrian intervention in Jordan had been a bloodless coup on the 14th November—the twenty-first in 21 years—when Hafez Assad took power, leading the military element against the civilian one. On the 18th Assad formally became Premier and Secretary-General of the Baathist Party. Under his guidance his Government moved closer to Egypt, and there was talk of federation. Although he declared that the Palestine resistance movement must be strengthened, there was a marked falling off in supplies sent from Syria into Jordan for the guerillas. In Syria itself he took immediate steps to bring the Saiqa under firmer control. Many of its leaders were arrested and its field units placed under the command of regular officers. Operations on to the Golan Plateau had to be approved in advance by the Syrian army general staff, and precise details given. On the 15th December Assad declared that he would not allow the Palestine revolution to be liquidated, which the guerillas took to mean that in the event of another confrontation with the Jordanian army, Syrian armour and troops would come to their assistance as they had done before, which gave them confidence and made them bolder.

In November and December rumours flooded the Middle East of secret meetings between King Hussein, his representatives, and the Israelis, some allegedly held in Switzerland, and others nearer home on the border just north of Akaba in the desert.[1] Later[2] *Al Ahram* confirmed that King Hussein had met Ygal Alon, Israeli Deputy Premier in the Wadi Araba in October 1970.

The guerillas feared that Hussein might make a separate peace with the Israelis, and so leave them stranded. Their

[1] 'The latest of ten or so that have been held since September 1968, when Hussein met Alon and Israeli Foreign Minister Abba Eban in London.' *Time* of 23rd November 1970.

[2] 24th March 1972.

other fear was that the West Bank might be a bargaining counter as a possible buffer Palestine state. In November King Hussein was non-committal when questioned on this point, insisting on his sovereignty over the West Bank. Fatah condemned outright the reports of a campaign to establish a Palestine state on the West Bank as having originated in mere soundings of opinions which were somehow crystallizing into a plan. The Palestinians themselves were disenchanted with King Hussein after the September civil war, and were no more reconciled to his authority than formerly, although some thought a federation of West Bank and East Bank might be feasible. Few in the West Bank looked forward to returning to his rule again. It was thought and feared by the guerillas that the Israelis favoured such a federation and might, to make this possible, be willing to evacuate the West Bank under certain conditions, such as a peace treaty with Hussein.

In December 1970 the Jordanian army decided that the guerillas should be moved from Jerash, and started to squeeze them out. In the resultant fighting about 100 men, mainly from an Iraqi PLA formation, were killed, and it was alleged that another 200 were killed after the troops had taken the town. Again, after a Jordanian patrol had been fired on near Jerash and one soldier killed and two others kidnapped, the army attacked guerilla positions near the town to search for the kidnapped men, and a six-hour battle ensued, in which there were many civilian and guerilla casualties. Two days previously, in Amman, guerillas had attacked a Jordanian police station, and in the fighting, that lasted for two hours, three were killed and nine wounded. Had the Fedayeen stayed passive they might have been allowed to remain where they were, but their abrasive attitude provoked the Bedu soldiers, and whenever there was an incident swift and deadly retribution followed. Mainly it was the Fedayeen militia causing trouble, aided at times by the PFLP. A 'Free Jordanian' movement appeared and claimed responsibility for several incidents, but it was only a shadowy front for such guerillas as were desperately determined to cause trouble.

On the 10th January 1971 the Jordanian army surrounded the Bakaa refugee camp and arrested many guerillas, deporting

384 of them. PFLP claimed that while this incident was in progress there was a mass walk-out from the camp, which then contained about 32,000 refugees, towards Israel as they said that they would rather live 'under the oppression of an enemy than the oppression of a brother'. The Jordanian government denied the mass walk-out, but there was certainly a large demonstration. Jordanian artillery had been shelling guerilla positions for the third successive day in northern Jordan, as FM Majali, once again the Commander-in-Chief, worked to ease the guerillas from the towns they had filtered back into, it being alleged by them that he was obstructing the Arab truce commission. In London, where he was receiving medical treatment, King Hussein rejected the mediation requests of the Arab truce commission, saying that it was doubtful whether his army was in fact attacking guerillas in areas the Fedayeen expected to have to themselves. In short, he strongly backed Wasfi Tal and FM Majali, and military pressure was maintained. On the 11th the Jordanian Government announced that a further 100 Syrian Saiqa members had been deported.

On the 12th January, as the result of consultations between Wasfi Tal and Ibrahim Bakr, spokesman for the central committee of the PNC, a joint statement for a cease-fire was made, which can be referred to as the disarmament agreement. Both said that they would disarm their militia, which were largely blamed for the recent disturbances, especially in Amman, and agreed that this should be completed by the 22nd January—the first instance of a time limit being specified. Arms were to be held at collecting points. On the following day the army took action against PFLP snipers in Amman, and a combined force of about 50 PFLP and DPF members attacked a police station in the capital. The army at once moved back into Amman, removing recently erected road blocks, and in this fighting at least 20 guerillas were killed. An area by area disarmament of the militia followed, in conjunction with army checks and searches. Already in six days of fighting at least 60 people had been killed or wounded, and at least 400 guerillas had been arrested. The Jordanian soldiers, now once again proud and confident, were poised to hit back at the slightest provocation. The headquarters of all guerilla organizations, including that of the PFLP, had moved from Amman out to Jerash; Wasfi Tal allowed the PASC office in Ramtha to re-open.

The 13-point disarmament agreement of the 12th, the fourth agreement since the end of the civil war, brought about a precarious truce. The guerillas were required to evacuate all towns at once and move to designated areas in the Jordan Valley which they reluctantly agreed to do. In return the Jordanian Government said that it would discontinue anti-guerilla propaganda on the radio. Fatah, thinking primarily of self-preservation and recoupment, evacuated the towns. The PFLP and the DPF refused to accept the truce, but as they had only a small number of armed guerillas in the towns this did not worry the Bedu soldiers. Arafat could not control the PFLP or the DPF, and his general influence over them had been weakened by defeat. George Habash threatened to take his men underground and to embark on a campaign of assassination and terror against the Jordanian army.

By the third week in January the Jordanian army had cleared the guerillas from the last piece of territory adjoining Israel, causing Arafat to complain bitterly that it was 'paralyzing movement and stifling attacks on Israel'. By the 17th Ajlun was cleared by the army, and the guerillas were all driven into the broken country formed by the triangle of Ajlun, Jerash and Irbid; afraid to enter towns for fear of being arrested or even killed, they mainly sheltered in caves. The Jordanian winter, together with a shortage of food, money and arms, lowered Fedayeen morale. Dispirited, they began to squabble amongst themselves, while Arafat frantically tried to unify and cheer them.

There had been a decline in Pan-Arabism since the death of President Nasser. Particularly was the Lebanon, complaining of rocket attacks made on Israel from its territory, losing patience with the guerillas. A party of Saiqa attacked a police post in Beirut on the 1st January 1971, and two policemen were killed. Although there had been friction and many incidents since the (Lebanese) Cairo Agreement, none had really been of a serious nature until this happened. The Lebanese Premier refused to meet Saiqa leaders to discuss the matter, so Arafat hastily denounced the attack. Arafat realized that with many of his men being elbowed out of Jordan, he had only the Lebanon left to operate in, and he saw that to continue to do so he must walk cautiously.

The guerillas themselves were carrying out self-criticism. On the 4th January 1971, at a refugee camp near Beirut, Abu Iyyad,[1] generally recognized as one of the senior Fatah leaders in the field, admitted that the civil war had cost them at least 200 centres in Amman alone, and he hinted at some high level changes, advocating less ostentation and a return to secrecy. Some minor guerilla leaders had taken to riding in cars through towns with guerilla escorts, and had posed before television cameras, welcoming personal publicity. Money was proving a difficulty and strict economy had to be exercised; on the same day it was announced that all the PLO offices in the Lebanon, except the main one in Beirut, would close. Saeb Salim, the Lebanese Premier, considered this to be due to his pressure on the Fedayeen, but lack of money may have been the real cause. Arafat was bending with the wind, and on the following day, the 5th, when a Jordanian officer was kidnapped and held for eight hours in Beirut by guerillas, he was quickly released when the Lebanese Government insisted.

In January (1971) Ghassan Kanafani, spokesman of the PFLP, said that George Habash, who had been re-elected leader of the PFLP on the 12th November 1970, realized that the mass hijackings in September (1970) had been wrong, and had directly led to guerilla setbacks in Jordan. A power struggle developed within the PFLP leadership, when abortive attempts were made to oust Habash, but an extremist faction, determined to discredit him, continued to provoke trouble. An attempt by PFLP frogmen to kidnap an Israeli from an off-shore island just south of the Lebanese border on the 15th resulted in an Israeli reprisal raid on Sarafand, on the coast about 25 miles north of the Lebanese frontier, by heliborne troops; a four-hour battle ensued, in which Israeli naval support was given. Sarafand, which had a large Palestinian population, was a guerilla naval base. A few frogmen were trained there, and it was also the supply and training depot for the guerilla seaborne forces and a guerilla smuggling point

[1] His real name was Waled Ahmed Nimer.

for arms brought in by sea. The Israelis stated that at least 10 guerillas were killed and many wounded.

On the 17th a shouting match occurred between the Fatah and the PFLP. To the surprise of many, George Habash had agreed to the 13-point Amman Agreement of the 12th, which included a time-table for disarming the Fedayeen militia, obviously to his disadvantage. It had always been a PFLP pre-condition to any agreement that a firm guerilla base should remain in Jordan. In his first statement since the civil war, Habash declared that he would work for the downfall of King Hussein and his replacement by a left-wing government. He also said that his militia would not hand in their arms, while Ghassan Kanafani, in Beirut, went further by saying that weapons would only 'be taken from their dead bodies'. Fatah, which previously had preached co-existence with King Hussein in Jordan, now also declared that it must work for his removal. Kamal Adwan, the Fatah spokesman, heavily criticized the PFLP, accusing its members of fleeing without fighting when the Israelis attacked Karameh in March 1968, and Habash of hiding himself away in North Korea instead of being in Jordan during the civil war. He added that Fatah would use all necessary force against the PFLP to protect the Palestine resistance movement, and that the PFLP members who ambushed a Jordanian patrol would be brought before a guerilla court. Kamal Adwan denounced Habash for not co-operating by disarming his militia. Ghassan Kanafani hit back too, saying that it was the lack of a combined plan that caused the PFLP to take such extreme action in September 1970. There was talk about going underground, forming cells and carrying out scorched-earth tactics.

In January 1971 Egypt was deeply involved in the Rogers Peace Initiative and did not want to be embarrassed by any outrageous acts by guerillas. After a series of meetings of the PNC central committee to determine future policy, Arafat announced that the guerillas would not obstruct Egyptian peace moves. On the 20th the Egyptian newspaper, *Al Ahram*, reported that the guerillas were ready to accept a political solution to the Palestine problem; but this was too much, and both Fatah and the PFLP issued frantic denials, insisting that an 'armed struggle' was the only way. On the 27th the newspaper *Fatah*[1] suspended publication, following a PNC Central committee decision, because of 'financial and technical difficulties'.

The Jordanian Government stepped up its propaganda against the guerillas and made personal attacks on Arafat. Fresh warnings were given by Wasfi Tal on the 31st, after nine tons of arms and explosives had been seized in night raids in Amman. On the 1st February there was a two-pronged Israeli raid across the Lebanese border in reprisal for nine guerilla attacks between the 10th and 29th January.[2] One prong struck at Khyam, where a guerilla recruiting office and camp were blown up by Israelis, who landed by helicopter, and the other hit at Kafr Kala where there was some fighting. The Israelis lost one officer killed and suffered three wounded.

Early in February King Hussein had a secret meeting with Saleh Mardi Ammash, the Iraqi Vice-President, after which most of the Iraqi division was withdrawn from Jordan. This was another blow to the guerillas, as while they had had no support from the division its very presence was a dark shadow over the Jordanian Government. On the 11th fighting broke out in Amman over the collection of arms from the Fedayeen militia, which went on for six days. The Government alleged that guerillas were bringing more arms into the city, and that arms held centrally under the Amman Agreement were being redistributed to the Fedayeen militia. On the following day there was fighting around both Jerash and Ajlun, as the army tried to prevent guerillas from re-entering those two towns. It was also able to enforce the order that guerillas must not fire into Israel from Jordanian territory, but must cross the River Jordan to carry out operations against the Israelis. Jordanian estimates at this time put the guerilla strength in Jordan at about 5,000, excluding the militia.

Despite their leaders' appeals the Fedayeen militia refused

[1] It had first appeared in June 1969, and had a reputed circulation of 32,000.

[2] An Israeli reprisal raid had been almost daily expected since the 25th December 1970, when guerillas killed a Druze on the Golan Plateau and took back his severed head.

to hand in their arms. By the 16th, when the fighting died down, the guerillas alleged that 100 people had been killed, including 15 guerillas. The Jordanians admitted that three policemen had been killed and six wounded. Joint Jordanian-Fatah patrols began to disarm the Fedayeen militia. During the previous day, the 15th, the DPF had wrecked a Jordanian DC-3 aircraft at Amman airport by rocket fire. On the 11th February the Israelis claimed to have broken a PFLP cell at Nablus, and on the 15th to have arrested an underground Fatah group in East Jerusalem.

On the 21st Brigadier Yahya, of the PLA, openly criticized the guerillas for failing to unite in the previous September, and he called for reform of the Palestine National Council. In his attack on Arafat, the first major one to be made, Brigadier Yahya demanded that the Asifa of Fatah, that is the military arm, be dissolved and all guerilla fighters put under his command.

On the 25th February the PNC met in Cairo. Although its transactions lasted several days, the main items discussed being unity and the possibility of a Palestine state, on neither issue was any progress made. The PNC was divided on whether to support the Egyptian peace moves. It accepted that part of the PFLP programme which called for a pro-guerilla government in Jordan, postponing the implementation of Arafat's plan to amalgamate all the guerilla groups. Finance was discussed and the PNC appealed for more funds from Arab governments, which were already some £16 million in arrears on their promises; it was stated that if money was not quickly forthcoming the PLA would have to be disbanded. The PLA strength had shrunk to about 5,000. There remained the two brigades in Syria, a unit in Egypt serving in the Suez Canal zone alongside Egyptian troops and for which the Egyptian Government paid £30,000 annually, and the Salehad Brigade in Iraq. Iraq decided to discontinue payments to the PNC, but to retain the Salehad Brigade under its control. On the 28th President Sadat, in an address to the PNC, told them that Egypt would not make a separate peace with Israel; this assurance mollified most of the guerillas. It was reported on the 1st March that Colonel Gaddafi, of Libya, promised to give £300,000 to the PFLP. Both Kamal

Adwan, of Fatah, and Ibrahim Bakr, of the PNC central committee, said that they would not oppose a Palestine state, and for the first time King Hussein admitted that he would accept one provided Palestinians chose it.[1]

The Egyptian diplomatic offensive and the Jordanian military squeeze forced Fatah to veer towards PFLP provocative tactics. There was now less reluctance than formerly, as despite its pleas of poverty and neglect, Fatah had been rearmed and re-equipped to a degree, and its morale was recovering. On the 7th March it was announced that a 'General Command' would be set up to embrace the PLA and 'elements of the popular militia'. Arafat, as chairman of the PLO, was to be the 'General Commander', and Brigadier Yahya, of the PLA, to be the Chief-of-Staff. The only permitted guerilla organizations were to be Fatah, Saiqa, PFLP, DPF and the Arab Liberation Front (the ALF, sponsored by the Iraqi Baathists), and there was to be one spokesman for all. This grand façade was maintained for a while, but the organization never really worked.

Sparse Syrian aid and support for the guerillas, formerly so generous, had disappointed them, as had the Government's cautious utterances, but on the 22nd February Hafez Assad assumed presidential powers in Syria, and stated that the 'armed struggle is the sole way for liberating occupied Arab land', which made the guerillas feel better. Already many hundreds of guerillas, squeezed out from Jordan, had taken refuge in Syria, the offices of the PNC and the PASC had moved to Damascus, and most of the attacks on Israel now came across the Syrian border. During March President Assad[2] tried ineffectually to re-establish the eastern front against Israel, which had abruptly collapsed after the civil war.

Kamal Nasser, spokesman for the PLO, stated that there would be a National Unity Charter, to unify all the guerilla groups, as proposed by Arafat; thus a single political and military policy would be pursued, and any group which deviated would be regarded as a dissident. The implementation of this PNC decision was left to the PLO. Again it was all façade, as the extremist PFLP and DPF had no intention of submitting to

[1] Interview in the *Observer* of 28th February 1971.
[2] The title Head of State is frequently used as well.

Arafat's leadership, and neither had the Syrian Government any intention of allowing its Saiqa to be taken from its control. Kamal Nasser also voiced the PLO's opposition to the creation of a Palestine state, but wanted a united front of Palestinians and Jordanians. He added that there would be no more aircraft hijackings, that the guerillas would strike deeper into Israel, and that the 'Palestinians had no other alternative but to wage a people's armed struggle against Israel'. It was all a sign that the guerillas, especially Fatah, were becoming more confident and aggressive.

On the 23rd Colonel Gaddafi, of Libya, called upon the Jordanian army to overthrow King Hussein, and said that if Libya had had a common frontier it would have intervened on the side of the guerillas in the civil war. Egypt now also openly supported the guerillas and was influencing other Arab countries against King Hussein's treatment of them. On the 30th the PLO and Fatah were again allowed to broadcast from Cairo. As the guerillas seemed to be growing in power again, President Sadat felt that it would be better if they were with him rather than against him; nor did he want them to fall under Iraqi influence. On the 31st Egypt withdrew its officers from the Arab Truce Commission because it considered King Hussein was hampering its activities and because Premier Wasfi Tal was regarded as having pronounced anti-guerilla views.

Meanwhile incidents increased, as did clashes between the guerillas and the Jordanian Army. From the 26th March there were three days' fighting in and around Irbid as the army tried to prevent the guerillas seeping back into the town; over 60 casualties were reported, the Jordanians admitting to eight soldiers killed and 20 wounded. A large contingent of guerillas established in the adjacent refugee camp (containing about 13,000 refugees) was becoming active. On the 29th a Jordanian army patrol was ambushed near Salt. The guerillas everywhere were attempting to swarm back into the towns of Jordan, and to forestall them the army progressively moved into Irbid, Zerka, Jerash and now Salt. Guerilla positions near Ajlun were shelled by the army. Disturbances spread to Amman, and the army again entered the capital. Arafat, loudly alleging that the soldiers had been sent into Amman to massacre

173

guerillas, demanded that the Arab Truce Commission, which had collapsed when the Egyptians pulled out, should return to investigate alleged killings in Irbid the previous week. The Fedayeen claimed that 200 guerillas and civilians had been killed in ten days and 400 wounded, but the Government's figure was only 18 dead.

So far, mainly because of weakness and low morale, the guerillas had invariably retreated from Jordanian army pressures. Now, being stronger, and encouraged by Arab support, they decided to fight back. On the 1st April 1971 Arafat announced the setting up of a new military command at Jerash, which would be responsible for the confrontation with Jordan, and on the next day the guerillas blew up part of an oil pipeline near the Zerka refinery. A spate of small incidents followed in the ensuing days in which a number of Jordanians were killed and wounded. The newspaper, *Fatah*, was again published in Damascus. The PLA moved close to the Jordanian border, and for the first time since the previous September the Government accused the Syrians of aiding the guerillas. The PLA, having been reorganized, was now some 6,000 strong in Syria and consisted of three brigades, the Kadesiyah, the Egyptian and the Yarmuk, the last-named having been formed since September 1970 by enlisting deserters and those dismissed from the Jordanian army.

Despite the decision to fight back, the Fatah still hoped for a negotiated settlement or, more realistically, to put off the evil day of confrontation as long as possible so that more strength could be gained. Frequent consultations took place between Arafat and the Jordanian Government. Differences within the leadership remained. On the 5th Arafat, with some difficulty, persuaded all the regular guerillas to evacuate the Wahdat refugee camp, near Amman. This action was more than had been specified in the 13-point Amman Agreement, but it was done partly to prevent them being liquidated by the army and partly as a grand gesture to encourage the Government to release some of the detained guerillas—but it did not.

The PLA had been shelling spasmodically across the frontier for several days. On the 6th the guerillas shelled the Jordanian air base at Mafrak, damaging two planes; while in Amman

King Hussein warned all guerillas to have all weapons out of the capital within two days—the first indication of any dead-line. So far the Jordanian army had seized over 30,000 weapons, mostly in Amman and district. On the 11th, in further house searches in Amman, more arms were found. That day there was more fighting in the north, and the army was provoked into firing shells into the Palestinian refugee camp near Jerash. On the 16th King Hussein said that the guerillas had been brought under complete control.

On the 2nd April Ygal Alon, Israeli Deputy Premier, warned Syria and Iraq not to interfere in the Jordan fighting, after there had been a report that the Syrians had told King Hussein that unless he stopped firing at the guerillas the PLA would invade Jordan. On the 7th Hussein rejected an Egyptian call for a conference on the situation in his country, saying that he would not tolerate any outside interference. Standing firm in the face of Egyptian pressure, he sent Abdul Moneim Rifai (a former premier who advocated reconciliation with the Fed-ayeen) with a small delegation to Cairo to try to improve relations between the two countries. On the 8th a Syrian military delegation, led by Major-General Talas, the Chief-of-Staff, arrived in Amman to seek to arbitrate between the Jordanian Government and the Fedayeen. On the following day it was announced that a six-man committee was to be set up for this purpose. On the 11th King Hussein cabled Arab heads of state meeting in Cairo that he would not accept any further deals with the guerillas. A federation of Egypt, Libya and Syria was announced on the 17th, with a policy of sup-porting the guerillas in Jordan against Hussein, which further emboldened the Fedayeen.

The guerillas in the field in Jordan needed encouragement as, although they were armed and better organized than they had been before, they were fewer in number, they had been driven from the towns and, even though some had succeeded in fighting their way back, most were on the barren hillsides. Heavy casualties had been suffered, and they no longer had their numerous well-equipped field hospitals in the refugee camps and elsewhere. Chinese support had fallen off sharply after the civil war. China had insisted that the guerillas should merge into only two organizations, one political and the other military, like the Viet Cong. However, from the 7th to the 14th April they held a Palestine week in Peking, to which they invited leaders of the main groups, that is Fatah, PFLP, DPF, Saiqa and the ALF. Arafat, slighted, did not attend because he thought that he alone should be invited to represent the Palestine resistance movement, but others went.

On the 12th May there was a three-hour battle near Ramtha. On the 16th PLA formations opened fire at a Jordanian village from Syrian territory, and a section of the railway from Amman to Damascus was sabotaged near the Jordanian border. On the 17th Abdullah Salah, the Jordanian Foreign Minister, accused Fatah of planning a campaign of assassination of leading Jordanians. On the 24th the guerillas mounted a small operation against Israel in the Jordan Valley, the first from Jordanian soil for three months, when rockets were fired in the direction of a kibbutz in the Beisan Valley. This had been done reluctantly, partly because their attention was directed on King Hussein and his Government, but mainly because Colonel Gaddafi, of Libya, had said firmly: 'No action against Israel—no money'.

On Jordanian Independence Day, the 25th May, King Hussein held the biggest military display he had ever staged, showing his 250 armoured vehicles, guns and British Tigercat rockets in a seven-mile long procession that took two hours to pass the saluting dais. Sixteen planes flew overhead, and his special troops of the Saiqa Brigade did an exhausting 'battle run', passing the King at the double in full equipment. It was clearly a demonstration of strength aimed at the Fedayeen.

On the 30th fighting again broke out in the north. It lasted for three days, consisting mainly of short, sharp clashes, in which at least four people were killed, four kidnapped and seven wounded, including a Jordanian officer. The Jordanian army put on display arms seized in northern refugee camps, while guerillas claimed that crops were deliberately burned by napalm and incendiaries. On the 31st the army moved in force into the Wahdat refugee camp, and with bulldozers levelled defences and blew up a monument on the tomb of the 'unknown Fedayeen', which had been erected over a mass grave of 175 guerillas and civilians killed in the civil war. On that day the army ordered the guerillas out of the town of Jerash, where they had infiltrated, bombarded their bases nearby and accused the Fedayeen of sabotage at the phosphate mines at Russeifeh. It was estimated that there were about 3,000 regular guerillas in the hills in the triangle formed by Irbid, Jerash and Ajlun. During June the Jordanian army kept up steady pressure on the guerillas who admitted that they were short of ammunition and could not fight a sustained war. The Fedayeen were making an attempt to purge their leadership. Some junior commanders were removed, but Arafat, despite a few anxious moments, retained his position as chairman of the PLO and leader of Fatah. He attempted to expel those with 'dual loyalties', such as those who looked to, or were controlled by, Syria or Iraq.

On the 4th the Jordanians attacked guerillas in the Salt area. A few days later the Fedayeen near Jerash were forced into the hills and surrounded by Jordanian soldiers, who blocked all movement, refusing to allow any food or supplies to reach the guerillas. Only individuals were able to slip through the cordon by night. Arafat complained that Hussein was preventing operations against Israel, and again Fatah came out demanding the King's overthrow. For the first time all the guerilla organizations urged the formation of a national union government, to include their representatives, to rule Jordan. Discussions were held, in which the Jordanian Government expressed its willingness to allow the guerillas freedom to resume operations against Israel if they promised not to molest Jordanian villagers, not to demand food and shelter of them, and not to fire rockets from Jordanian territory. Arafat would not agree. On the previous day Fatah had appealed over its Cairo radio for the 'entire Arab nation' to help to topple King Hussein. For good measure it also accused the PFLP of conspiring to destroy the Fatah movement. This charge was in reply to a mysterious broadcast on Radio Amman, purportedly by a group of Fatah commanders calling themselves 'free officers', who announced themselves as the new command of Fatah and denounced Arafat as a 'hireling tied to world imperialism'.

For some time King Hussein had been worried in case Egypt,

in its search for a peaceful solution in the Middle East, might make a deal with Israel and, ignoring Jordan, agree to the establishment of a West Bank state. On the 2nd June Premier Wasfi Tal accused the guerillas of plotting to set up such a breakaway state, and broadcast that King Hussein had ordered him to take 'bold, decisive and tough action against the handful of professional criminals and conspirators who use the commando movement to disguise their treasonable plot'.

While Fatah had been dwindling in numbers and activity through lack of funds the PFLP claimed to be in the ascendant and to have just acquired 300 new recruits. It was known that Colonel Gaddafi gave money to the PFLP, as he considered it the only guerilla organization that achieved anything, and so George Habash was able to continue with his policy of deliberately increasing tension that would provoke Israeli reprisals. His underground cells in Israel and the occupied territories instigated incidents that caused loss of life and injury. He realized that too many pressures were against him to repeat aircraft hijackings, but his eyes were still on the world stage. He again hit international headlines on the 11th, when four PFLP members fired rockets from two small speed-boats, which had been launched from a fishing boat in the Bab El Mindab Straits of the Red Sea, at the 78,000-ton Liberian tanker, *Coral Sea*, carrying Persian oil to the Israeli port of Eilat, to be pumped through the oil pipeline to Ashdod. Fires were caused but were extinguished and the ship made port safely. However, immediately after the incident the PFLP personnel were chased by Ethiopian gunboats, and were forced to take refuge on shore in the Yemen, where they were arrested. Although the Israelis feared more similar attacks on their shipping, this PFLP act was extremely unpopular with Arab states as well as with other nations. The PFLP afterwards said that this project had been under consideration for two years, but had been delayed as they were not sure how the Yemeni Government might react in the event of Israeli reprisals.

On the 26th June 1971, the day the Israelis claimed to have killed eight guerillas on the Golan Plateau in two encounters, King Feisal, of Saudi Arabia, who was visiting Cairo and President Sadat, sent messages to King Hussein offering to mediate between him and the Fedayeen. A few days later Hussein rejected their offer and plan for co-operation.

Towards the end of June the guerillas were entrenched in the areas of Jerash and Ajlun, preparing to resist a Jordanian attack. They suffered another unexpected blow on the 4th July, when the Syrian Government seized a quantity of arms, that included tanks, guns and other equipment for a new mechanized brigade of the PLA which it was planned to form, on the grounds that such arms were not suitable for guerilla warfare. The Syrian Government was reluctant to release the arms, which had been sent from Algeria, partly because the arms would make the PLA too powerful and partly because it was enjoying a rare moment of almost-friendly relations with Jordan. The arms were eventually returned to Algeria. The Kadesiyah Brigade and the Yarmuk Brigade were near Dera, while the Egyptian Brigade lay farther in the rear. The Salehad Brigade was in Iraq, but close to the border. Arafat had moved his headquarters to Dera. On the 6th July the PLA Chief-of-Staff, Colonel Osman Haddad, announced that four officers and others had been dismissed from the PLA for 'attempting to take over forces in Jordan', which indicated the uneasy state of its leadership.

Another conference of the PNC began in Cairo on the 7th July, the day King Hussein hanged a Fatah member who had placed a bomb in a phosphates factory—the first time he had enforced capital punishment against guerillas.[1] Arafat was re-elected chairman of the Central Committee, the fiction of the 'General Command' was maintained, and he was also given the title of Supreme Commander. Despite deep differences between the guerilla groups, all seemed to accept, although with reservations, the principle of a central field command under Arafat. The main item on the agenda was shortage of funds, the only contribution received by the PLO in the preceding year being £62,500 from Qatar in January. Arafat bitterly complained of the attitude of the Arab press which, he said, before September 1970 had nothing but good to say of the Fedayeen,

[1] On the same day, the 7th, the PFLP fired four rockets into Petah Tikva, killing two Israelis and wounding 18, this being the first such incident in the Tel Aviv area since November 1970.

but since could find nothing right with the guerillas. On the 13th the conference was hastily abandoned to enable members to return home quickly, as King Hussein had mounted an all-out attack on the Fedayeen in Jordan.

Apparently influenced by the abortive coup on the 11th July against King Hassan of Morocco, King Hussein moved his army on the 13th against the guerillas in Jordan in a concentrated effort to clear them out. His army moved willingly, operations lasting for almost a week. Throughout this period the Jordanian authorities remained silent about the course of the fighting as they feared intervention if they prematurely boasted of successes.

On the first day Jordanian armour and troops surrounded and attacked Karameh, recently reoccupied by guerillas, and also positions near Ajlun and Jerash. There was hand-to-hand fighting in the Jerash refugee camp. When he realized the purpose and intensity of the Jordanian offensive, Abu Iyyad, left behind in charge of operations, appealed desperately to the Syrians to send in armour and the PLA as they had done in September 1970. The Syrians hesitated, and instead sent their Chief-of-Staff to contact the Jordanian Chief-of-Staff to advise him to settle his difference with the Fedayeen amongst themselves. The guerillas accused King Hussein of having launched an offensive with a force of 'one division, two brigades, three regiments, tanks and planes' against their base at Jerash, but the Government formally denied this in a reference to 'routine daily skirmishes not worth talking about'.

On the 14th Jordanian troops dislodged guerillas from several places they had refused to evacuate voluntarily, and according to the guerillas they suffered 'several hundred' casualties. To all Fedayeen allegations of massacres, the Jordanian Government remained silent. That night Arafat arrived at his headquarters near Dera and gazed into Jordan where the enemy was using flares to light up the battlefield and aircraft were dropping phosphorus bombs. On the following day, the 15th, government troops continued to push the guerillas northwards and westwards into the region of waterless wadis[1] running into

[1] Dry, and often wide and deep water courses, that briefly flooded in the short rainy season.

the Jordan Valley. In the Ajloun area, under the direct command of Abu Iyyad, of the original 800 guerillas only about 50 remained holding out, and they were short of water and ammunition.

Arafat formally declared war on the Jordanian Government, cabling that he would attack with all his forces, but they were empty words. On the 16th there was heavy shelling of guerilla positions, and many near Ajloun and Jerash were hastily abandoned, while those near Karameh were encircled. Guerillas from the Salt area were being driven from the forests north into arid wadis where there were no villages at all. Forest fires were burning and a pall of smoke hung over places where there was fighting. Triumphantly the Jordanian Government declared that it considered both the (Jordanian) Cairo Agreement and the Amman Agreement null and void, and that there would be no new agreement with the guerillas. By the 17th the guerillas had definitely started to crack, and the first group, of 16 men, crossed the River Jordan and gave themselves up to the Israelis. During the following day another party of 31 did the same.

On the 19th Premier Wasfi Tal held a press conference at which he said that 2,300 guerillas had been captured and that only 200 remained at large; they would soon be arrested. The captured Fedayeen were being held in army camps at Irbid and Mafrak. Another 17 Fedayeen fighters crossed into Israel, bringing up to 72 the numbers of those who chose Israeli detention rather than stand up any longer to the Jordanian army. Premier Wasfi Tal said that no more guerilla bases existed in Jordan, but the Fedayeen more doubtfully claimed to be still fighting back hard. He also related that during the 20 days prior to the 13th July the guerillas several times attacked army convoys; in the fighting the army lost 16 killed and suffered 19 wounded, and 20 civilians were killed and 50 injured. Anxious to avoid trouble, Syria hastily and firmly closed its frontier with Jordan. Thus many guerillas were prevented from escaping to that country, and so perhaps were forced to flee into Israel.

On the 20th the Syrians accused the Jordanians of shelling the Dera area from Ramtha, Iraq called for the expulsion of

Jordan from the Arab League, and the Sudanese Government said that it would allow the guerillas to recommence broadcasting from Omdurman. The Syrians sent a delegation to mediate, but it was ignored and had to return. On the 21st the Jordanian Government stated that of the captured guerillas only 39 wanted to continue fighting as Fedayeen, 1,539 were 'cleared' and another 831 were 'sent home', of whom 311 were deported to foreign countries and another 397 to Syria. That day another 14 guerillas sought refuge in Israel, making a total of 91 who chose to enter an enemy state rather than take their chance with an Arab government. It was later admitted that the Fatah commander in Jordan, Abu Iyyad, was among those killed, it being alleged that a letter was found in his pocket indicating that a large sum of money had been recently received from an Arab state. Fatah alleged that Abu Iyyad[1] had been captured and almost immediately killed by Jordanian soldiers, being dragged along behind a tank, after which his mutilated body was displayed from town to town. Another Fedayeen leader killed was Musa Khalili, the Fatah commander in the Dibbin Forest area. Jordanian official figures quote its losses as being 20 dead, but this is generally regarded as being far too low.

The guerillas claimed that wounded were killed by Bedu soldiers and point to the fact that no wounded guerillas had been captured. The Jordanians were silent on the number of guerillas killed (or wounded), but as they had estimated that there were over 3,000 in Jordan just before their last offensive began, this leaves a silent, unaccountable figure of 500, of whom, of course, a few may have been able to break through the closed Syrian frontier.

In one week King Hussein had completely cleared his country of hostile Fedayeen: his army was victorious, his Government jubilant, the Palestinian refugees cowed, the guerillas beaten and the Bedu soldiers elated. Other setbacks for the guerillas followed. On the 25th July an underground group was detected in Nablus and an arms cache found, and the Israelis announced

---

[1] John Bullock wrote in the *Sunday Telegraph* on the 10th September 1972 that 'Abu Iyyad, a one-eyed, bald-headed giant of a man in his mid-forties who called himself the Arab answer to Moshe Dayan, kept them fighting to the end.'

that they had exposed the guerilla ring responsible for bomb explosions in Haifa and Tel Aviv between July 1969 and September 1970. Nablus became a centre of discontent, not so much hostile to the Israelis as to King Hussein because of his treatment of the Palestinian guerillas. Arab states professed horror at King Hussein's action. On the 26th Syria again closed its border with Jordan after having opened it briefly to take in the deported Fedayeen. On the 30th certain Arab heads of state met in Tripoli, where they condemned Hussein and discussed possible economic sanctions against him, but little came of this. George Habash was reported to have said: 'We are beaten. We are having a very hard time. But from these hard times we will build a real underground'.[1]

Colonel Gaddafi, of Libya, wanted an advanced base to be formed near Dera, in Syria, from which to launch armed forces into Jordan. Indeed, in anticipation of this, formations of the Jordanian army were moved into the northern part of the country, but Syria was reluctant to become the springboard for an Arab war against Jordan, although it too moved three or four brigades southwards. Arafat was in a 'wait and see' mood as he had many fences to mend himself, and did not like the new Syrian Government's attitude towards the guerillas, but he maintained a diplomatic silence. The PFLP was less tactful and loudly complained that the Syrian Government was insisting that guerilla operations must be carried out at least ten miles inside Israel, and had banned all such incursions into Jordan completely. A paradox, perhaps peculiar only to the Middle East, occurred when, despite the closed frontier, Jordanians were allowed into Syria to take delivery from Latakia of a number of Land-Rovers with recoilless rifles, which drew bitter comment from the PFLP. Additionally, the Syrians hindered free movement of the guerillas, compelling them to buy their food and supplies in Syria at high prices. The Government also rigidly purged its Saiqa, members being confined to camps, and some being arrested.

Border friction erupted into a three-day fight on the 12th August, which involved guns, tanks and aircraft across the frontier in the region of Dera and Ramtha, in which the Syrians

[1] *Time* of the 27th September 1971.

claimed to have destroyed four Jordanian tanks. President Sadat personally intervened to persuade President Assad to end the fighting, which largely involved PLA formations, as it marred his projected federation with Syria, and the cross-frontier firing died down. Syria broke off diplomatic relations with Jordan, as had Libya a few days previously. The Jordanians said that 14 Syrian tanks had invaded Jordan, of which five were destroyed. Later both sides raised their claims to nine tanks each destroyed. On the 18th a Jordanian truck hit a mine near Ramtha, injuring the driver.

Meanwhile, US military equipment was sent to Jordan. Mainly flown in from Turkey, it reportedly included some 65 aircraft (mostly F-104s) and a radar network to cover the north-eastern parts of the country—that is, those facing Syria and Iraq. On the 11th August the Government had closed down all Red Crescent offices in Jordan on the suspicion that the organization was over-sympathetic towards the guerillas, even to the point of actively helping them, and so some 30,000 people a year were deprived of free medical treatment.

Both Saudi Arabia and Egypt worked hard to try to settle the differences between the Jordanian Government and the guerillas. While Arafat agreed to the terms they put forward, King Hussein, who did not, demanded the restoration of subsidies from Libya and Kuwait and acknowledged authority over both the West and the East Banks. The Saudi Arabian subsidy had continued throughout. The guerillas demanded to be allowed to re-enter Jordan and re-establish both a political and military presence there, which Hussein would not permit. King Hussein secretly invited President Sadat, Colonel Gaddafi and President Assad to come to Jordan to see the situation for themselves, but they did not respond

On the 19th August the leaders of Egypt, Libya and Syria had secret talks with Arafat, and on the following day, the 20th, the Damascus Proclamation was announced declaring the federation of those three countries, with a total population of 42 million people. The Jordanians and the guerillas were invited to attend a meeting in Saudi Arabia early in September. King Hussein sent a delegation, but as soon as the guerillas knew of this they boycotted it, although the PLO had agreed to send one. Talks were postponed, the Jordanians waited a while and then returned home. This prompted King Hussein, on the 8th September, to propose the formation of his country into the National Union of Jordan, to be composed of both the West and the East Banks, on a federal basis. He thus made his bid to continue to speak for all Palestinians.

On the same day a Jordanian aircraft on a regular flight between Amman and Beirut, with 83 people on board, was hijacked by Fatah members and flown to Benghazi in Libya.[1] Despite his strong opposition to King Hussein, Colonel Gaddafi detained the two hijackers and returned the plane and everyone else on board to Jordan within the hour. To national governments everywhere this was an extremely hopeful sign, as if all would deny refuge and help to hijackers, as countries did to pirates in olden days, the problem could be brought under control to a degree. This incident caused reconciliation negotiations to collapse.

On the 9th September the TAPLINE oil pipeline was sabotaged in Jordan near the Syrian frontier, and again on the 14th. On the 16th September a Fatah member failed to hijack a Jordanian airliner between Amman and Beirut, being overpowered by the security guard,[2] and during the following day an attempt to blow up the Intercontinental Hotel was foiled when a bomb was discovered in time. On the 17th the Jordanian Government announced that it had invited guerilla representatives to Amman for talks to help them operate against the Israelis. Instead, on the 20th representatives of Jordan and the PLO met Saudi Arabian and Egyptian mediators at Jedda, but the talks were inconclusive; King Hussein would not readmit the Fedayeen into his country. On the 4th October three PFLP members were executed in Amman for killing civilians in September 1970, making a total of 15 guerillas executed in Amman since the beginning of the year.

On the 28th November 1971 Premier Wasfi Tal, who was also Defence Minister, and was in Cairo at the Arab League Joint

[1] On the 25th August 1971 a bomb had exploded in a Jordanian airliner at Madrid after everyone had disembarked, and so no one was injured.

[2] A Lebanese, he was sentenced to death on the 7th October 1971.

Defence Council meeting to try to establish military co-operation against Israel, was killed on his hotel steps by guerillas who claimed to be members of the Black September Group, the BSG.[1] Abdullah Saleh, the Jordanian Foreign Minister, who was with Wasfi Tal, was wounded. All four assailants who were captured had Syrian passports. For long Egypt had declared that it would not admit Wasfi Tal into the country because of the part he played in defeating the guerillas in Jordan, his attitude to the Palestine problem, and his constant criticism of Egyptian policies. One senior Israeli officer once said to me: 'Wasfi Tal killed more guerillas in one year than we did in ten'. The guerillas alleged that Wasfi Tal had killed 10,000 Fedayeen in all. To the Bedu element in Jordan and the army he was a hero, and apprehension descended on the refugee camps in Jordan, damping down the jubilation generally felt in the Arab world at this assassination.

This was the first mention in public of the existence of the Black September Group, and Fatah denied all knowledge of or connexion with it. The BSG consisted of a small body of extremists (perhaps all Fatah members) formed just after the guerila defeats of September 1970, determined to avenge their setbacks. This particular attack was stated to be in revenge for the killing of Abu Iyyad on the orders of Wasfi Tal.

King Hussein appointed as Premier Ahmed al-Lawzi, who was not so hostile towards the Fedayeen, for what he intended to be an interim period until Jordan was received back into the Arab fold. The new Premier at once flew to Cairo to take Wasfi Tal's place at the Arab League Joint Defence Council meeting, which ended on the 30th without a communiqué being issued, although Lieutenant-General Saad Adin Shazli, Egyptian Chief-of-Staff, said that a number of secret resolutions had been adopted. Hussein appointed Mohammed Rasoul Kailani, a former Minister of the Interior, to be his special adviser on security, with the task of reorganizing the army special branch and the police. King Hussein said that there would be no more

[1] The BSG members were brought to trial in Cairo on the 20th February 1972, and bailed on the 29th, since when they have been living in comfort in Cairo at the expense of the Government of Libya. *Sunday Express* of the 6th November 1972.

talks with the guerillas, while Ahmed Lawzi warned them of the strongest action if they disrupted the peace. There was a further clash on the Jordan-Syria border on the 30th November, when one Jordanian soldier and two guerillas were killed. On the 12th December King Hussein declared that the Arabs were not ready for war with Israel, and that he would not let his country be involved at that time.

Meanwhile the guerillas had again been indulging in self-criticism. As Arafat now had to rely much more on Egyptian support, he dismissed the editor of the newspaper, *Fatah*, a former member of the Muslim Brotherhood, who had criticized Egyptian policies at times. Other former Muslim Brotherhood members were removed from influential positions in Fatah, which caused President Sadat to smile on Arafat. But Arafat had enemies, and on the 5th October an attempt was made to assasinate him on his way to inspect guerillas near the Golan Plateau. His driver was killed, but he was not hurt. Two days later Kamal Adwan, spokesman of the 'General Command' of the PLO, said that the assailants were members of a Fatah splinter group (vaguely indicating the Black September Group), which had not yet come into prominence, and that senior members of the PLO may have known little or nothing about it.

Arafat had lost much of his popularity by adopting such a moderate line towards Jordan throughout the negotiations, and had alienated sections of the Fedayeen. At the Fatah conference held in Damascus in July 1971 he had been heavily criticized for his insistence on continuing to search for an agreement with King Hussein. The younger members had complained that senior positions, both political and military, had been held continually by the same people, and that it was time for changes. At the next Fatah conference, in September 1971, Arafat introduced some amendments enabling a few younger members to be brought on to the central committee of Fatah. There was talk of going underground again, but the drawback was that most of the guerillas, especially the leaders, were well known to the various authorities; too much secrecy had been cast off for this to work successfully.

There were also several cracks in the façade of PLA unity. The continuing feud between the Commander, Brigadier Yahya,

and his Chief-of-Staff, Colonel Haddad, had come to a head
back in July 1970, when Brigadier Yahya, with Arafat's support
as chairman of the PLO, tried to dismiss Haddad. But neither
was strong enough. Colonel Haddad had gained the support
of the Syrian Government, which allowed him to announce
from Damascus that Brigadier Yahya had been dismissed from
the PLA. However, this had been patched up—at least on the
surface—and the two retained their respective positions, but
owing to their inability to get on together the PLA suffered in
organization, performance and morale. Now having gained more
Egyptian support, Arafat was in a stronger position, and on
the 7th October 1971 he announced that both officers were
removed from their positions, together with some 29 other
PLA officers. This latest crisis within the PLA had been caused
by the death of a PLA officer, who allegedly had been tortured
on the orders of Colonel Haddad, when Haddad had ordered
a clamp-down on the extreme Leftists in the PLA. Arafat
insisted that Haddad must go, but the Syrians, whose policy
had changed since President Assad had come to power, only
agreed if Brigadier Yahya went too. The PLO appointed
Brigadier Midhat Budeiry,[1] a Syrian regular officer, to be the
Chief-of-Staff, with powers to act as the Commander, a situation
the Syrian Government accepted.

A large number of guerillas ejected from Jordan had moved
into the Lebanon. Although for a while border incidents with
Israel did not noticeably increase, at dawn on the 9th August
the Israelis struck with armour and aircraft into the Lebanon,
and a six-hour battle developed. On the 18th Moshe Dayan
again warned the Lebanon against harbouring guerillas. The
newly elected Premier, Saeb Salim, was determined to keep as
firm a grip on the Fedayeen in his country as possible, and
after a series of meetings with Arafat the PLO announced on the
23rd that it was closing down its offices in the Lebanon,[2]
except for one in Beirut, enabling the Premier to boast that:
'There will be no trouble with the guerilla commandos next

[1] He had previously briefly commanded the PLA, being dismissed in
June 1969.

[2] Most had been closed down previously, but many had gradually
reopened.

autumn'. Arafat loudly complained of the presence of some 40 commandos of the Jordanian Saiqa Brigade in Beirut, but the explanation was that they were there to protect the Jordanian Embassy. Arafat adopted a very cautious and conciliatory attitude in his dealings with the Lebanese Government, as he realized that this was the last remaining country in which guerillas had some freedom of movement and freedom to operate against Israel. He had no wish for a confrontation with the Lebanese army, which was being equipped with US M-16 rifles and was negotiating with the French for light armoured vehicles. Previously, in July (1971), a Lebanese military mission had visited the Soviet Union, and it was to obtain some Soviet military material. On the 26th August the Government had announced a £26-million five-year programme to strengthen and re-equip the Lebanese army. On the 24th July 1971 Major-General Njeim, the Lebanese army Commander, had been killed in a helicopter crash, and had been replaced by Major-General Iskandar Ghanem.

President Suleiman Franjieh, who had been in office for about a year, had made it plain that, in any confrontation, the Lebanon would be considered first and the guerillas second. Small raids, mainly rocket attacks, were made from the Lebanon on to Israeli territory, provoking the Israelis on the 2nd September to launch a ground attack on the villages of Kafr Hamam and Rashaya el-Foukhar (where guerilla bases were), which developed into a five-hour exchange of artillery and mortar fire. Then there was a comparative lull until December, when on the 20th the Israelis alleged that there had been four rocket attacks during the previous few days aimed at Israeli settlements.

Other Fedayeen ventures during the latter part of 1971, which were mostly unsuccessful, included a plot to blow up an El Al aircraft, which misfired; the attempt was revealed by the Israelis on the 9th September, but no technical details were given. PFLP members had persuaded two girls, one Dutch and one Peruvian, unwittingly to take on board the aircraft a suitcase containing explosives, but responsibility was denied by the PFLP and some suspicion fell on the BSG. Already, in August, the Israelis considered the security situation on the

West Bank to be so good that they began to allow deportees, who had been expelled to the East Bank during the last five years, to return. On the 30th September some 90 Fatah suspects were arrested in the Hebron area, the Israelis claiming to have broken another underground group of cells, but in October, on the 10th, a grenade explosion near the Wailing Wall injured 13 people, and on the 19th three other people were injured in a bus explosion in Haifa. The Egyptians deported 15 Iraqi students, alleging that they had set up secret guerilla cells. The year 1971 ended on a flat note for the guerillas everywhere, except in the Gaza Strip, where their activities had been the focus of Israeli attention for some months.

# 9. *The Gaza Strip*

While it could be said that the Israelis were having more than moderate success in keeping order on the West Bank, they were experiencing greater difficulty in the crowded, discontented and unruly Gaza Strip. In 1968 they had formulated a plan to 'thin out' the refugee camps and to resettle a proportion of the refugees on the West Bank where the economy was better able to support them, but there had been combined resistance to this. 'Resettlement' was a dirty word among Arabs and so the plan had to be quietly postponed. Under political and terrorist pressures the refugees themselves were against it as it would have deprived them of their refugee status and UNRWA rations. The inhabitants of the West Bank wanted no additional burdens on their economy; their standard of living was higher than that in many Arab states and, despite the Israeli occupation, it was steadily improving. To the Fedayeen it would have meant the removal or weakening of convenient guerilla bases and centres of support. Towards the end of 1968, and throughout 1969, both Fatah and the PFLP infiltrated into Gaza City and the main refugee camps in the Gaza Strip; they consolidated their forces while maintaining an intermittent campaign of petty terrorism against the occupation authorities and such Arabs as collaborated with them.

Early in 1969 the Fedayeen began a civil disobedience campaign, when in February schoolgirls were used in a series of demonstrations lasting a week, which were followed in March by other student demonstrations in Gaza. After a short while these died down as the Israelis closed the colleges and schools, so the only people who suffered were the students, whose educa-

191

tion ceased, and the teachers, who were unemployed. As more arms, mines and grenades were obtained by the Fedayeen, incidents causing loss of life and injuries became frequent. For example, on Israeli Independence Day, the 15th May, grenades were thrown in Gaza; on the 5th June three Israeli soldiers were killed in the Gaza Strip; on the 5th July nine people were injured by grenades; and a few days afterwards the Israeli Government announced that 13 residents of the Gaza Strip had been killed and 200 wounded by grenade and mine incidents since the end of the June War of 1967.

The catalogue of petty terrorism continued. The curfew on parts of Gaza was extended on the 10th August, after four Israeli soldiers had been wounded in an ambush, and was further extended to cover the whole of the city on the 12th, a situation that lasted for a month. It should be explained that since the end of the June War there had been an almost perpetual partial curfew in force somewhere or other in the Gaza Strip, varying only in degree and application. On the 16th September two people were killed and 14 wounded when a grenade was thrown in a crowded street; on the 30th October the Israelis demolished eight houses after the murder of an Israeli shopkeeper;[1] and on the 8th November the PFLP claimed to have executed an Arab for spying for the Israelis. On the 15th November the Israelis said that in that month so far there had been a dozen terrorist attacks resulting in seven Israeli soldiers and 24 Arabs being wounded, as well as seven petrol bomb attacks, one murder, one attempted murder, and a number of vehicle ambushes. On the following day a grenade thrown at the Israeli Military Governor's car bounced off without exploding. That was a summary of the pattern and type of incidents that continued throughout 1969; later (on the 4th March 1970) Moshe Dayan stated that during the course of that year Arab guerillas had killed 18 Arabs and wounded 308 in the Gaza Strip.

The year 1970 was one of struggle between Fatah and the PFLP for dominance within the refugee camps and there was some internecine fighting, but at the same time terrorist incidents continued. On the 10th February, for example, 32 Arabs

[1] In this instance the Israelis for the first time provided some accommodation for the people whose homes had been demolished.

192

and one Israeli soldier were injured by grenades thrown in
Khan Yunis, that being the biggest single casualty toll of this
type in the occupied territories since the June War. On the
27th, in another grenade incident in Gaza, an Arab boy was
killed and 39 others, including three Israeli soldiers, injured.
On the 24th April some 50 guerillas were arrested in Gaza,
among them the local PFLP commander, and dumps of arms were
discovered. On each of the twelve succeeding days at least one
guerilla was killed in clashes with the security forces. The

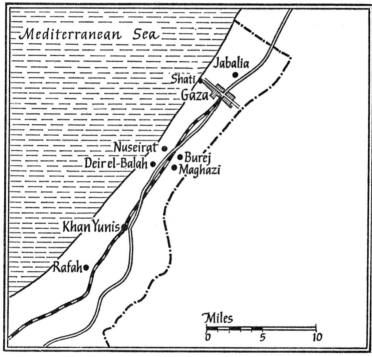

The Gaza Strip

Fedayeen became more active against Israeli patrols, seldom a
day passing without a sniping or grenade incident occurring.
They also launched a campaign to terrorize and even assassinate
Arab informers and collaborators, and to deter the many Arabs
who daily left the Gaza Strip to work (mainly on farms and

building sites) in Israel or on the West Bank. The fighting across the Suez Canal and events in Jordan all tended to overshadow guerilla activities in the Gaza Strip. A number of suspects were arrested on the 13th September as counter-hostages (although the Israelis denied this) at the time of the PFLP hijackings to Dawson's Field, but were released after a few days.

After a comparative lull while the Jordanian civil war was being fought out (17th - 25th September) guerilla activity was resumed with greater intensity, terminating in the Arovo murders, in late December, when two Israeli children were killed in an ambushed car. It was later stated that during 1970 20 Arabs and 20 Israelis had been killed in the Gaza Strip, and 650 Arabs and 50 Israelis wounded. During the year Fatah and the PFLP struggled with each other for supremacy in the various refugee camps; by December one or the other had become dominant in each of the major camps, having driven out or eliminated its rival. These were the only two guerilla organizations operating in the Gaza Strip. Although there were remnants of the old PLA, a left-over from the June War, in some camps, they remained passive.

The Israelis made proposals for improving the refugee camps by providing roads, electric light and running water, but all these were resisted by suspicious and distrustful Arabs. On the 11th March the Israelis had denied a report in the Egyptian *Al Ahram* that they planned to transfer 300,000 Arabs from the Gaza Strip to the West Bank and to bring Israeli settlers in their place. Since the June War the Israelis had appeared to take little action to better the lot of the refugees. The Israeli plan to 'thin out' the camps remained, but was baited by economic incentives, either encouraging the refugees to travel to work in Israel or on the West Bank, or encouraging work, such as tailoring, to be brought to the camps, the material being sent in from Israel. Also, they encouraged the refugees to develop local industries, such as tile and brick making. Then without much warning, on the 7th December 1970, they opened the first Israeli settlement in the Gaza Strip, known as Kfar Darom after a former settlement that had been evacuated in the 1948 War in the face of the Egyptian advance. It was not until the 10th January 1971, on which day the Israelis killed three PFLP members and other grenade explosions wounded another 12 people, that Moshe Dayan announced that more Israeli settlements would be made in the Gaza Strip.

1971 had begun with the dismissal of the Arab Mayor of Gaza on the 4th January for non-co-operation with the Israeli occupation authorities. On the following day the Shati refugee camp, containing some 27,000 refugees, was sealed off and house-to-house searches were made in one section containing some 12,000 people—an operation that continued for some days. The four-mile long road from Shati refugee camp to Gaza had become known as 'Grenade Alley'. The Arab Mayor of Gaza had been appointed by the Egyptians when they were in control, and he had stayed on in office under the Israelis. On the 15th February the Israelis dismissed the remaining members of the Egyptian-nominated municipal council of Gaza, and the Israeli Military Governor took over all powers.

Tired of the lawlessness that was fast developing, and perhaps also slightly piqued because this was the only part of the occupied territories in which the guerillas were really defying him, Moshe Dayan, the Defence Minister, launched a large-scale security campaign in the Gaza Strip, which lasted several months. It began on the 16th January, when detachments of Druze border police were drafted in to the city. They were used because they were more ruthless and indifferent towards Arabs generally; in the past many Israeli soldiers had been reluctant to fire at terrorists in case they hit innocent people. The Druze moved in with a heavy hand and within a week had shot 12 Arabs for not halting when challenged, killing five of them. They beat up many more. Although it seemed that this security drive had been prompted by the Arovo murders, this was not so. It had been planned as soon as it became evident that the Suez Canal cease-fire had become more stable and, indeed, the campaign had been approved by the Israeli cabinet on the 20th December 1970. In addition to the Druze border police, many Israeli army units were moved into the Gaza Strip to saturate it, and within days the number of incidents was reduced considerably. On the 25th Dayan had announced that since the June War 132 residents (including 20 children and 31 women) had been killed by guerillas, and some 979 wounded. The lull was broken on the 1st February, when a grenade exploded in Gaza, injuring 61 Arabs.

At least 700 suspects had been taken from the refugee camps and held in make-shift camps in the desert, while at the Shati refugee camp a road-widening programme was begun to sectionalize the camp to facilitate better security measures. By the end of January at least 13 houses had been demolished in the camp. As soon as the lull descended, complaints began to pour in about the conduct of the Druze, and a senior military officer was appointed to hear them. Israeli soldiers had also been heavy-handed in their methods, and on the 10th February the Israelis admitted that there had been some unnecessary violence, that some officers and soldiers had been punished, and that at least 30 people had been injured by the Druze border police. There had been instances of looting, and it was later stated that any stolen goods would be restored to their owners.

Despite complaints this hard security policy continued. Measures included removing families of 'wanted men' from the refugee camps as they were suspected of helping their menfolk, and some—about 60 families in all—were moved to Abu Zneimeh, a small, deserted manganese mining port in the Sinai. During January and February, it was stated by the Israelis, 150 guerillas were arrested, many weapons were discovered, and grenade incidents, which had averaged about 18 a month during the latter part of 1970, dropped to five in February and in March respectively. However, other figures released on the 9th March indicated that there had been 71 incidents since the security drive began, and that about 320 people were held in camps in the Sinai because other detention camps were full. Intensive measures restricted, but did not completely stop terrorism; on the 13th five Arab women, wives of alleged collaborators, were murdered, and in April a former PFLP commander of the Gaza area was arrested.

Gradually the strict Israeli measures had effect. By June some 30,000 Arabs daily crossed the 'Green Line' (the pre-June 1967 border) to work in Israel, but incidents continued. On the 4th two Arabs were killed by guerillas; another three were killed on the 6th; and on the 11th two Arabs were killed and 81 injured in grenade attacks on people waiting for buses to take them to work in Israel. June was a bad month. On the 23rd grenade attacks in Khan Yunis market place killed two Arabs and an Israeli and wounded 44 Arabs. But these came to be the exception as the guerillas' power over the inhabitants lessened. There were no more student demonstrations, and shopkeepers' strikes ordered by the guerillas were hardly observed except in token, but the Israelis still relentlessly demolished houses that sheltered terrorists. The Israelis calculated that there were about 100 men on their 'wanted list' at any one time, and perhaps another 100 Fedayeen operating underground in the Gaza Strip whom they did not know much about. Captured guerillas seemed to talk readily, informing on their colleagues (who in turn were arrested) and excusing their betrayal by alleging that they were tortured. The guerillas became less bold and resorted to paying teenage boys to throw their grenades for them. The culprit in the Arovo murders was detected and arrested; he was a 15-year-old boy who had been paid £6 to throw the grenade.

Perhaps the most troublesome refugee camp was that at Jabalia, about five miles to the north of Gaza, which contained about 36,000 refugees, where it was estimated that about 40 murders had been committed in the first six months of the year. The Israeli security forces descended on Jabalia refugee camp, and after a thorough house-to-house search began bull-dozing houses to make way for straight, wide roads so that it could be sectionalized. By July 1971, some 400 houses had been demolished and some 1,200 refugees moved out, many to El Arish, where there were empty dwellings vacated by the with-drawing Egyptians in 1967. Three 'wanted' guerillas were killed in a bunker on the 3rd August after refusing to surrender. In Shati refugee camp, near the sea shore, houses were demolished for the same purpose. Dayan explained that the policy was to 'thin out' the four main refugee camps in the Gaza Strip so that the remaining inhabitants could become workers and not refugees, and that a long-term plan existed to move Arab families to the West Bank. He admitted, however, that so far only about 200 had volunteered to go. Egypt protested and asked the UN to prevent refugees being moved from camps, but the UN declined to take any action.

On the 12th July an Israeli soldier was killed in ambush near Gaza. Responsibility was claimed by the PFLP, which also boasted that it had placed explosive charges under an Israeli helicopter that had crashed a few days before; the Israelis, however, denied that the accident could have been caused in this way. On the 25th five members of the PFLP were killed in a gun battle in a school where they had taken refuge when their refugee camp hide-out was discovered, bringing the number of Fedayeen killed that month in the Gaza Strip to 13. Arab demonstrations followed the incident, but they barely lasted two hours before the city went back to normal, whereas six months or so earlier strikes, demonstrations and protests would have dragged on for days. On the 16th August 23 Arabs were injured by grenade attacks when out on the streets in defiance of a guerilla order to strike. This time shops had remained open as the Israelis threatened to close permanently any that shut, and buses continued to run as the Israelis said that if they did not alternative transport would be brought into the Gaza Strip and would remain there, so depriving many locals of a livelihood.

On the 18th August, the day when the bulldozers moved into the Rafah refugee camp to clear the way for wider roads, Moshe Dayan stated that in the absence of prospects of peace with the Arabs, Israel should take over the occupied territories, but on the 22nd, under cabinet pressure, he had to tone this statement down considerably. Dayan's policy in the Gaza Strip was a bold one in that he was attempting to change the status and outlook of the people from that of helpless refugees to workers. If this could be achieved the Arabs would be able to earn a wage and gain some self-respect, instead of having to live on UN charity. He would have liked to take over the administration of the refugee camps where, under weak UN control, terrorism and corruption tended to flourish. Ignored by the Egyptians for 19 years and by the Israelis for four, UNRWA had been feeding and educating refugees who had no hope of ever obtaining a job. Dayan thought the spur of incentives might eventually work, and what had started as a large scale heavy-handed security operation, with more than a slight punitive element, might develop into a resettlement programme, under which the Israelis planned to move out up to one-fifth of the refugees from the camps and to split the camps themselves into smaller, self-supporting villages.

Dayan persevered with his plan, and in the ensuing months made periodic progress reports. On the 31st August he announced that 13,336 persons had been moved from the Jabalia, Shati and Rafah refugee camps, and of that number some 2,000 had been 'resettled in El Arish'. Another 1,300 had moved to the West Bank, the others remaining in the Gaza Strip. Next he startled the Arabs by saying that a number of Israeli settlements would be established in the central sector of the Gaza Strip, the first within a fortnight (on the 18th October). On the 24th October there was fighting during clearing operations at Jabalia refugee camp in which four guerillas were killed by the Israelis and two Arab girls were killed by a guerilla grenade, but by this time the first phase of the plan was under way. The second phase, that of rehousing the refugees in small detached newly-built houses was set in motion. These houses were to be the nucleus of new camps, each of about 100,000 inhabitants, which would become viable as their economy developed. This was a much tougher proposition, there was opposition, and a spate of terrorist incidents followed. Two Arab girls were killed on the 22nd, four guerillas were killed in a clearing operation in Jabalia refugee camp on the 24th, and on the 26th, in a grenade incident in Burej refugee camp, about 10 miles south-west of Gaza, two guerillas and an Israeli were killed during a search. On the next day, the 27th, the deputy commander of the PFLP in the Gaza Strip was killed in a camp search. Intensification of searching continued, and during the last few weeks of the year there were almost daily reports of arms being discovered in refugee camps and of Fedayeen being killed, captured or wounded.

More figures followed on the 2nd November, when the Israelis announced that the first stage of road construction in the Jabalia, Shati and Rafah refugee camps had been completed, that 1,857 buildings had been demolished, and that 1,900 families had been moved, of whom 250 had gone to El Arish and 30 to the West Bank. On the following day, the 3rd, it was stated that some 8,000 acres of land near Deir al-Balah, just south of Gaza, were to be used to establish six Israeli settlements, and that already security fencing had been erected round 1,000 acres. More figures given out on the 9th December[1] indicated that recently 627 convicted prisoners and detainees had been released after review, of whom half were from the Gaza Strip. Some 400 still remained in 'administrative detention' (the figure had been 1,300 twelve months previously) and about 3,500 'security prisoners' were still held, of whom 250 were from within Israel itself.

After much searching and lobbying the Israelis, in May 1971, appointed Rashid al-Shawa[2] as Mayor of Gaza. As the situation in the Gaza Strip improved the Israelis slightly relaxed their ban on political activities. They did nothing to discourage vague talk of a Palestine state among young intellectuals and politicians, or to prevent the Palestine National Alignment which aimed at a Palestine state, from coming into being. The ban on political meetings as such remained; in the previous year (1970) they had refused Sheikh Jabari, Mayor of Hebron, permission to hold a conference of Arab notables to talk about a West Bank state of some sort. However, as all was going well in the occupied territories, the Israelis allowed Arab mayors to meet together for the first time on the 28th August 1971; officially this was only to discuss economic matters, politics being forbidden, but there was much backstage discussion. On the 18th October Mayor Jabari, of Hebron, and 20 other Arab personalities were allowed to visit Rashid al-Shawa to congratulate him on his appointment. On this occasion there was discussion amongst them of the feasibility of calling a Palestine congress to discuss the possibility of a Palestine state or of a West Bank federation with Jordan.

Throughout the summer the new Mayor of Gaza seemed to be co-operating reasonably well with the Israelis until suddenly,

---

[1] Another fact released by the Israelis was that there had been a riot at the Askelon prison in October, when half the 480 prisoners held there had to spend up to 23 hours a day in their cells. The Israelis claimed that there had been reforms since.

[2] His brother had been Mayor of Gaza in 1956, and had remained at his post when the Israelis occupied the Gaza Strip, but when the Israelis withdrew in 1957 the Egyptians imprisoned him for collaboration, and he died while still in detention.

on the 21st November, it was announced that Abu Nimer (his real name was Said al-Husseini), commander of all the PFLP forces in the Gaza Strip, had committed suicide in the Mayor's house. Exhausted and desperate, he had been driven to this by constant Israeli patrols and searches. He had taken refuge there on the 11th November and terrorized Rashid al-Shawa into concealing him. The Israelis knew that Abu Nimer was in the Mayor's house, and allowed him to enter into secret negotiations with them for a safe-conduct for himself and about 40 of his PFLP members to an Arab country.

The Israelis played for time, and eventually the guerilla leader shot himself. The Mayor was placed under surveillance for a while. Realizing that they would have difficulty in replacing him, the Israelis after investigation accepted his explanation and Rashid al-Shawa continued in office.

In four months the Israelis had killed over 40 guerillas and captured over 350, grenade incidents were down to about three a month, and as the Israelis almost completely denied freedom of movement to the guerillas, the three-year long period of murder and terrorism had almost come to an end.

On the 27th March 1972, the day before municipal elections were to be held on the West Bank, the Israelis announced that the Gaza Strip would be incorporated into Israel and that Israeli settlement would continue. A group of 200 students, about half from the Gaza Strip, travelled to the Damascus University on the 15th June, being the first Arabs since the June War to be allowed to cross from the occupied territories into Syria.

By August the situation in the Gaza Strip was even better from the Israeli point of view, despite the underlying fact that it was widely regarded as a pawn in protracted peace negotiations. Over 40,000 Arabs travelled daily into either Israel or the West Bank to work, mainly on farms and building sites. Those admitting to earning more than the equivalent of £10 per week were struck from the UNRWA lists as no longer entitled to free subsistence rations, which caused Mayor Rashid al-Shawa to declare bitterly that the time would come when the Israelis would be able to say: 'We have no refugee problem'. Home industries were slowly developing, the will to work seemed to revive among the Arabs, and the Israelis were anxious to employ them as cheap and menial labour. There was talk by bolder refugees of merging the refugee camps with the adjacent towns. Wide roads driven straight through the refugee camps had enabled the Druze border police[1] to crush the Fedayeen operating underground in them, and incidents remained less than half-a-dozen a month. From the beginning of August 1971 until the end of July 1972, for example, there were only 25 Israeli casualties (of whom five had been killed), 98 Arab casualties and 69 guerillas killed, as compared with 130, 649 and 49 respectively during the previous twelve months. On the 25th August there occurred the first grenade explosion of any magnitude for some time, when 18 people were injured, and on the 30th another grenade killed one Arab and injured two near Khan Yunis. On the 15th August the curfew, which had been in force in one form or another since the June War, was lifted, and vehicles were allowed to move along most roads throughout the night.

The main result of the removal of the major terror threat in the Gaza Strip was to allow a moderate political Arab leadership to emerge timidly. On the 16th, with Israeli permission, some 45 Arab personalities led by Mayor Rashid al-Shawa visited Amman, ostensibly to give their condolences to King Hussein on the death of his father.[2] While there they talked about the King Hussein plan for federating the East and West Bank. The discussions covered the Gaza Strip and envisaged an Israeli concession of a 'corridor' to link it with the West Bank, all of which seemed to find favour with al-Shawa's delegation. This was not quite how the Israelis had visualized things working out. As a counter to the King Hussein plan, on the 24th Premier Golda Meir said that she thought the Gaza Strip should be incorporated into Israel—a view she had previously voiced on the 16th March and which had been officially endorsed by her Government some eleven days later. When questioned on the 27th August Moshe Dayan was non-

[1] The Druze border police were moved from the Gaza Strip to Tel Aviv in August 1972 to cope with an outbreak of violent crime.

[2] King Talal, Hussein's father, had died in an institution in Turkey on the 8th July 1972, having become insane in 1951.

committal on a report of an Israeli scheme to establish a new Israeli town, of about 250,000 people, with its own airport in the Gaza Strip to be called Yamit (of the sea). His reticence was taken by the Arabs to indicate merely that the time was not yet ripe for such a project.

As well as visiting Jordan, Mayor Rashid al-Shawa had been touring other Arab states asking for investment in the Gaza Strip, which caused him to be unpopular with the Fedayeen, who did not want the refugee problem to be solved by economic means. On the 4th September they made an unsuccessful attempt to assassinate him. The 'General Command' of the guerillas claimed responsibility, saying that he had 'worked against the interests of the Palestine revolution'. This coincided with a minor wave of violence, which was put down to students being on holiday.

The Israelis made another move in their efforts to turn refugees in the Gaza Strip into citizens when, in August, they ordered municipal councils to provide water, sewerage, refuse clearance and other services for the refugee camps in their areas. All began to comply with the exception of that of Gaza, whose Mayor objected because he felt that the Military Governor's order foreshadowed political changes that would prejudice the refugee status of the people. There were rumours that the Israelis intended to thin out the Jabalia and Shati refugee camps by some 15,000 people each, and Mayor Rashid al-Shawa, who had previously objected to this policy, had been told firmly on several occasions that he must not make political statements. Also, he openly supported the King Hussein plan. The order for municipal councils to provide services for the refugee camps had been made by the Egyptians in 1966, when they were in occupation, but had never been enforced until the Israelis chose this moment to revive it to improve living conditions. On the 22nd October the Israelis dismissed Rashid al-Shawa from his position as Mayor of Gaza for refusing to supply municipal services to the Shati refugee camp, and the whole of the Arab council resigned. The Mayor was replaced by a senior Israeli official.

Two days previously, on the 20th, it had been reported in the Israeli press that the Shati refugee camp was the first to elect democratically its own camp council, which replaced the hereditary or traditionally selected 'mukhtars'. To find a new mayor and council for Gaza, the Israelis announced that they intended to hold municipal elections in the Gaza Strip.

Such elections would shatter the age-old political pattern and social system, as the purpose was to invite refugees to forget their long-lost, distant homes in what is now Israel, and to become voting residents and permanent inhabitants with a long-term interest in the Gaza Strip.

# 10. *Flickering Embers*

The year of 1972 saw dramatic changes in Fedayeen methods, as the guerillas in the field were kept out of Jordan, controlled in Syria and progressively restricted in the Lebanon, bringing home to them the painful fact that they were having little success against the Israelis with their vaunted revolutionary guerilla warfare techniques. It was a year in which new terrorist tactics were tried, that included more hijacking, more killing of hostages and the commencement of a letter-bomb campaign, in which the Israelis also surreptitiously joined.

About 9,000 guerillas escaped from Jordan during 1971, mostly to Syria, where they were kept on a very tight rein. When this became apparent many began to move into adjacent Lebanon, where for two years, since the (Lebanese) Cairo Agreement, the situation had been comparatively quiet, the Lebanese army successfully penning up the Fedayeen in Fatahland. During that year there had been a number of small hit-and-run raids by the guerillas, who probably had a strength of about 2,000, and in reprisal the Israelis launched occasional attacks, blowing up in all some 200 buildings, but these were given little publicity. A guerilla build-up began in November 1971, and continued until there were at least 4,000 fighters in Fatahland, who included a detachment of about 100 Libyans, allowing Arafat to boast that Libyan guerillas were fighting alongside their Palestinian brothers in the field. The Lebanese army had been unable to stop this influx. Raids from the Lebanon into Israel had been limited in scope as the Israelis were in good positions in overlooking hills, and in fact had constructed a road to supply them, a mile or so of which actually lay within Lebanese territory.

Fedayeen attacks from Fatahland increased in January 1972, there being at least 13 in the first ten days of the month; one on the 6th, involving the killing of a civilian who was decapitated and whose head was carried off by the attackers, provoked a two-pronged Israeli raid supported by artillery fire. One prong hit at Bint Jebeil, when four guerillas were killed, and the other struck Kfar Hamman, farther north in the Mount Hermon foothills, where houses were demolished, two Israeli soldiers being killed and one wounded in this operation. On the following day, in what was becoming a customary immediate reaction, guerillas fired rockets into Israeli territory, this time at a school in Kiryat Shimona, but there were no casualties. On the 14th the Israelis again raided into the Lebanon, striking at Kafra, a village some six miles over the border, blowing up houses. As small guerilla attacks continued on the 18th, the Israelis threatened to occupy part of the Lebanon if the Government did not control the Fedayeen in its territory.

The adjacent Syrian frontier with the Israeli-occupied Golan Plateau became troublesome. There had already been 14 incidents in January (1972), when on the 24th Israeli aircraft raided Dera, near the Jordanian border, striking at a guerilla encampment. On the same day three guerillas were killed on the Golan Plateau, and one was killed and eleven captured by Israeli patrols in caves in the Upper Jordan Valley. Israeli aircraft also made a strike into Lebanese territory, the first for 19 months.

Then followed a lull until a guerilla raid on the 24th February, in which two Israelis were killed, caused the Israelis to launch a major ground and air operation that lasted for four days, during which time Lebanese territory was occupied and held. On the first day Israeli troops, with armour and artillery support, crossed the frontier and attacked the village of Ainta, near Bint Jebeil, about three miles over the border, killing five guerillas. Twenty-one houses were demolished in this guerilla base, and five Fedayeen were captured, as well as quantities of arms and ammunition being seized. Israeli aircraft struck at Bint Jebeil and other villages in the area.

On the second day, the 26th, Israeli aircraft again struck into the Lebanon, hitting targets as far as 25 miles from the border. Then, under cover of air and artillery support, Israeli soldiers were lifted by helicopter to attack a guerilla base to the north at Habbariya, through which supplies passed from Syria to Fatahland. The fighting lasted for over two days, and the guerillas admitted having over 60 casualties. On the same day, too, another Israeli ground force, with 30 tanks, penetrated nine miles into the Lebanon to become involved in fighting at the village of Rashaya, which lasted for two days. Generally, the guerillas were pushed back from the border in these three areas to a distance of up to ten miles in places, the fighting devolving into a series of running battles. By the end of the fourth day, the 28th, the Israelis had withdrawn. Casualty figures differ, but the Israelis admitted losing three killed and having eleven wounded, while claiming to have inflicted many guerilla casualties.

Watching on the fringes of the fighting during this four-day raid, the Lebanese army did not become involved, except for the exchange of a few impromptu shots, but as soon as it was seen that the Israelis were withdrawing, the army promptly moved into their retreating footsteps, forestalling the Fedayeen who, after being driven back, were regrouping preparatory to returning to their former bases. In this way Lebanese troops occupied large sections of Fatahland. On the 1st March they were busy consolidating, letting it be known that they fully intended to stay, and blocking the return of the guerillas. The (Lebanese) Cairo Agreement was brushed aside, and talks between Arafat and Lebanese Premier Saeb Salim brought no comfort to the guerillas.

On the 1st March Syrian aircraft raided Israeli settlements on the Golan Plateau, this being the first major Arab move of this nature since the cease-fire of the 7th August 1970, and in retaliation Israeli planes bombed guerilla camps near Dera. The Fatahland border with Israel remained quiet for a few days until raids on the morning of the 9th provoked Israeli aircraft to strike at the village of Kafr Zayit, four miles north of Fatahland, where guerillas were concentrating.

Meanwhile, the guerilla organizations themselves splintered and shook, and the former tough and virile PFLP, which had

207

so dramatically held the world to ransom by hijacking airliners in September 1970, was in a decline. When it held its third congress at Tripoli during the first week in March (1972) differences were aired. Despite argument and increasing unpopularity, George Habash was re-elected leader of the PFLP, but by a narrow margin. The PFLP declared that it had given up hijacking, as such tactics created a 'revolutionary élite', which was much admired but which did not enable the masses to participate in the liberation of Palestine as was desirable.

At the congress a splinter movement led by Abu Shihab broke away from the PFLP. It called itself the Revolutionary Popular Front for the Liberation of Palestine, the R-PFLP. Although extremely violent in attitude, it did not expound a positive platform. On the 20th March Habash was expelled from the Arab Nationalist Movement, of which he was secretary-general and founder, for 'subversive and deviationist activities,' and its central committee announced its support for the new splinter R-PFLP instead of its long-time guerilla arm, the PFLP. The PFLP decided to go it alone, and its leading personalities were now George Habash, Wadi Haddad (commander in the Gaza Strip), Ghassan Kanafani (editor of the PFLP weekly Al Hadaf) and Abu Riyad (commander in the Lebanon).

The tenth congress of the PLO opened in Cairo on the 6th April 1972, but attendance was poor. The Israelis forbade Palestinians in territory under their control to go. The Jordanian Government said that 80 per cent of PLO members in Jordan did not want to attend, and that it had advised the remainder not to do so. Those at the congress were dissatisfied with the way PLO affairs had been handled and with Arafat as a leader, complaining that he was arbitrary, secretive and unpredictable; but Arafat remained chairman. Proposals were put forward that a Palestine government-in-exile should be formed; these were favoured by Arafat and others, but were opposed by a powerful section of Fatah, led by Khalid al-Hassan, and also by Egypt, so they were not carried. When addressing them, President Sadat told members that Egypt had severed diplomatic relations with Jordan over the King Hussein plan, while Arafat announced that the all-out policy of Fatah was now to overthrow the King Hussein régime. Previously Arafat had not been so pointed and definite in this view. A surprise speaker at the congress was Ahmed Shukairy, the former chairman of the PLO, who was trying to make a political comeback, and who was given some support by Egypt to counter-balance the almost absolute control that had been wielded by Arafat for some time. Shukairy put forward many proposals, and regained an element of his former popularity.

Elections were held in the Lebanon on three successive Sundays in April 1972, after which Saeb Salim, remaining as Premier, turned his attention to bringing the Fedayeen in his country under firm control. Military pressure on the guerillas was maintained by the Lebanese army until at the beginning of June both Premier Salim and Major-General Iskandar Ghanem, the army Commander, claimed to have restored their writ in Fatahland. They said that since the Israeli four-day raid in February there had not been a single Fedayeen attack on Israeli territory from the Lebanon, and not a single Israeli reprisal. This was not completely accurate as, although the raids came mainly from Syrian soil, the Israeli air force had made a reprisal attack on positions in Fatahland on the 2nd May. The Premier said that road blocks were now manned by Lebanese soldiers, guerillas were not allowed to wear uniform, carry arms or live in villages, and the 400 Christian inhabitants of Rashaya, a former guerilla centre, were now freed from intimidation. The army Commander stated that out of some 3,000 Fedayeen in the Lebanon, only about 100 remained. The Israelis were not convinced of the correctness of this statement, insisting that there were still 5,000 Fedayeen near their northern borders, being mainly Fatah in the Lebanon and Saiqa in Syria. The right-wing Christian Falangists demanded a formal end to the (Lebanese) Cairo agreement, while the Israelis wanted the Fedayeen to be completely rooted out from the Lebanon.

Fedayeen attacks were mostly sprung from Syria, and on the 15th June, in a clash on the Golan Plateau, four guerillas and two Israelis were killed. The lull on the Lebanese-Israeli border was broken on the 20th, when guerillas ambushed an Israeli bus and wounded two people by rocket fire. On the following day Israeli aircraft struck at Hasbaya, a Druze village some seven miles inside the Lebanon, where the previous day's

209

raiders had been based, and in the bombing several houses were demolished and damaged and a number of people killed and injured. The Lebanese Government stated that all the casualties were villagers, and eventually gave the figure of 48 killed. It appeared that in response to urgent requests and pressure from the villagers, the guerillas who had been living in Hasbaya were prevailed upon to leave, and had just assembled outside the village when the Israeli air attack was made on the village itself. The Israelis had claimed to have killed 30 guerillas and 14 civilians, but later (on the 26th) the error was admitted by Ygal Alon, the Deputy Premier.

On the same day, the 21st, an Israeli patrol crossed into the Lebanon near the village of Amiyeh, only ten miles from the coast, and in a fight with a Lebanese patrol captured five senior Syrian officers who were visiting the Lebanese army, as well as a Lebanese officer and four Lebanese soldiers (one of whom later died of wounds), and wounded a Syrian officer. The Lebanese Government, which had just returned two Israeli civilians who had strayed across the border on the 10th, admitted to having nine killed and 18 wounded in this engagement. The Syrian officers were a brigadier, two colonels of the intelligence branch and two lieutenant-colonels.

President Franjieh summoned an emergency cabinet meeting, and Premier Salim met Arafat, demanding that guerilla raids into Israel cease. Arafat was anxious to fulfil this condition, but he was losing, or had lost, control of an extremist section of his Fatah, which would no longer listen to him. Arafat appreciated that only in the Lebanon did the guerillas have some last vestige of freedom of movement, and he desperately wanted to preserve this advantage until fortunes changed. He was particularly anxious not to provoke a head-on clash with the Lebanese army, which could only mean a repeat performance of the Fedayeen disaster in Jordan. After a meeting of the Higher Committee for Palestine Affairs, the coordinating body set up when the (Lebanese) Cairo Agreement was signed in November 1969, it was announced that measures were being taken against the Fedayeen, but no details were given. Nearly half the members of the recently elected National Assembly were demanding that this agreement be scrapped.

On the 23rd June the guerillas struck again at dawn, firing rockets at Kiryat Shimona which provoked Israeli air attacks on several villages. The Fedayeen themselves admitted heavy casualties near Hasbaya, Masnaa and Deir al-Asayir, the latter being a smuggling and guerilla staging point on the rocky slopes of the Mount Hermon range. The Israelis had been successful in turning the Druze villagers of Hasbaya against the Fedayeen. Lebanese pressure was now heavy on Arafat, who cabled urgently to President Sadat for support, but received none. On the 25th a spokesman of the 'General Command' claimed that its gunboats had been in action against Israeli naval craft and helicopters near Nahariya, on the northern part of the Israeli coastline, for the second day running, and there was another on the following day. Already there had been a minor clash at sea on the 8th, when Israeli craft intercepted guerilla boats attempting to smuggle in arms. On the 26th June there were reports of firing between the Lebanese army and the Fedayeen.

Representatives from both Kuwait and Saudi Arabia went to Beirut to help Arafat negotiate with the Lebanese Government. While Arafat was prepared to agree to a temporary 'freeze' of guerilla activity in the Lebanon as a matter of simple expediency, the PFLP and the extreme section of Fatah were not. Neither did Arafat have any authority over Saiqa, as a visit to Damascus indicated clearly. The Lebanese Government wanted to deal directly with any guerilla organization for an infringement of any 'freeze', but despite his lack of complete control over guerillas in the field, Arafat was able to uphold the fiction of the authority of the PLO umbrella, and he refused to allow this. He said that he was prepared to accept a temporary halt of guerilla movement and activity, but not total evacuation from the Lebanon.

After hesitation, on the 28th June Arafat agreed to the Lebanon's minimum demand, as he feared that its army was becoming impatient to march against the Fedayeen. He announced that the guerillas would 'freeze' all operations in and from the Lebanon and move back from the border with Israel, but would continue to maintain a presence near the frontier. This was not a popular decision with the guerillas, and there were mutterings against it, and also against Arafat. President

211

Franjieh called it a 'preservation of brotherly co-existence' between the Lebanon and the guerillas which 'guarantees the interests of both sides'. In fact, it meant that the guerillas had lost out and were forced to back away. On the 30th June the bulk of the guerillas in Fatahland moved away from the frontier region and their places were taken by Lebanese troops, only a few, mainly hard-line Fatah and PFLP, remaining to hide in the rugged terrain. The inhabitants of southern Lebanon were glad to see them go. On the 2nd July some Egyptians were urging the guerillas in the Lebanon to go underground, but all seemed to be dazed. Deputy Premier Ygal Alon stated that Israel would like to sign a treaty with the Lebanon to prevent further guerilla attacks from that country, but the Lebanese Government would not go as far as that and rejected the offer, calling it an abortive attempt to sow dissention between the Lebanon and its sister Arab states.

In July 1972 the Russians began their exodus from Egypt, which altered the balance of power in the Middle East. On the 21st Arafat went to Moscow, but returned empty-handed and disappointed; the Soviet Union had no interest in the Arab Fedayeen movement. On the 11th the PFLP claimed responsibility for a grenade explosion at the Tel Aviv bus station, which wounded 11 people. This was the first such attack in the Tel Aviv area for nine months, and was the exception in Israel rather than the rule.[1] Fedayeen activity generally subsided to a new low, as it had become obvious that guerilla warfare and terrorism as practised since the June War had failed to gain the desired effect, causing despondency to overtake the Fedayeen leaders and their followers. On the 2nd August it was announced that Egypt and Libya were to be federated—a different pattern of power in the Middle East was emerging.[2]

Another form of terrorism began to develop amongst ex-

[1] On the 1st April 1972 a PFLP member had been killed in Amman when trying to blow up FM Majali's residence.

[2] At about this time the Israelis were trying to arrange an exchange of prisoners. They held 108 Arabs (being three Lebanese, 45 Syrians and 60 Egyptians), while Syria held three Israeli pilots and the Egyptians ten Israeli soldiers. The Syrians considered that their five officers seized on the 21st June 1972 had been kidnapped and not captured, and so no agreement was reached.

tremists, that of sending parcel-bombs; it was not new, but while the Fedayeen had appeared to be a force in the field and until the illusion that revolutionary guerilla warfare might win the day had been shattered, this had hardly been thought necessary. This phase of terrorism could be said to have really begun in January 1972, when parcel-bombs were sent from Austria to prominent personalities in Israel. The parcels were all detected before delivery, which gives an indication of the high quality of Israeli intelligence, the only casualty being an explosives expert who was injured when one exploded.

Attempts had been made on the lives of various Fedayeen leaders, including Arafat, from time to time, but they had been spasmodic and put down as much to personal hatreds as ideological vengeance. A change in emphasis became apparent. The leadership of the PFLP, for example, seemed to take some hard knocks. It was reported that Habash suffered from a heart complaint that restricted his activity, and so he progressively took a lesser part in directing the affairs of the PFLP. On the 9th July Ghassan Kanafani was killed in Beirut in his car by a bomb that was wired to its starter; on the 19th a parcel-bomb injured Anis Sayegh, a senior PLO official and a PFLP member; and on the 25th Bassam Abu Sharif, the PFLP spokesman in Beirut, was partially blinded by a parcel-bomb. Then partly because of acute internal dissension and partly because of this spate of parcel-bombs sent to guerilla leaders, Wadi Haddad, who was actually the deputy leader of the PFLP, was reputed to have moved in secrecy to eastern Europe for safety, and so he also became largely ineffective. At first the PFLP blamed the Israelis for sending the parcel-bombs in reprisal for those sent to the Israelis in January, as the Palestine News Agency (the WAFA) reported that a piece of paper found at the scene of Kanafani's death had on it the Israeli symbol of the candelabrum and the words in English; 'With the compliments of the Israeli Embassy in Copenhagen'. The Israeli police stated that Kanafani's wife was Danish and that he had a brother in Denmark. The Israelis denied complicity, when suspicion fell on the break-away R-PFLP, which in turn also denied responsibility. Apprehension continued to be felt by guerilla leaders, who suspected each other as well as the

213

Israelis, causing some to go into hiding and others to shun publicity.

Comparative calm and economic progress on the West Bank caused the Israelis to decide to hold elections. On the 9th February 1972, two days after seven guerillas had been captured near Hebron, the Arabs were given permission to hold political meetings and to start electioneering campaigns. The mayors and other office holders had been in their positions for nine years, and although there seemed to be no general sign that the people wanted a change, the Israelis were anxious to make this political test. The only new political force in the field was the rather timid and immature Palestine National Alignment. On the following day, the 10th, travel restrictions were eased by both Israel and Jordan.

On the 23rd March the Israelis put pressure on the Arabs after some candidates had withdrawn. There was apprehension in case the Fedayeen would terrorize the people into boycotting the elections, but although they expressed disapproval they took little action. On the 28th municipal elections were held in towns in the northern part of the West Bank, Judea, which were conducted calmly; despite a call for a boycott by the Jordanian Government, there was a reported 80 per cent poll. On the 24th April the Israelis allowed the Arabs in the Gaza Strip to travel into Israel without special passes. On the 2nd May polling took place in towns in the southern part of the West Bank, Samaria, again without trouble, and with a high percentage poll. Most mayors were returned to office, the only dispute being at Jericho, where two antagonistic factions had arisen. These results amounted to a rejection by the people of the West Bank of the King Hussein plan for federating it with Jordan, indicated that the majority were seemingly content with the way affairs were progressing, and showed that the electorate did not pay heed in practice to the calls and threats of the Fedayeen.

The Black September Group struck again in December 1971 when two of its members tried to assassinate Said Rifai, the Jordanian Ambassador in London, a close adviser to King Hussein during the civil war. He was only wounded. Parcel bombs sent to members of a Jordanian mission to Geneva were also generally put down to the BSG. On the 6th February 1972 five Jordanians, believed to be intelligence officers who had been active in the civil war, were killed in Cologne by two men who raided their flat and machine-gunned them. The BSG claimed responsibility, and later two men were arrested by the West German police in connexion with this incident.

On the 22nd February five members of the BSG hijacked a West German jumbo jet after take-off from New Delhi, landing it at Aden airport, where they threatened to blow up the aircraft, together with the 171 persons on board, if the two Arabs held by the West German police were not released. After some negotiation the passengers were released, but not the crew of 14. On receipt of a coded message from the BSG leadership, in return for a ransom of £2 million the hijackers released the aircraft and crew, which flew off with the passengers on the 24th. The five BSG members, who had been taken into custody by the authorities, wereset free on the same day; in return, it is generally believed, the Government of South Yemen took about £400,000 of the ransom money.

Through these activities the BSG came into fuller prominence, and although it remained shrouded in secrecy, a little more came to be known about it. It consisted basically of a group of about 60 people, all Fatah extremists[1] formerly associated with Abu Iyyad (alleged to have been murdered in Jordan on orders of Wasfi Tal) who, disgusted at Arafat's moderate line, decided to take direct action to revenge themselves for their defeat in Jordan. Sinking behind a deep veil of secrecy they recruited selected personnel, and formed themselves into small cells each of up to six individuals, only one of whom was the contact with the leadership, the others knowing only each other but no one else in the BSG movement. Dedicated to achieve their object by violent means, they swore to avenge the death of Abu Iyyad. Their primary targets were King Hussein, his Government, and those who had primarily contributed to the guerilla defeat, but as the King was so well guarded Wasfi Tal had become their first victim, and he was followed by lesser known personalities.

[1] At the initial hearing at the trial in Cairo of the killers of Wasfi Tal, one of them referred to Fatah as 'our mother group'.

No one, not even guerilla leaders, knew for certain who led the BSG or where its headquarters were. Not even Arafat knew, and when he and the Fatah leadership, whose fortunes were at a low ebb, denied all knowledge of this newly-formed guerilla organization, they were being truthful. According to the Israelis, the leader of the BSG was Abu Hassan (real name Ali Hassan Salameh), who had been in charge of the recruiting and security department of the PLO, responsible for intelligence, fund raising and also for politically vetting recruits to all PLO guerilla organizations, and so he was able to select and recruit for the BSG. Abu Hassan had a close liaison with Major-General Bakr Younes, the Libyan Chief-of-Staff, a contact that resulted in funds being given to the BSG. The BSG drew heavily on expatriate Palestinians (there being some 70,000, for example, in Germany) and the many branches and offices of the two large Palestinian organizations, the General Union of Palestinian Students and the General Union of Palestinian Workers to one or the other of which practically all expatriates belonged. They provided a ready made intelligence-gathering medium and labour force.

At first Arafat did not take much notice of the BSG, assuming that it was just a small group of embittered guerillas who would either eventually reveal themselves or break up and fade away, but when they hijacked the West German airliner to Aden he sat up and took an immediate interest. Being an astute politician, he wanted to be associated with their success and popularity and also to use them for his own purposes if possible. He tried to make contact, but had initial difficulties as no one seemed to know anything about the BSG, or would admit to knowing anything, even within Fatah. Eventually he discovered that one of the leaders was a sister of Abu Iyyad, and a contact was made with her through Abu Jihad, a senior Fatah leader trained in Peking who became the official liaison officer between Arafat and the BSG. Arafat offered all the resources at his disposal to the BSG, on the condition that it diverted itself from the narrow aim of vengence on Jordan to the greater one of the Palestine cause as a whole. The BSG seemed to have accepted this offer, and the character of the attacks it made changed. Arafat did not attempt to probe too deeply, and it was doubtful whether for many months he knew any details about the BSG.

The change of aim was demonstrated on the 8th May, when four members of the BSG hijacked a Belgian Boeing 707 after it had taken off from Brussels and landed it at its scheduled destination, which was Lydda. Once on the ground the 95 persons on board were kept as hostages for 22 hours, while the Israelis negotiated with the hijackers, who demanded the instant release of 100 Arab guerillas held in Israeli detention. Moshe Dayan, the Defence Minister, came on to the scene and personally took charge. The Belgian Government indicated that it was willing to offer up to £1 million for the release of the hostages, but Dayan would not allow this. He played for time for a while, and then suddenly the aircraft was stormed by soldiers dressed in mechanics' overalls. Two of the hijackers, both men, were killed, and the other two, both girls,[1] were wounded, as were two Israeli soldiers and two passengers, one of whom later died. The hijackers had been under orders to blow up the aircraft, and the people on board, including themselves, if attacked, but at the last moment had hesitated and so were overcome. The International Committee of the Red Cross, whose representatives had been involved in negotiations between the Israelis and the hijackers, accused the Israelis of deceit. This attempt by the BSG to obtain the release of Arab prisoners, in which it had boldly put its head in the lion's mouth, had been foiled by an equally bold and astute Dayan, but it drew gasps of admiration from the Arab masses. The PFLP initially falsely attempted to claim credit for this exploit, but although the BSG did not make any formal claim openly for responsibility, all Arabs and others seemed to be instantly aware who the authors were.

The next major terrorist attack was more deadly and fanatical. On the 31st May, three Japanese who had just arrived at Lydda airport on an Air France Boeing 707, having boarded it in Italy, calmly opened their suitcases, took out sub-machine guns and grenades, and commenced shooting and throwing grenades at the passengers in the crowded terminal, killing

[1] They were sentenced to life imprisonment by the Israelis on the 13th August 1972.

26 and wounding 72 people. Two of the terrorists were killed and the other overpowered.[1] The survivor said that he belonged to the 'Red Army' and the attack was one in a series 'to bring about world revolution'. He said that he and his companions had spent some time in a guerilla camp near Beirut, where they had been trained to kill, and that an Arab guerilla contact had visited their organization in Japan. It was known that various Arab guerilla groups, especially the extreme, left-wing ones, had wide contacts with many revolutionary bodies, both national and international, in Europe and the Americas, but this employment of Japanese terrorists came as a surprise to practically everyone. The PFLP hastily claimed responsibility, pointing out that it indicated the amount of international support the Palestine cause attracted, but there were doubts as to whether the PFLP or the BSG were the organizers of this terrorist act of such magnitude.

The Israelis blamed the Lebanese, called for an international boycott of Beirut airport, demanded that the Government should instantly bring all guerilla activities in that country to an end, and threatened reprisals. Fearfully, thinking back to the Israeli raid on Beirut airport in December 1968, Premier Salim stated that while the PFLP had an office and printed a newspaper in Beirut, the location of its headquarters was not known, but that he was taking immediate steps to curb PFLP propaganda. This terrorist attack on Lydda airport obviously did much to stimulate the Lebanese Government to crack down further on the guerillas, which action resulted in the agreement of the 28th June, previously mentioned, when they had to withdraw from the area of the Israeli border. Farther removed from Lydda, Egyptian Premier Aziz Sidki openly approved of the raid, as did other Arab leaders, the only dissenting voice being that of King Hussein, who declared it 'a sick crime committed by sick people which had nothing to do with the Arab world'.

On the 4th August the oil storage tanks at Trieste were blown up and 200,000 gallons of oil were set on fire, the damage amounting to over £2 million. Some thought this act might have

[1] The survivor pleaded guilty and was sentenced to life imprisonment by the Israelis on the 17th July 1972.

been committed by German urban guerillas or Croatian nationalists, but the BSG claimed responsibility, saying that it had been done because the bulk of the oil, which came from Libya, went into refineries in Austria and Germany, countries which were sympathetic to or were helping Israel.

Next, on the 16th August, a bomb exploded in an Israeli Boeing 707, just after it had taken off from Rome for Lydda. The explosion was a minor one, no one was hurt and the aircraft was able to land safely. The bomb, an 'altitude' one, had been concealed in a tape-recorder given by two members of the BSG at the last moment to two British girls they had briefly made friends with in Rome; the girls took the present not knowing its contents. The two Arabs were arrested by the Italian police.

Both Israeli and Arab national teams competed at theWorld's 21st Olympic Games at Munich which opened at the beginning of September 1972. Suddenly, at dawn on the 5th, eight BSG members entered the quarters of the Israeli team, killed two of them and held the other nine as hostages, demanding that 200 Arab prisoners be released by the Israelis. They were besieged in a building in Olympic Village throughout the day by German security forces while negotiations were in progress. That afternoon the Egyptian team withdrew from the Olympics and a group of 50 Israelis staged a sit-down demonstration there. Certain German politicians volunteered to take the place of the hostages, but their offers were refused, as were large sums of money offered by the German Government. The BSG commandos demanded that an aircraft be made ready to fly them to an Arab country.

In the late evening the BSG members and their hostages were taken in three helicopters to the nearby Fürstenfeldbruck military airfield where, after a confused pause, firing broke out just after midnight. When it was over five of the Arabs had been killed, the other three were captured, and one helicopter had been blown up by a grenade. All nine Israeli hostages had been killed, one having been suffocated in the burning helicopter and the remainder shot. One German policeman was killed. Realizing why they failed at Lydda in May, this time the BSG made their ruthlessness and determination evident. After a brief adjournment the Olympic Games were resumed, ending on the 11th, by which time the Israeli and Arab teams and nationals had quietly departed, as had some Jewish competitors, but the BSG had brought the Palestine cause dramatically to the attention of the world.

There was criticism, especially by the press, of the German authorities' handling of the affair. At one point it had been wrongly announced that the hostages were safe. Throughout the Israeli Government was adamant that it would not release any Arab prisoners in exchange for the hostages, and it was later leaked to the press that the German Government had turned down an offer by Moshe Dayan to direct the rescue operation personally. It seems that the West Germans were equally determined not to allow the BSG members to leave Germany, in support of which claim they pointed out that the guerillas and hostages had been taken to a military and not a civilian airfield. The unfortunate result was sparked off by premature firing by marksmen detailed to pick off the BSG members, who in turn became alarmed and killed the hostages.

The bodies of the five dead BSG guerillas were flown to Libya on the 11th, where they were given a heroes' funeral, while the three survivors were detained by the West German police. On the same day a member of the Israeli diplomatic staff was lured to a café in Brussels and shot, although only wounded. The BSG were suspected of this act, but no one was quite sure. The aim of the BSG action at Munich had been to negate what it called the Egyptian 'European offensive' aimed at friendship with Germany, and all Arab states were forced to criticize strongly the German methods used. Moderate Fedayeen leaders, like Khalid Hassan, the PLO delegate to the Arab League and a Fatah member who had formerly criticized the BSG, were now silent. All, including Fatah moderates, were compelled to praise the BSG and its activities.

However, after a pause some Fedayeen leaders had second thoughts, and on the 14th September, in Damascus, Arafat said openly that the PLO disclaimed any responsibility for the Munich killings. He said this to try to ward off any action by the Israelis, which might include the assassination of guerilla personalities, so many of whom had become well known and generally identifiable. The Israelis published certain information which they had gleaned about the BSG, confirming that its European wing was led by Ali Salameh.

Immediately after the Munich incident Arab states tensely waited for the anticipated Israeli reprisals. On the 8th September the Israelis launched a 100-plane raid into Syria and the Lebanon that lasted for about 20 minutes, hitting at ten guerilla bases, some in or near refugee camps. The Syrians estimated that 300 people were killed, 70 in one single building in a refugee camp, and many injured, while the guerillas themselves said that they had 66 killed and 220 wounded. The Israelis stated that only 200 were killed, of whom 60 per cent were guerillas, but denied that this was a reprisal for the Munich killings. On the following day, the 9th, the Israelis claimed to have shot down three Syrian aircraft over the Golan Plateau and to have hit a fourth. A later Syrian claim to have brought down two Israeli aircraft in this air battle was denied.

The Lebanese Government hastily allowed the press to visit the frontier area, generally forbidden to them, in an attempt to show that the guerillas had left and that the Lebanese army was in control, but the Israelis were not impressed; they estimated that there were still up to 5,000 guerillas in Fatahland. On the 16th September, the day after two Israeli soldiers had been killed on the Golan Plateau, the Israelis launched a dawn attack with (according to the Syrians) an armoured brigade and three aircraft squadrons, that penetrated to within 15 miles from the border. The Israeli ground forces engaged did not withdraw until 36 hours later. The Israelis occupied 16 villages, cleared nine guerilla camps in the Mount Hermon foothills, destroyed two bridges across the Litani River, demolished 150 houses and seized quantities of arms and ammunition. Generally, the guerillas fell back before the Israeli onslaught, the only serious opposition being put up near the village of Juwaya, at the north-west tip of the penetration.

The Lebanese army became involved when a unit in the path of one of the Israeli drives made a stand near Beit Yahoune, and aircraft were brought in against this position. Later the Lebanese admitted that in this clash they lost three tanks, an armoured vehicle, other vehicles and three guns, while casualties included 17 soldiers killed and seven wounded. As the Israelis withdrew, the Lebanese army quickly filtered into the area left vacant, this time erecting barriers and check-points to prevent the guerillas returning to that part of Fatahland. The Israelis admitted three killed and six wounded, but claimed to have killed 60 guerillas and captured an unspecified number. Premier Salim declared a state of emergency, but later denied that he had given the Fedayeen an ultimatum to leave his country. Over their radio transmissions from Cairo and Damascus the guerillas complained that the Lebanese army was obstructing them in the fighting, and demanded that the state of emergency be rescinded.

As the Lebanese army stood firm against the guerillas there was fear that fighting between them might erupt, although the Premier hastily denied that there was any tension, but extreme tension nevertheless existed. By the 20th September the guerillas were slowly giving way, and on the following day the army was given authority to censor any newspapers that 'refused to censor themselves'. The Lebanese army had gained more prestige and respect. Clearly the Fedayeen wanted to avoid a Jordanian type confrontation in which not only the Lebanese army but also the Falangist militia would be against them, and the refugee camps would become battlefields. Under the continuing quiet pressure the last of the guerillas pulled out from the frontier areas in the Lebanon by the 4th October.

*Al Ahram* reported on the 27th September that the guerillas in the Lebanon had agreed to 'freeze' their activities and adhere to the (Lebanese) Cairo Agreement—but there was more to it than just that. The Lebanese Government wanted total restrictions put on the Fedayeen, and Arafat had been compelled to agree, which caused internal trouble as he tried to enforce this condition. A breakaway group of the PFLP, led by Ahmed Jabril, who was now backed by Colonel Gaddafi of Libya, rejected it completely, but after some scuffling the discontented guerillas moved over the border into Syria. Arafat also had difficulty with Fatah, and on the 15th October, when a detachment refused to withdraw from a frontier village in Fatahland, there was an outbreak of fighting in which at least two guerillas were killed and half-a-dozen wounded, while the besieged 'rebels' held hostage three senior Fatah members sent to negotiate. The main complaint was of weak Fedayeen leadership. The Yarmuk brigade of the PLA, in Syria, came out openly on the side of the 'rebel' Fatah detachment, but made no move to help it. Arafat had to compromise, and he reshuffled a few posts within Fatah. The Lebanese army was slowly enforcing the 'new agreement', which the Lebanese Government announced on the 19th October, until by the end of the month only a handful of Fedayeen remained at large in the rougher terrain of Fatahland. Most had moved back from the frontier into Syria or had gone underground; in any case, winter was approaching. For the time being the Lebanese Government could justify its claim that it had the guerilla problem under control, and that Fedayeen raids from the Lebanon into Israel had ceased.

Meanwhile a new extension of terrorism in the form of the letter-bomb appeared on the scene, and on the 19th September 1972 an Israeli diplomat was killed by one in London. In this initial wave the letter-bombs were posted from Amsterdam, being sent to Israelis and Jews. The BSG was blamed. By the new technique a small amount of explosive contained in an ordinary air mail envelope automatically detonated when the letter was opened and certain pressures were released. It was a refinement and improvement of the parcel-bomb or book-bomb. By the 24th[1] some 42 letter-bombs had been discovered in eleven of the world's capitals.

Terrorism breeds counter-terrorism everywhere, and Israel was no exception, as was disclosed on the 21st September when the Israeli Minister of Police warned the right-wing Jewish Defence League (the JDL) that he would not allow any organization to carry out acts of sabotage against anyone. Two members of the 200-strong JDL were arrested within days of each other on suspicion of smuggling arms and explosives out

[1] It was revealed on the 24th September that the son of the Jordanian Ambassador to France had been kidnapped in Paris on the 30th August, when an immediate ransom of £15,000 was paid for his release. This incident was kept quiet as it was not certain whether the Fedayeen were involved in any way.

of Israel for terrorist purposes. One was reputed to be a former member of the Irgun Zwi Leumini, a Jewish terrorist organization active in the days of the Mandate, and the other to have been imprisoned in America for taking explosives aboard an aircraft—it was said that he was going to hijack an Arab plane in retaliation for Arab hijacking of Israeli aircraft. Yet another member of the JDL, who admitted that his organization accepted full responsibility for trying to smuggle arms out of Israel, was arrested, but all three were quickly released.

On the 1st October Rabbi Meir Kahane, the leader of the JDL, was arrested and held for a few days. He was an extremist, who allegedly had fermented trouble between Israelis and Arabs in the Hebron area, causing the Government to ban him from that sector. Meanwhile the Israeli police confirmed that there was an illegal flow of arms and explosives from Israel for the anti-Arab campaigns abroad. Sudden thoughts must have struck Arab guerilla leaders, making them wonder if indeed the Israelis had not been sowing dissension between them by acts of violence which each thought the other might have perpetrated When released on the 6th, Rabbi Meir Kahane stated that his JDL would take political action and contest the following year's elections.

Discussion continued on the possibility of a Palestinian state, and indeed of the acceptability of the King Hussein plan. On the 28th September, the second anniversary of the death of President Nasser, President Sadat called upon Palestinians to set up a government-in-exile. This was an immensely unpopular statement, denounced by the Jordanian Government, which considered King Hussein to be the spokesman for all Palestinians, and also by the Fedayeen which, because it did not recognize Israel, could not negotiate with that country, whereas a government-in-exile might do just that—perhaps successfully. The PLO central committee was divided on this issue, but after deliberation on the 2nd October it formally rejected Sadat's suggestion.

With the Lebanese Government clamping down firmly on the guerillas within its territory, Israeli attention began to turn towards Syria, as its frontier with Israel was now the only one along which guerilla incidents occurred and across which the Fedayeen still raided. Also, there were large numbers of guerillas camped close to the border. On the 28th September it was reported that the Soviet Union delivered some 12 tons of small arms, machine guns and mortars direct to Fatah in Syria, the first-ever open delivery to the Fedayeen, except for the arms given to the PLA. These Soviet arms and ammunition were taken to the Fatah base at El Hamma. In October Soviet military material began arriving in Syria, including elements of an air defence system, which was based on SAM-3s and modern radar. The Syrian army became abrasive and went into action against the Israelis as well as did the Fedayeen, guns firing fairly frequently on to the several new Israeli settlements established on the Golan Plateau since 1969. For example, on the 9th November there was fighting all day along the length of this front, with an air battle overhead much of the time, in which the Israelis claimed to have shot down two Syrian MiGs.

Meanwhile terrorism continued. On the 4th October 1972 there was an explosion in the Palestine Information Centre and library in Paris, when responsibility was claimed by the Massada Action and Defence Movement, an organization about which little or nothing was known, or admitted, by the Israelis. On the 9th there were two explosions in Beirut, one at the PLO headquarters, which injured one person, and the other at the PFLP headquarters in a nearby refugee camp; both organizations blamed the Israelis. On the 17th gunmen killed a senior Fatah member in Rome, and again the Israelis were blamed.

From the 25th October more letter-bombs were sent to Fedayeen leaders, injuring six, while early in November there was a counter-wave of letter-bombs addressed to Israelis and Jews. On the 10th a letter-bomb injured a Jew in London, and 12 other letter-bombs were detected in time in that city and two others in Glasgow. All had been sent from India, apparently addressed at random, the names being taken from the *Zionist Year Book*. By the 12th the Indian police had detected a total of 51 letter-bombs.

On the 29th October two members of the BSG boarded a West German Boeing 707 at Beirut, due to fly to Ankara with some

20 people on board. Once in the air they hijacked it, ordering the pilot to fly first to Zagreb, in Yugoslavia, for fuel. The hijacked plane then flew on to Munich to circle overhead for two hours, while the hijackers negotiated for the release of the three BSG members held by the German police for the Munich killings in return for the safety of the aircraft and the persons on board. The West Germans agreed and flew the three captive Arabs to Zagreb airport, where they were taken on the hijacked Boeing, which had followed and landed there. The German airliner then took off with the hijackers and the three released Arabs to Tripoli, in Libya, where all were greeted as heroes. The Israelis were extremely angry, especially as the West Germans had given way so soon, and they accused the Germans of being glad to escape the embarrassment of a trial with an inevitable blaze of propaganda, publicity and the attendant danger of more hijacking and terrorism. The Fedayeen were jubilant, and praises of the BSG were on all Arab lips.

On the following day, the 30th, Israeli aircraft struck at four guerilla bases in Syria (two belonged to Fatah, one to Saiqa and the other to Ahmed Jabril's breakaway group of the PFLP), and also at a regular armoured unit near the Lebanese border. Later the West German Government banned the General Union of Palestinian Students and the General Union of Palestinian Workers and closed down their many offices in Germany.

From the 11th November 1972 onwards over 100 officers of the Egyptian armoured corps were arrested for alleged complicity in a coup against President Sadat planned for the 16th, and all transport and some aircraft were grounded for several days. On the 18th the Egyptian Government declared that it would reopen the war across the Suez Canal if there were any major invasion by the Israelis of Syria, and the three squadrons of Egyptian MiGs in Syria were placed under Syrian command. On the same day, the 18th, when over 300 Jordanian officers were arrested on the discovery of a plot against King Hussein, the pilot of a Jordanian Starfighter, also in the plot, attempted to kill the King by rocket fire at the helicopter at the Basman Palace just as the King was about to enter it. The King was only slightly wounded; he spent three days in hospital. On the

21st fierce fighting flared up across the Syrian-Israeli border. On the 22nd the French lifted their ban on arms to the Middle East. On the 26th there was more border fighting between the Syrians and the Israelis. The age-old turbulent pattern of the Middle East did not change.

# 11. Retrospect and Prospect

In brief retrospect we have seen the phenomenon of the sudden and unexpected emergence of Arab Guerilla Power, which grew in strength until it shook Arab governments. Initially the purpose of the Fedayeen was to carry out revolutionary guerilla warfare on the Algerian and Viet Cong patterns inside the Israeli occupied territories, but when this failed its objectives became blurred and diverse. The mystique of the Fedayeen fighter swept through an Arab world smarting under yet another humiliating defeat by the Israelis in battle, evoking hysterical enthusiasm. The Fedayeen took full advantage of this popularity to consolidate, to expand and to exact privileges. Many Fedayeen fighters were dedicated idealists. Soon they were joined by thousands who went along for the ride, who sought to share the popularity but who had little intention of getting themselves hurt. Several Arab states attempted to control the Fedayeen or bend them to their own national purposes, but failed. When governments realized that their national interests and policies were being eclipsed by Arab Guerilla Power, each did what it could to bring the guerillas in its territory under control and took measures which, as in Jordan and the Lebanon, included armed force, until the huge, gaudy balloon of Arab guerilla power was deflated.

The main achievement of Arab Guerilla Power was to give a beam of hope, and a sense of unity and purpose to the Palestinians, refugees, expatriates and those living under Israeli occupation, who lacked national cohesion and leadership. The refugees in particular had been contemptuously neglected and used as pawns in the Middle East power struggles; at last it seemed as though someone was doing something for them. Wildly optimistic and inaccurate communiqués were eagerly and implicitly believed. It seemed to them that a bright new era was dawning and that a new-found flame of energy had broken through the lethargy, throwing up a young, dedicated leadership. Seeing how Arab governments quarrelled, prevaricated and put self-interest always first, the Fedayeen leadership decided that the only way to achieve its ultimate aim of an Arab-controlled Palestine and the elimination of the state of Israel was to reach past governments and appeal directly to the people. It set out to stand above Arab rivalries and to be completely independent of Arab national influence.

Arab Guerilla Power failed in its objective completely as Israel not only remains on the map but also retains a strong grip on its occupied territories. A state of terrorism has existed at times in the occupied territories, expecially in the Gaza Strip, while acts of terrorism have been committed in Israel itself. The many guerilla incursions have caused Israeli and other casualties, but none of these have given the Israeli Government any serious anxiety about its own security or led it to doubt its ability to cope with them. Briefly, the main reasons for the failure of Arab guerilla power were lack of comprehension of revolutionary guerilla warfare; mushrooming of so many guerilla groups, independent of, and frequently antagonistic to, each other; the absence of an outstanding leader who might have unified them; and lack of appreciation that governments would not willingly tolerate a cuckoo in the nest, or any organization they could not control, or allow any group to have power without responsibility.

Dazzled by the success of the Chinese, the Algerians and the Viet Cong, Fedayeen leaders were fascinated by the theory of revolutionary guerilla warfare, and they saw no reason why it should not be imported and applied equally successfully to the occupied territories, but it was soon obvious that the smaller, less populous cockpit of the Middle East was not nearly so suitable for the 'fish' and the 'sea' techniques as were the jungles of Vietnam. Although there were 1·3 million Arabs living under Israeli control the requisite mass feeling of antagonism could not be whipped up, despite terrorist and other pressures, as individual survival, material well-being and traditional Arab lethargy were too strong a combination to overcome. Prompt and efficient Israeli counter-measures contributed as much to this guerilla failure as did guerilla lack of appreciation.

Lesser men attempted to emulate the seeming instant success of Asifa, the military arm of Fatah. Their efforts resulted in a multiplicity of guerilla organizations, many of which merely sought to cash in on the popularity of the Fedayeen movement. Others were motivated by personal ambition or selfishness. Some were sponsored by national governments, such as the Syrian Saiqa, with the intention of influencing Arab Guerilla Power generally and thwarting any plans that might be contrary to their national interest. Others had ideological aims, some quite extreme, such as the PFLP and the DPF. Attempts were made at times by President Nasser, Arafat, the Arab League, the PLO and others to combine them in one unified organization, but without success. That numbers were whittled down from about 20 to half-a-dozen was due as much to some smaller groups being greedily gobbled up by larger ones, than a calculated design to benefit Arab Guerilla Power as a whole. Fighting often occurred between the groups, as exemplified by the Fatah struggle with the PFLP for domination in the refugee camps in the Gaza Strip. Right to the end, until it fell to pieces, the PFLP took its own line of action without consultation or thought for the others, while the newer BSG is just another instance of this acute independence.

Fatah had an unfortunate leader when it was first launched; Ahmed Shukairy lacked many of the necessary qualities. Since rising to power Yassir Arafat has managed to keep the majority of the guerilla groups in the PLO and PASC, but he too has limitations in this respect. Had any outstanding personality been thrown up to weld the groups together, he might have been able to negotiate with Arab heads of state from strength to determine the best use of Arab Guerilla Power to achieve its ultimate aim. Such a leader has yet to arrive on the Middle East scene.

The other main drawback was the failure to appreciate that there can be no power without responsibility. The Fedayeen demanded freedom of movement, support, money, supplies, arms, training and base camps near the Israeli border, and headquarters and offices in cities and towns, but did not want any interference at all in their affairs by national security forces. They wanted to be able to do exactly as they pleased, and to be above the laws of their reluctant host countries that bore the brunt of the Israeli reprisal attacks they provoked and were expected to provide the defensive screen behind which the guerillas irresponsibly operated. The guerillas gained only as much of these demanded freedoms and privileges as governments could not prevent them taking. For example, the Fedayeen-dominated areas in northern Jordan and Fatahland in the Lebanon were established only because of national military weaknesses, and not because the governments concerned were in favour of them. It should be noted that there was never any hint or possibility of a 'Fatahland' developing in Egypt where Nasser had a strong political and military structure, or in Iraq, or even as yet in Syria.

This struggle for 'power without responsibility' came to take up the major portion of Fedayeen effort, resources and energy, leaving only a fraction for its avowed aim of ultimately eliminating Israel. Blind arrogance and bad judgement provoked the clash with the Jordanian army which resulted in the guerillas being eventually ejected from that country, and military pressure gradually squeezed them out from Fatahland in the Lebanon, so depriving them of the power to terrorize and blackmail. In Syria regular officers controlled Saiqa, in which organization there were frequent purges, and the rusting PLA was kept inactive. Arab guerilla power was deflated and almost destroyed, not by its official enemy, Israel, but by Arab Governments.

Attitudes towards the Fedayeen varied, but the overriding one was that all Arab governments wanted the guerillas to prosper in, and operate from, any Arab country other than their own. None advocated the formation of a Palestinian government-in-exile, and most were heavily against the idea of allowing the Palestinians to speak up for themselves and decide their own fate. Caught in the coils of their own anti-Israeli propaganda, they were forced to praise the guerillas and give them money, arms, supplies and facilities, but they (including Syria) gave not an inch or a dinar more than they thought expedient. President Nasser tried to control the Fedayeen movement, seating the PLO at Cairo under his eyes. but it frequently disregarded his advice and was unpredictable in its decisions. He never allowed the guerillas any of the freedoms they demanded in Egypt, and he gave some behind-the-scenes support to other régimes, in difficulties with them, such as King Hussein's, to make a balance of power acceptable to himself. For much of the time Nasser was mainly preoccupied with his war of attrition with the Israelis across the Suez Canal, and so the Fedayeen had a lesser priority, but he did not forget or neglect them. To Nasser the Fedayeen were a weapon he anticipated using from time to time for his own ends and he did not want them to be completely obliterated; indeed, his last political act was to bring about a cease-fire in Jordan to prevent them from being annihilated or driven from that country completely. The attitudes of King Hussein and the Lebanese leaders were quite clear. Despite lip-service to Fedayeen ideals, they wanted to oust guerillas from their territory as soon as possible, being only hampered in accomplishing this by pressure of Arab opinion, threats of sanctions and loss of subsidies from Arab countries.

The Soviet view on the Fedayeen movement was equally clear and cold. Strongly disapproving all guerilla organizations, the Soviet Union withheld recognition despite visits by Arafat to Moscow to plead for it, and aid sent was infinitesimal. China, prompted by its differences with the Soviet Union and its inherent faith in guerilla warfare, held the opposite view. Some support was given and supplies and arms were sent, but China was far away from the Middle East, and so gained comparatively little credit for this help; nor was it able to influence Fedayeen policy at all.

The popularity of Arafat, the Fedayeen leader and once the idol of the Arab world, has declined considerably, but despite criticism from many quarters for the failures of Arab Guerilla Power, he must be given credit for keeping the Fedayeen movement, such as it was, viable, although he has maintained his leadership with difficulty. Arafat is an astute politician forever angling for more power, rather than a wise statesman planning for a sound future; he longed to win the reputation of a victorious field general, but his military capabilities are considerably less than his political gifts. A conservative co-ordinator rather than a dedicated revolutionary, Arafat was overwhelmed by his own verbosity; applause went to his head as he became deeply immersed in his own personality cult. In many ways he falls short of being a great leader. An advocate of power without responsibility, he sought to use governments while striving to remain independent of them. A resilient political figure, he bowed with the changing Arab winds and switched policies to fit shifting Arab opinions; after the civil war in Jordan, for example, he allowed himself to be seen and photographed shaking hands with King Hussein, a thing he had many times previously sworn he would never do.

Pressures and threats from Arab governments ensured that the PFLP did not repeat their dramatic hijackings of September 1970 or their attack on a ship bound for Israel in June 1971. This restraint tended to hamstring the guerilla extremists, and as the guerillas were progressively restricted in countries adjacent to Israel, their activities against Israel became almost negligible. With Arafat's conservative outlook, and his dependence for support on Arab states, it seems as though, paradoxically, Arab Guerilla Power was being nullified by the Arabs themselves. This situation gave rise to the secret BSG, which used violent and dramatic methods, that included hijacking, shooting hostages and rescuing captured members, against the Israelis on the world stage. The book-bomb has given way to the more sophisticated letter-bomb, and one waits apprehensively for the next development.

Arab Guerilla Power largely failed to become an effective instrument because the Arabs, as ever, quarrelled amongst themselves. Practically every country can throw up a few dedicated fanatics in times of stress, but this is not enough. To become a real power they must have a leader who will unite, rouse and vitalize the masses. The belief that revolutionary guerilla warfare and commando incursions would create such a condition of chaos as would force the Israelis to hand over power to the Palestinians has proved false, and it remains to be seen whether there will be a revival of the guerilla movement.

Within Israel, counter-terrorist measures have been reasonably effective, but Israeli and Jewish personalities, in Israel and abroad, have been the recipients of letter-bombs, so the possibility cannot be excluded that the Israelis, for self-protection, may be involved in some form of counter-terrorism against the Arabs. If so, they will obviously not admit it, either officially or unofficially, but the Arabs recall the Israeli terrorist campaign, mainly using parcel-bombs, that drove German scientists and technicians from Egypt in the early 1950s, and also the notorious Lavon affair, in which Israeli agents were alleged to have been sent to carry out acts of terrorism in Egypt. The Arabs claim that Israeli agents have recently been responsible for sending letter-bombs to, and attempting to kill guerilla personalities; in support of these allegations they quote the activities of the Jewish Defence League. Finally only time will tell whether Arab-Guerilla Power is durable, or whether it was a brief phenomenon that will not recur.

# Index

The following words are not included in the Index as they appear on so many pages:
Arab(s), Arab-Israeli, Israel (i)(s), Fatah, Guerilla(s), Palestine (ian)(s), Lebanon(ese), Syria (n)(s), Jordan(ian)(s).

235

157, 158, 164, 178, 183, 212, 226, 228–30, 232
Miza, 98
Mokkadem, Farouk, 101
Morocco, 180
Moscow, 44, 77, 81, 123, 124, 212, 232
Movement for the National Liberation of Palestine, 26
Mufti, of Jerusalem see Husseini (al-), Haj Amin
Munich (airport), 12, 118, 219, 221, 226
Muscat and Oman, 124
Muslim(s), 61, 67, 71, 85, 92, 95, 96, 98, 101, 105
Muslim Brotherhood, 31, 52, 53, 57, 187

Nabatiyah, 108
Nabhani, Sheikh Takieddin, 85
Nablus, 77, 80, 128, 171, 182, 183
Nahariya, 211
Nasser, President Gamel Abdul, 12, 17, 19–23, 25–7, 31–3, 35, 37, 52, 53, 55–7, 59, 63, 65, 70–2, 74, 76, 81, 84, 101, 103, 106, 114, 123, 131–5, 137–9, 147, 150, 151, 155–8, 162, 167, 224, 230
Nasserites, 22, 23
Nasser, Kamel, 130, 172, 173
National Bloc Party, 102, 105
National Guard (of Jordan), 25
National Liberal Party, 102
National Liberation Front (NLF), 32
National Union of Jordan, 185
National Unity Charter
Negev, 43, 60, 126
Neguib, General, 17, 19
New Delhi, 215
New York, 138, 139
Nida (al-), 75
Nimer, Abu, 200

Nimer, Waled Ahmed see Iyaad, Abu
Njeim, General Jean, 107, 108, 112, 189
Nouri (al-), Major-General Mohammed, 133
November Agreement, 64–6
November Resolution (Security Council), 37
Numeiry, President, 153, 154
Nuri Said, 17
Nuseirat, 42

Omdurman, 182
Olympic Games (Village) (21st), 219, 220

Palestine Armed Struggle Command (PASC), 75, 86, 90, 113, 122, 123, 141, 167, 172, 230
Palestine Day, 78
Palestine Government in Exile, 208
Palestine Information Centre (Paris), 225
Palestine Liberation Army (PLA), 23, 25, 26, 32, 33, 37, 38, 41, 50–2, 55, 70–2, 75, 86, 89, 100, 123, 128, 150–3, 157, 158, 165, 171, 172, 174–6, 179, 180, 184, 187, 188, 194, 208, 209, 223, 225, 231
Palestine Liberation Front, 163
Palestine Liberation Movement, 123, 200, 214
Palestine Liberation Organization (PLO), 23, 25, 26, 31, 33, 37, 38, 52–5, 63, 70–2, 76–8, 86–8, 98, 100, 106, 108, 113, 116, 123, 124, 130, 131, 137, 141, 146, 154, 155, 162, 163, 168, 172, 173, 177, 179, 184, 185, 187, 188, 212, 213, 216, 220, 224, 225, 230, 232
Palestine National Alignment, 200, 214
Palestine News Agency (WAFA), 213

T.W.A. (airline), 117, 138, 139
Tyre, 112

U.A.R. (United Arab Republic),
see Egypt
Unified Arab High Command, 23
Unified Command (of PFLP), 118,
122–5, 128, 141, 163
United Nations, 19, 21, 23, 36, 37,
56, 135, 197, 198, 201
United Nations Emergency Force,
21, 41
United Nations Relief and Works
Agency (UNRWA), 18, 43, 50,
98, 158, 191, 198
United Nations Security Council,
69
Upper Jordan Valley, 16, 206

Vanguards of the Popular Liberation War (VPLW), 70
V.C.10 (Airliner), 140
Vietnam(ese) (style), 20, 35, 38,
42, 124, 133, 229
Viet Cong (pattern), 11, 16, 38,
39, 77, 83, 89, 157, 163, 176,
228, 229
Voice of Fatah, 59, 61
Voice of the Palestine Revolution,
146

Wadi Araba, 164
Wahdat (camp), see Jebel Wahdat
Wailing Wall, the, 78, 190
'Wars of Liberation', 123

Wazir, (al-) Khalil, 26–8, 216
West(ern) (Powers), 20, 21, 44,
157
West Bank(ers), 17, 22, 25, 35,
39, 40–4, 58, 77, 86, 89, 90, 125,
135, 144, 165, 178, 184, 185, 190,
191, 194, 197, 199, 200–2, 214
World War I, 15
World War II, 16, 18, 139

Yabis, 79
Yafi (al-), Premier Abdullah, 91, 92
Yahya, Brigadier, (Major) Abdul
Razzak, 38, 55, 86, 100, 171,
172, 187, 188
Yahuda, 79
Yamit, 203
Yanta, 100, 102
Yariv, Major-General Ahron, 139
Yassin, Subhi Mohammed, 56
Yemen(i), 178
Yemen (South), 215
Yifta, 30
Younes, General Bakr, 216
Yugoslavia, 122, 226

Zagreb, 226
Zahrur, Ahmed, 72
Zeayean, Yussef, 149
Zerka, 122, 127, 128, 130, 135, 143,
148, 149, 152, 173, 174
Zionist, 36
*Zionist Year Book*, 225
Zneimeh, Abu, 196
Zurich (airport), 72, 118, 138

## Formations, Aircraft, Weapons and Armour

**FORMATIONS**
*American*
82nd Airborne Division, 130
6th Fleet, 151, 152

*Iraqi*
Iraqi Brigade, 33
Salehad Brigade, 171, 179

*Jordanian*
3rd Armoured Brigade (Royal),
121, 128–30, 135, 145, 146
40th Armoured Brigade, 148,
150, 153
60th Armoured Brigade, 148,
152, 153

# INDEX

*P.L.A.*

Egyptian Brigade, 151, 158, 174, 179
Hittin Brigade, 150, 151
Kadiseyeh Brigade, 55, 174, 179
Yarmuk Brigade, 174, 179, 223

AIRCRAFT

Alouette (helicopter), 96
F-104, 184
Hawker Hunter, 96
MiGs, 73, 80, 81, 103, 111, 114, 225, 226
Mirage, 96, 98
Phantom, 117

Skyhawk, 126
Starfighter, 226
Sukhoi 7, 81
Vampire, 19, 96

WEAPONS AND ARMOUR

A-K 47 (Rifles), 49, 88
A.M.X. 13 (Tanks), 96
Katyusha (Rockets), 88
M-16 (Rifles), 189
SAM (Missiles), 114, 225
Tigercat (Rockets), 176
T-34 (Tank), 89, 151
T-54 (Tank), 151
T-55 (Tank), 150, 151